Economic Calculation
Under Inflation

Economic Calculation
Under Inflation

Introduction by Helen E. Schultz

Liberty*Press*

Indianapolis

HF
5657
E26.

Contents

Economic Calculation
Under Inflation

Introduction

Helen E. Schultz, President
LIBERTY FUND, INC.

Liberty Fund, Inc., was created by the late Pierre F. Goodrich to encourage the study of the ideal of a society of free and responsible individuals. This ideal is not a utopia but rather a polestar in a world of imperfect human beings where choices must be made among imperfections.

Choices are made more difficult by the presence, in the United States and throughout the world, of inflation—the decrease in the purchasing power of the medium of exchange caused primarily by governments which spend more than they can obtain through taxation or through borrowing from savers.

For example, the United States dollar, which has been the historical measuring unit used in financial accounting and reporting, lost 76 percent of its purchasing power in the years 1935–1974, and during 1974 it lost 12.5 percent of the purchasing power it had at the beginning of the year. Obviously, dollars representing transactions made in previous years, or even at the first of 1974, were not the same measuring units as those expended or received at the end of 1974. It appears the purchasing power decline in 1975 will be approximately 6.5 percent. Using historical dollars distorts financial information and the business decisions made as a result of that information.

In 1954 Mr. Goodrich, as President of Indiana Telephone Corporation, started that corporation computing and reporting the effects of the declining purchasing power of the dollar by price-leveling its financial statements. Indiana Telephone Corporation has been the only company in the United States which has consistently given its stockholders this information. During this time very few businessmen recognized the importance of being better informed about the effects of inflation on their respective companies.

The discussion among accountants and economists as to whether all corporate financial statements should be restated to reflect the effects of inflation accelerated as double-digit inflation arrived in the United States and triple-digit inflation arrived in other countries. Great Britain, Chile, Argentina, and Brazil took steps to introduce price-leveling into corporate financial statements.

In the United States the Financial Accounting Standards Board (FASB) held hearings in April 1974 on its Discussion Memorandum, "Reporting the Effects of General Price-Level Changes in Financial Statements." Subsequently, on December 31, 1974, the FASB issued its Exposure Draft, "Financial Reporting in Units of General Purchasing Power," and invited comments thereon.

In February 1975, Liberty Fund invited a group of people who have been thinking, writing, and teaching about various phases of accounting and economics to enter into a seminar discussion on "Economic Calculation Under Inflation."

Although the basic issue for the majority of businessmen

and accountants has been and continues to be, "*Should* we account for the effects of inflation?" the question of "how?" is a very integral part. Methodology is especially important to those who have made the decision that price level accounting should be used. Several major controversies have arisen which were included in the discussion.

One of the most universal questions concerns the use of current value accounting versus price level accounting. As is emphasized by the Financial Accounting Standards Board in its Exposure Draft, the two are not alternatives but actually serve two different purposes. Each method is important in its own time and place. Price-leveling involves indexing of historical dollars in order to determine a unit of general purchasing power which can be compared with a similar unit at other times. It tells how much of the apparent gain in value may have been caused by inflation.

Current value accounting requires a variety of specific indices and appraisals which attempt to reflect changes in specific prices or values. By its very nature, current value has to be a subjective figure. A market price is determined solely by a willing buyer and a willing seller. It would be mere coincidence if the current value of an account were the same as the price-leveled value. Current value reflects other causes of change besides inflation, such as supply and demand. When the rate of inflation is zero, there is no need for a price level adjustment but there may very well be a need for an adjustment to current value.

Price level reflects what has happened to the general purchasing power of the dollar. Current value reflects what has happened to particular prices at particular locations.

Determining whether a company is receiving a return of, and a fair return on, the purchasing power of the dollars which it has invested is a wholly separate thing from determining what it would cost to replace obsolete equipment with technologically advanced equipment and from the shareholder's determining whether to continue his investment in a company.

Should a general index of the purchasing power of the dollar or specific indices be used? If the object is to determine what has happened to the purchasing power of dollars, a general purchasing power index should be used. The Financial Accounting Standards Board stated that the best index currently available is the Gross National Product Implicit Price Deflator. The inclusion of a number of specific indices does not accomplish the above purpose. Specific indices, however, do have a place in specific instances. Their purposes and uses vary in the same way as do the purposes and uses of price level and current value accounting.

How should corporations account for the gain or loss on long-term debt? There are three major positions: (1) The position of the Financial Accounting Standards Board in its Exposure Draft, that all general price level gains and losses should be reflected in current income. (2) The position that gains and losses related to long-term debt should be adjustments of the carrying amount of fixed assets acquired with the proceeds from the sale of long-term debt. (3) The position that gains and losses relating to long-term debt should be deferred in the general price level statements until such time as the debt is retired and not refinanced.

Indiana Telephone Corporation takes the third position because in a highly leveraged corporation, the Financial Accounting Standards Board's recommendation that gains and losses should be reflected in current income will create and require current reporting of earnings, which may be illusory, as if they were fully realized. This will cause investors to expect increased dividends, regulators and customers to expect reduced sales prices, taxing authorities to expect increased taxes, and employees to expect increased wages and salaries. If such a corporation were to be forced to accede to any of these expectations, which would have to be paid out of paper profits, the results could and very likely would be disastrous.

The position that gains and losses related to long-term debt should be adjustments to the carrying amount of fixed assets acquired with the proceeds from the sale of long-term debt, assumes that the assets and the debt used to purchase the assets will continue to be specifically related. Actually, the term of the debt will only by coincidence be the same as the life of the investment.

Through the use of indices, what has happened to the purchasing power of the dollar in the past and what is happening currently can be approximated, but the purchasing power of the dollar when long-term bonds mature cannot be foreseen. Therefore, holders of the third position maintain that only when that debt is retired and not refinanced is the resulting gain or loss in purchasing power known, and only then should it be reflected in income in the financial statements. The gain, if any, belongs to the equity holders; they are the owners, and they are the risk takers. The bondholder has only those rights set forth in the debt agreement.

These questions and others were not definitely answered but the papers and discussions provoked thought and further refinement of positions. The directors and staff of Liberty Fund appreciate the cooperation of these people in our attempt to study this facet of the ideal of the society of free and responsible individuals. This book includes the papers and pertinent parts of the discussion, all of which have been edited and updated through the efforts of Mr. William Rickenbacker, publisher of the *Rickenbacker Report,* and Mr. David Franke and Mrs. Anne Lawrason of the Liberty Fund staff.

Since the conference, the Securities and Exchange Commission has made recommendations for replacement cost accounting. The long awaited Sandilands Report has been published in Great Britain. The Financial Accounting Standards Board has not yet announced its final position.

February 5, 1976

Conference Participants

Dr. William T. Baxter, London School of Economics and Political Science, London, England

Mr. Albert Bows, Arthur Andersen & Co. (retired), Atlanta, Georgia

Professor Bryan Carsberg, Department of Accounting and Business Finance, University of Manchester, Manchester, England

Dr. Sidney Davidson, Center for Advanced Study in the Behavioral Sciences, Stanford, California

Professor Thomas R. Dyckman, School of Business, Cornell University, Ithaca, New York

Mr. C. Leon Earl, Operating Vice President, Indiana Telephone Corporation, Seymour, Indiana

Dr. Solomon Fabricant, National Bureau of Economic Research, Inc., New York, New York

Mr. William H. Fletcher, Financial Vice President of Liberty Fund, Inc., Indianapolis, Indiana, and Executive Vice President of Indiana Telephone Corporation, Seymour, Indiana

Mr. Paul Grady, Price Waterhouse Company (retired), Boca Raton, Florida

Mr. W. W. Hill, former Chairman, Public Service Commission of Indiana; now with United Telecommunications, Inc., Kansas City, Missouri

Mr. John Kohlmeier, Arthur Andersen & Co., Chicago, Illinois

Dr. A. Neil McLeod, Executive Director, Liberty Fund, Inc., Indianapolis, Indiana

Mr. Chester May, Standard Oil of Indiana, Chicago, Illinois

Dr. David Meiselman, Virginia Polytechnic Institute & State University, Reston, Virginia

Professor Maurice Moonitz, School of Business Administration, University of California, Berkeley, California

Dr. William A. Paton, Graduate School of Business Administration, University of Michigan, Ann Arbor, Michigan

Dr. William A. Paton, Jr., Graduate School of Business, Washington State University, Pullman, Washington

Dr. Benjamin A. Rogge, Distinguished Professor of Political Economy, Wabash College, Crawfordsville, Indiana

Mr. Fred W. Ruebeck, Director, International Pharmaceutical Marketing and Development, Eli Lilly & Company, Indianapolis, Indiana

Mr. T. Alan Russell, Controller, Indiana Telephone Corporation, Seymour, Indiana

Mr. John L. Ryan, formerly with the Public Service Commission of Indiana; Indianapolis, Indiana

Professor W. Allen Spivey, Graduate School of Business Administration, University of Michigan, Ann Arbor, Michigan

Dr. Robert T. Sprouse, Financial Accounting Standards Board, Stamford, Connecticut

Mr. George Terborgh, Machinery and Allied Products Institute, Washington, D.C.

Professor Richard F. Vancil, Harvard Business School, Cambridge, Massachusetts

Mr. Hendrik Vermeulen, North American Philips Corporation, New York, New York

Mr. Claude M. Warren, Sr., Attorney and specialist in regulatory issues, Warren, Snider & Warren, Indianapolis, Indiana

Professor William J. Wrobleski, Graduate School of Business Administration, University of Michigan, Ann Arbor, Michigan

Dr. Stephen A. Zeff, Graduate School of Business Administration, Tulane University, New Orleans, Louisiana

I

Economic Calculation Under Inflation: The Problem in Perspective

Solomon Fabricant

I

O ur subject is economic calculation under inflation, not the whole problem of inflation. But it is well to start with some discussion of the larger problem, for the importance of our particular subject derives from the importance of that problem.

We cannot recall too often, these days, Lord Keynes' warning:

> There is no subtler, no surer means of overturning the existing basis of society than to debauch the currency. The process engages all the hidden forces of economic law on the side of destruction, and does it in a manner which not one man in a million is able to diagnose . . . [The] arbitrary rearrangement of riches [caused by inflation] strikes not only at security but at confidence in the equity of the existing distribution of wealth. . . . All permanent relations between debtors and creditors, which form the ultimate foundation of capitalism, become so utterly disordered as to be almost meaningless; and the process of wealth-getting degenerates into a gamble and a lottery.

Writing shortly after World War I, Keynes of course had in mind the severe wartime inflations, a few of which were already escalating in Europe into "hyperinflation." Inflations today here and abroad have been less rapid than those of World War I, or World War II. But they have persisted over a longer period. Their cumulative effects have too frequently already reached orders of magnitude similar to those of wartime. And they show no encouraging signs of coming to an end.

Chairman Arthur Burns of the Federal Reserve Board sees good reason to echo Keynes' warning. His remarks, pointedly entitled "The Menace of Inflation," also deserve to be quoted:

> Concerned as we all are about the economic consequences of inflation, there is even greater reason for concern about the impact on our social and political institutions. We must not risk the social stresses that persistent inflation breeds. Because of its capricious effects on the income and wealth of a nation's families and businesses, inflation inevitably causes disillusionment and discontent. It robs millions of citizens who in their desire to be self-reliant have set aside funds for the education of their children or their own retirement, and it hits many of the poor and elderly especially hard.
>
> In recent weeks, governments have fallen in several major countries, in part because the citizens of those countries had lost confidence in the ability of their leaders to cope with the problem of inflation. Among our own people, the distortions and injustices wrought by inflation have contributed materially to distrust of government officials and of government policies, and even to some loss of confidence in our free enterprise system. Discontent bred by inflation can provoke profoundly disturbing social and political change, as the history of other nations teaches. I do not believe I exaggerate in saying that the ultimate consequence of inflation could well be a significant decline of economic and political freedom for the American people.

In the light of these warnings, we can begin to see the social and political implications of our subject—a subject that at first sight might seem purely technical, and narrow even in that regard. Consider, for example, the reluctance, or at any rate the failure, of corporate officials to correct reported business profits for inflation, or to supplement the conventional figures with figures expressed in terms of general purchasing power; or of the auditors who certify corporate financial statements to draw attention to this lapse. As a consequence, during recent years the daily newspapers have published a flood of reports of large percentage increases in profits, almost always to new highs. Because these reports are generally limited to prior-year comparisons, newspaper readers are not reminded of the cyclical and other factors that make for large fluctuations in reported profits. The blinkers thus placed on them contribute to the impression of "unseemly" gains in profits. During most of the postwar period, however, inflation has been the major source of overstatement of profits.

It does not help the situation that the public reports on business income are in striking contrast with public reports on other kinds of income.

Efforts to measure and report labor income free of the effects of changes in the prices paid by workers have, in fact, a long history. Indices of food prices at retail became available in the United States around 1900. Comparison of changes in wages and salaries with changes in the food component of the cost of living promptly followed. A more comprehensive measure of change in consumer price levels, covering also non-food items, was demanded and became available during the great inflation associated with World War I. This consumer price index, applicable to urban wage earners and clerical workers, has been available on a regular basis ever since, and it has been gradually improved in coverage and accuracy. Indices of wage and salary income are now as a matter of course accompanied by this index of consumer prices and attention is paid not less to real than to money labor income in discussions of the changing economic status of labor. In a word, "deflated" wages and salaries are a commonplace.

Systematic allowance for change in prices paid when assessing the economic wellbeing of farmers came later, in the 1930s, when the "parity" idea was introduced and implemented under the Agricultural Adjustment Act. Like labor income, farm income—the return from capital investment and "entrepreneurship," as well as labor—is now regularly reported in constant as well as current dollars.

In contrast, corporate reports on profits earned during the year or quarter, whether made to stockholders, tax collectors, public utility commissions, "cost of living councils," or the public at large, are calculated on the basis of "generally accepted accounting principles," on which the dollar is assumed to be a stable unit of measurement.

Even the information on profits that is currently prepared by economists and statisticians for use in following the changing economic situation is deficient in this regard. The first appearance of a deflated corporate profit series in the monthly *Business Conditions Digest* and other publications of the Department of Commerce occurred only a couple of years ago. (Even this series exaggerates the rise in profits, because it is profits *before* the inventory valuation adjustment that the Department of Commerce makes in its national accounts.) No deflated corporate profit series yet appears in *Economic Indicators,* prepared by the Council of Economic Advisers for the Joint Economic Committee of the Congress. This monthly periodical, distributed to all members of Congress, and presumably widely used by them, publishes deflated income series only for labor and farmers. Such components of property income as dividends, interest, and rents are shown, in both *Business Conditions Digest* and *Economic Indicators,* deflated not separately but only in combination (along with labor and farm income) in the aggregate of personal income.

It is hard to overestimate the impact on public opinion of the exaggerated reports on profits. Indeed, the situation may have become such that the belated rush to the "last-in-first-out" (LIFO) method of costing inventory withdrawals could even strike some citizens, reading one news story after another about it, as only a subterfuge to conceal excessive profits and evade corporate income taxes. In any case, the well-nigh universal failure to adjust business financial statements for the depreciation of the dollars in which they are expressed can hardly have been other than misleading. It must have contributed to the public misunderstanding of the causes and consequences of our current economic situation. And to the extent that it did, it has made more difficult the task of choosing wisely and applying effectively government policy to deal with inflation—a task that would have been difficult enough under any circumstances. The consequences, social and political as well as economic, must be viewed as serious.

II

The sharp warning that debasement of the currency disturbs the economic arrangements and calculations that underlie our society suggests another and broader theme. The theme is complex as well as broad, relating as it does to a number of major historical developments. Economic historians have made these developments crucial factors in their delineation of the process of economic growth.

There is, first, the introduction and spread of money in the economy. As Wesley C. Mitchell put it in his beautiful essay, "The Role of Money in Economic History":

> By giving economic activity an immediate objective aim, and by providing a common denominator in terms of which all costs and all gains can be adequately expressed for business purposes, the use of money provided a technically rational scheme for guiding economic effort. . . .

The spread of the money was accompanied by—indeed, it stimulated—technical and managerial innovations that brought greater precision of measurement, greater ease of calculation, and vastly improved economic information. Werner Sombart's enthusiastic emphasis on one of these advances, the rise of systematic bookkeeping, as a decisive factor in the development of capitalism—"the complete rationalization of economic life became possible only through the advent of double-entry bookkeeping"—is now taken with a large grain of salt. But he did succeed in drawing attention to the significance of rational economic calculation. Max Weber widened the view of the development of economic calculation to include also such items as the final acceptance in Europe during the fifteenth and sixteenth centuries of Arabic numerals in place of the Roman.* And John A. Hobson widened it still further:

---

* Weber's comment on the displacement of Roman by Arabic numerals is worth a footnote: "It was at first viewed as a disreputable means of securing an immoral advantage in competition, since it worked in favor of the competitors of the virtuous merchant who disdained its use. Consequently it was first sought to exclude it by prohibitions. . . ."

The development of bookkeeping accompanied as it was by a
wide general application of rational and mathematical system
throughout commerce in the shape of exact measurement of time
and place, forms of contract, land surveying, modern methods of
weights and measures, city plans, public accounts, was at once
an indispensable tool and an aspect of modern industry.

An economic historian writing today would, I suppose,
want to mention that the chart of accounts of today's large
business corporation is rather different from the simple
bookkeeping set forth in Pacioli's famous treatise. Pointing
to the greater power and precision of modern methods and
means of measurement and calculation, he might update
the list of examples to include such items as operations research, electronic computers, and the marketing and other
surveys that utilize small sampling techniques. And he would
not fail to draw out the implications of these developments
—for example, the increase in the average size of business
enterprise and the economies of scale to which this increase
contributes.

An economist, looking over the historian's shoulder,
would remind him of the contribution of economic theo-
rists. He would at least mention their recognition of the
complementary character of supply and demand in determining price, their discovery and refinement of marginal
analysis, and the distinction they draw sharply today between social and private benefits and costs. And the economist would point also to the invention and improvement of
such economic tools of analysis as index numbers, national
accounts, and econometric models.

Another development related to these was the widening
of economic, and inevitably also political, freedom. In
Mitchell's words:

When money is introduced into the dealings of men, it enlarges their freedom. For example, when a personal service is commuted into money payment, the servitor has a wider choice in the use of his income. By virtue of its generalized purchasing power, money emancipates its users from numberless restrictions upon what they do and what they get. As a society learns to use money confidently, it gradually abandons restrictions upon the places people shall live, the occupations they shall follow, the circles they shall serve, the prices they shall charge, and the goods they can buy. Its citizens have both a formal and a genuine freedom in these respects wider than is possible under an organization in which services and commodities are bartered.

In turn, freedom makes for greater efficiency, for in a free society, as was pointed out above all by Mises and Hayek, individuals have the authority and the incentives to use the particular knowledge which they—and only they —possess to adapt most economically to the incessant changes that go on in a dynamic world.* This stock of

---

* Many people are familiar with the idea that capitalism is efficient and free, at any rate relative to other systems, but not with the idea that capitalism is efficient in substantial part because it is free. The idea helps us to understand the difficulties encountered by Soviet Russia in its effort to reach a "Western"—a capitalistic—level of economic efficiency. I cannot resist the temptation to comment on it.

The analysis by Mises, mentioned above, was made shortly after World War I, in the course of a theoretical examination of the possibility of rational economic calculation in a socialist economy. Soviet Russia's experience since then has provided some concrete information on the relation between rational economic calculation and economic and political freedom, something that Hayek also had very much in mind, and to which Burns referred in his warning of the menace of inflation. Understanding has grown in Russia of the limitations of a centralized planning agency in acquiring and utilizing effectively all the information about consumer demand and production possibilities that is needed for the efficient allocation of resources. There has consequently been a good deal of discussion there about the desirability and feasibility of a system of decentralized decisions, and even some hesitant movement towards something like a profit incentive and freer price system. The trend has been hesitant because it is also real-knowledge includes detailed information that no central authority could ever hope to gather, digest and apply in formulating its plans and making its decisions. It is precisely because inflation biases the information in the hands of individual economic units and renders this information less useful, that inflation makes for inefficiency in the allocation of resources and inequity in the distribution of income and wealth.

Improvement in the technical means of economic calculation and in the information utilized in economic calculation has been made almost continuously over the centuries, and even at an accelerated pace in recent generations. In one significant respect, however, there has been little progress. The pecuniary unit, a necessary element in all economic calculations, has not been kept stable; and this instability has been generally ignored in business accounting. The contrast with the improvements made in other aspects of economic calculation is striking. The most sophisticated calculation using the latest generation of electronic computers cannot yield a truly rational result if the data fed into the computers are expressed in unstable units. "Garbage in, garbage out" has become a tattered cliché among computer men. But, worn and vulgar as it may be, it states our problem vividly, if not quite accurately.

III

The overstatement of increases in business profits because of inflation—or understatement of decreases—has

---

ized that such a move would lead to, and its success require, a degree of economic freedom incompatible with the tight control Party stalwarts feel to be essential.

worried thoughtful citizens. They are concerned about the implications of this overstatement for business decisions generally, investment in particular, and taxation, price and wage controls, and economic forecasting.

This concern has, of course, been intensified by the very rapid inflation that the American economy has been experiencing in recent years.

The failure of conventional accounting practice to deal adequately with changing price levels is an old worry, however. Over twenty-five years ago two outstanding accountants, George May and Percival Brundage, organized a "Study Group on Business Income" under the auspices of the American Institute of Certified Public Accountants (then called the American Institute of Accountants). Ten years ago the Accounting Research Division made another study of the question. Five years ago the Accounting Principles Board of the AICPA issued its "Statement No. 3" recommending—but not requiring—supplementary statements disclosing the effects of changes in the general price level on the financial accounting measurements. Yet these studies and statements have had hardly any effect on current accounting practice.

Only very recently has the accounting profession as a whole begun to recognize the need to allow for changes in the general price level, in business accounts, and to do something about it. Four years ago the Accounting Principles Board could still say that "the effects of inflation in the United States are not considered sufficiently important at this time to require recognition in financial accounting measurements." Now, however, its successor, the Financial Accounting Standards Board, considers it possible as well as desirable to propose a Statement of Principles that "would require supplemental disclosure of accounting information restated for changes in the general purchase power of the dollar." A similar proposal has been made in Britain and Canada. In a few countries—not many—some sort of adjustment for changes in the price level is already in fairly general use, as a recent compilation by Price Waterhouse indicates.*

The FASB's action, and the behavior of others throughout the economy, implies, of course, acceptance of the idea that inflation is and will remain "sufficiently important" for some considerable time in the future. It is worthwhile, however, to take a moment to clarify our notions of the magnitude of the inflation we have already experienced and of the prospect of inflation in the years ahead.

Over the 10 years since 1964, when the current inflationary episode is often said to have begun, the Consumer Price Index has risen by 66 percent. This seems like a big enough rise to be considered substantial by any standards. Its relative magnitude may be better appreciated, however, if we compare it with the increases associated with the two World Wars. In the inflation associated with World War II, counting from 1939 to 1946, the consumer price level rose by about 40 percent. In the inflation associated with World War I (1913–1920), the consumer price level rose by 100 percent. If the period associated with World War I is extended to 1922, the sharp decline after 1920 puts the net increase (1913–1922) at 70 percent. The price increase since 1964 compares "favorably"—if that is the right word —with the two wartime increases.

---

* Another valuable compilation is provided in George Lent's paper prepared for the International Monetary Fund.

However, the Consumer Price Index was rising before 1964. In fact, the period of inflation since 1964 is only the latest episode of a history that dates back to the period starting before World War II. Every one of the calendar years after 1939, except only two—1949 and 1955—saw a price index higher than it had been in the year before. With respect to the price level, our generation's experience has been almost nothing but inflation. The cumulative effect since 1939 has been a rise of 270 percent in the price level, equivalent to a reduction of almost 75 percent in the purchasing power of the dollar.

This suggests another comparison—namely, with the inflation dignified as "the price revolution" by historians. It resulted from the great transfer of gold and silver to Europe following the discovery of America, along with a substantial debasement of the currency. Despite reservations made necessary by the paucity of comparable data—only some wholesale prices are available for the early period—as well as by the vast difference in stages of economic development, the results are worth presenting. Over the sixteenth century, according to indices assembled by Anna Schwartz, wholesale prices in France and England rose at an average annual rate of only about 1 percent in terms of silver, and about 2 percent in terms of money on account. The latter, the more relevant, is much less than the 3.3 percent we have experienced over the 36 years since 1939. The whole of the sixteenth century saw a wholesale price level increase of some 600 percent. We have already come close to this —500 percent—in the twentieth century, despite the precipitous price decline during the Great Depression. And our century is not yet over.

Looking ahead, the prospects for a quick end to inflation

appear rather dim. If there are still some optimists among
us, they should ponder the reaction of the country to the
recession under way since 1973. Inflation is no longer the
nation's "number one" economic problem.

The rate of inflation will probably decline as the effects
of the spurt in petroleum and grain prices recede, and the
recession worsens, before efforts to turn the economy
around are agreed upon, are actually applied, and their
results finally materialize. Looking "over the valley" to the
expansion ahead, however, it is likely that the policies to
bring about revival in employment will also prevent the rate
of inflation from declining during expansion. These policies
may even result in some acceleration of inflation before or
after revival. Even if anti-recession policy should somehow
prove neutral with regard to inflation—which is hard to
believe—the coming expansion phase of the business cycle
will tend for other reasons to be accompanied by a rise in
the rate of change in the general price level, as Geoffrey H.
Moore has shown to be typical of cycles in the postwar
period, just as it was of the more violent business cycles before World War II.

The application of some form of incomes policy involving
controls over individual prices and wages at some later
date is, I suppose, not altogether out of the question, despite
Administration denials. But even a strong set of controls,
vigorously enforced, would have to be relaxed—perhaps
after a brief "freeze"—to permit some increases in prices
and wages. "Hardship cases" and other exceptions to "catch
up" will abound. Experience provides little reason to expect
that efforts to slow up wages that are already ahead of the
crowd, or to reduce the prices of industries in which productivity is rising rapidly and costs per unit are declining,

will be successful—if they are attempted at all. Yet these slowdowns or reductions are necessary in order to offset valid increases if the general price level is to remain stable.

What I see ahead, through 1976 and well beyond, then, is a rising long-term trend in the general price level, around which will be cycles of retardation and acceleration in the rate of inflation. Progress toward stabilization will gradually diminish the amplitude of cycles in the rate of increase of the price level and lower the level of the average rate of inflation. But I do not see inflation soon vanishing or the amplitude of fluctuations in the rate of increase in prices soon becoming negligible. Whether there would, in fact, be progress—a reduction in the amplitude of fluctuation and in the average rate of inflation—is not certain. It depends on how soon and to what degree anti-inflation policy is relaxed during a slowdown or recession. It depends on whether, and how strongly, the need to fight inflation is kept in mind during the earlier as well as the later stages of business expansion. It depends on the means used to moderate inflation and inflationary expectations. It depends on the success of continuing efforts to remove already notorious structural obstacles to price declines and fuller employment; to improve governmental organization; to expand tested economic knowledge; and to add to the flow of current information required to apply this knowledge effectively. And all this depends, in turn, and fundamentally, on how well the public is taught to understand the problem of inflation.

IV

My earlier remarks about the failure to adjust current business accounting in order to allow for inflation were not meant to imply that this adjustment is altogether simple and straightforward. I want, rather, to say the contrary.

Various problems, many of which are difficult, arise when one attempts to correct financial statements for inflation. The *Business Conditions Digest*'s simple deflation of the reported profit series is, no doubt, a major step toward recognizing changes in the value of money. The rise in corporate profits before taxes between 1966 and 1973, for example, reported in current prices as 40 percent, is under 10 percent when measured in constant prices. But how thoroughly this deflation corrects for reduction in the value of the dollar is a matter of considerable controversy. The *Business Conditions Digest* deflated series is derived simply by deflating profits as accountants calculate these profits.*

Four groups of questions arise about the validity and accuracy of the result. One concerns the current-dollar profit figure, reported in the usual corporate income account or profit and loss statement, that is deflated. Another concerns the deflator, that is, the index that measures the decline in the purchasing power of money. The third concerns the purchasing power gains or loses, realized or not, on monetary and non-monetary assets and liabilities when the value of money changes—gains or losses not covered in the deflation of the reported profit series. And the fourth concerns "current value accounting," a subject on which questions properly arise when the price level is stable, questions which—for good reason—become more intense

---

* More exactly, the Department of Commerce distinguishes between the two components of profits—dividends and undistributed profits—and deflates each separately. Dividends are deflated by the national consumption implicit deflator. Reported undistributed profits are deflated by the gross capital formation implicit deflator. The two deflated series are then combined to yield the deflated profit series.

when inflation occurs and the subject of "general purchasing power accounting" is brought up. All four groups of questions overlap, and are therefore difficult to keep apart. But it would be worse to consider them all together.

Reported profits, such as are shown in annual or quarterly reports and mentioned in the daily press, are not good measures even of profits expressed in current prices. The reason is well known to economists and accountants. Certain important elements of current cost are calculated in the prices paid in earlier periods, not in current prices or in original cost prices adjusted for change in the general purchasing power of money. When price levels are moving up, original cost prices may be significantly below the prices appropriate to the current period, the period for which profits are being measured.

One such element of cost is withdrawals from inventory of material, components, goods in process, and the like, in producing the goods or services sold. With the "last-in-first-out" method of costing inventory withdrawals, the charge to current operations is at something reasonably close to current prices. But LIFO is in fact used only to a limited (but, recently, a rapidly growing) extent in calculating corporate profits. When prices are rising fast, the underestimation of the cost of withdrawals from inventory may be large. In 1973 this cost may have been understated by some $15 billion.

Similarly, depreciation and obsolescence charges are generally based on the prices prevailing in earlier periods —indeed, periods far more remote than the corresponding periods for inventory. Yet accountants make no effort, when calculating business profits, to substitute for the original purchase price and equipment the current replacement price, or the original price adjusted for change in the general price level. The difference between original and current prices of capital equipment used up in any year may be greater or less than the difference in the case of inventory withdrawals; it depends on the course of the price level up to that year. In 1973 depreciation and obsolescence charged at original prices understated the current cost also by about $15 billion.

In the national income and outlay accounts prepared by the Department of Commerce, the cost of withdrawals from inventory is adjusted (approximately) to the current price level by means of the department's "inventory valuation adjustment" that I mentioned earlier. However, even in the national accounts an adjustment is not yet made for the fact that under current accounting practice depreciation and obsolescence are charged at less than current cost or original cost adjusted for inflation.

Returning to the profits reported in corporate financial statements, it appears that 1973 profits before income tax, reported as $118 billion, must have been overstated by as much as a third. Further, the degree of overstatement of profits in 1973, measured in 1973 prices, was greater than the degree of overstatement of profits in 1972, measured in 1972 prices. The deflation procedure followed in *Business Conditions Digest* putting profits in all years on the same price basis—that of 1958—does not correct this upward bias in the rate of change in profits.

Conventionally measured profits may suffer also from biases in the opposite direction—biases that understate rather than overstate both the levels and the rates of change of profits. If sufficiently strong, the downward bias could even provide some offset to the bias that results from calculating inventory withdrawals at original cost, although this offset could hardly be important in years when inflation is very rapid.

One such offsetting factor is provided by "accelerated" depreciation and obsolescence, which the Internal Revenue Service has permitted in recent decades. Speeding up the deduction for depreciation and obsolescence reduces the lag between the time when capital goods are acquired and the time when depreciation is charged, reducing also the difference between original and replacement cost. But accelerated depreciation does not make it possible to recoup more than the original cost. The difference can be reduced, not eliminated. Accelerated depreciation serves to eliminate *some* of the profits that reflect merely a rise in the general price level (profits on which corporate income taxes would otherwise have to be paid) but doe snot eliminate *all* the "profits" or the taxes due on these "profits." In addition, there is a question whether the accelerated charge for depreciation and obsolescence really represents a departure from the appropriate charge. In one view, which I tend to share, the accelerated charge is closer to and more representative of the underlying facts on depreciation and obsolescence than the charge permitted under IRS rules before the revision of these rules.

A more subtle and perhaps more powerful offset that some economists have worried about results from technical change. This tends to reduce the cost of maintaining the capacity of capital equipment to produce a given volume of output to less than the depreciation charged. They have worried also about growth in the capital stock. This growth also serves to make current depreciation charges higher than the amount needed to maintain current capacity on a replacement accounting basis. The issue, as I see it, is whether technical change and capital growth do in fact offset the understatement of depreciation and obsolescence in the calculation of business profits, if depreciation and obsolescence are viewed as measuring reduction in the private value of plant and equipment rather than reduction in the capacity of plant and equipment to produce. The issue involves a difference between two points of view, the social and the private. The issue merits more attention than it has received.

V

The second group of questions concerns the deflator used to convert business profits in current prices to profits in constant prices.

In a dynamic economy, prices are always changing in response to shifts in demand and supply. The prices of some products will tend to decline in relation to the prices of most other products when the industries producing them enjoy exceptionally rapid increases in productivity because of breakthroughs in technology, for example, or because cheaper sources of supply of materials have been discovered. The relative prices of some products will tend to rise when productivity in the industries manufacturing them advances less rapidly than in the nation as a whole. And the prices of still other products will tend to move with the general price average when productivity in the industries producing them keeps up with the national average. "Change in the general price level," then, must mean some sort of average of many different price changes. The problem of defining and measuring this average led to the invention of index numbers.

Many index numbers of prices have been devised. They

differ in the markets to which they refer, in the mathematical form of the averaging process used, and in the weights used to allow for differences in the relative importance of the various commodities and services—an importance that changes over time as the economy develops.

One of the issues here is what index should be used in deflating profits. If a single index is to be used for all companies, should it be the GNP Implicit Price Deflator or some alternative to it? Alternatives sometimes suggested are the implicit price deflator for private GNP, the "fixed weighted price index" for gross private product, the Consumer Price Index, the all-commodity wholesale price index, and the industrial-commodity wholesale price index. Most of these indices differ significantly over long periods as well as short. The two alternatives most often considered are the GNP Implicit Price Deflator and the Consumer Price Index, which differ rather slightly, on the whole. The error made in choosing between them, if any, is a trivial matter compared with the error of not deflating at all.

Another issue is whether a single deflator should be used for all companies, or deflators be tailored to the particular situation of each company. In the case of wages and clerical salaries, the common deflator used is the national Consumer Price Index, which reflects change in the average level of prices paid by all those in urban areas receiving this kind of labor income. It is known, however, that consumer price indices in different parts of the country do not move exactly parallel to the national average. Nor is it likely that consumer price indices applicable to workers at different income levels even in the same city would be identical. The question has usually been avoided, presumably on the ground that the differences are not large. Now, however, it is attracting attention because of the plans of the Bureau of Labor Statistics to broaden the coverage of its price index.*

A similar question arises in the case of profits. Companies differ considerably with regard to the goods and services on which their profits are expended—by stockholders with their dividends, and by the companies themselves with the money they retain to replace and enlarge inventory and capital goods as well as for other purposes. These differences among companies in the composition of expenditures must be far wider than among workers. The range is from the small, specialized firm in one tiny corner of the United States to the vast multinational conglomerate doing many different kinds of business in many different countries, countries in which price levels change at diverse rates, and between which exchange rates may fluctuate widely.

The use of deflators specific to each company would, however, tend to eliminate some of its profits or losses caused by changes in relative prices. The possibility raises another complicated issue. It involves a difference between those who think of the real profits of a company as measuring its contribution to the real national income and those who think of these profits as measuring the company's

---

* Old families living in their own homes with the mortgage paid off will not experience the same degree of inflation as young families in rented apartments, or only now acquiring their own homes.

Involved here is an important and difficult problem, but one seldom mentioned. If the price of housing services is based on rental equivalents in the case of owner-occupied houses, there will be no great difference in the prices paid (or imputed) for such services between owners and renters. But there will then be a difference in the income received (or imputed). It is, in other words, difficult to determine the effect of inflation on the economic position of a family without paying attention to its income as well as to its expenditures. The same difficulty arises in the case of business firms.

share in the real national income. Interestingly enough, the issue was raised in the very first Income Conference held by the National Bureau of Economic Research almost forty years ago, as well as in later conferences. But there continues to be much confusion about it—in the economic as well as the accounting literature.* The appropriate treatment in financial statements of changes in relative prices, when making adjustments for inflation, raises another issue that would warrant careful analysis.

VI

We turn to the third set of questions about the deflation of profits. In addition to the effects of inflation on the costing of inventory withdrawals and depreciation and obsolescence, economists and accountants naturally think also of the effects of inflation on other items in the income account and balance sheet.

Besides inventories and plant and equipment, the asset side of the balance sheet includes holdings of non-depreciable tangible assets such as land. Land and other tangible assets are carried on the books at original cost, less accumulated depreciation in the case of assets subject to depreciation. But their market value, or their original cost adjusted for inflation, may have risen substantially. This rise in value is not included in the conventional measure of profits until it is "realized." Realization may be through sale of the asset itself, as in the case of land. Or it may be through sale of the products, to the cost of which have been charged the

* Recall the Department of Commerce's deflation of undistributed corporate profits, referred to earlier, by the implicit deflator for gross capital formation rather than GNP.

materials drawn from inventory and the depreciation of
the plant and equipment used in producing the products.
The issue, here, hinges on whether realization of a profit
(or loss) during a fiscal period is considered crucial in the
decision to include it in the period's profit. The issue is old,
but it draws more than the usual amount of controversy
when inflation (or deflation) is rampant.

There are also monetary assets and liabilities, the "real"
values of which change when changes occur in the purchasing power of the money in which they are expressed.
Much the same issue arises in the case of monetary items as
in the case of non-monetary items. To illustrate: Is the loss
on the purchasing power of a bond investment to be charged
to the period in which the decline in purchasing power
occurs, or to the period in which the bond is finally re-
deemed? The answer to this question has implications for
the treatment of the interest received on the bond.

Let us suppose that inflation proceeds at a constant rate,
that it is fully anticipated, and that the coupon rate is therefore sufficiently high to offset the loss of purchasing power
of the principal. Suppose further that it is decided to charge
the purchasing power loss on principal to the last period.
The interest received in any period must then be considered
subject to a depreciation charge, which is to be credited to
a reserve for the depreciation of the principal's purchasing
power when it is finally realized. Even the precise form of
the method of depreciation is implied; it must be such as
to yield a net interest income constant in terms of purchasing power. If the treatment of the interest received,
under general purchasing power accounting, is made consistent with the treatment of the loss on bond investments,
it will not matter which of the two alternative answers is

given to the question posed. The point I have been making applies equally, of course, to the treatment of debts and interest paid on them.

In this discussion of the effects of inflation on the balance sheet, and through it on the income account, I have been concentrating on the accounts of business firms. The same questions arise—or should arise—also about the "accounts" of wage and salary workers and farmers. Although not as often pointed out in popular discussions of labor or farm income as they should be, to recipients of these types of income also, the balance sheet or wealth effects of inflation are of concern. Questions about capital gains, for example —real or nominal, realized or unrealized, and their bearing on income and income tax status—must give trouble to citizens receiving various kinds of income and standing at various levels in the size distribution of the nation's income.

VII

Another set of questions about the adjustment of profits for inflation revolves around the issue of "current value" accounting. The questions are essentially the same as those we have already discussed about the valuation of assets, but they are usually discussed in somewhat different terms and may therefore be worth some separate consideration.

Advocates of current value accounting would abandon the principle of historical cost and would value all assets and liabilities at current prices. Because the difference between current value and historical cost widens during inflation, the issue is brought closer to the boiling point.

Advocates of current value or historical cost accounting could and probably would agree on the usefulness of general purchasing power accounting. Those who favor current value accounting would make the adjustment for change in the purchasing power of money after converting historical costs to current values. Those who hold to historical cost accounting would make the adjustment for change in the general price level without converting historical cost to current value. If all prices moved closely together, the results would be essentially the same. But all prices do not move closely together. The results will therefore differ. However, they will differ by not nearly so much as they might if general purchasing power accounting did not eliminate a major part of the difference between current value and historical cost.

In the end, when assets are sold or have become fully depreciated, and when liabilities are finally settled, current values will have entered the books under either system of accounting, whether historical cost or current value.* But the periods in which current values are recognized and recorded will not be the same. Under historical cost accounting, the recording of any difference between original cost and current value will be delayed until final "realization." Under current value accounting, the gain or loss will enter the calculations in every period in which prices differ from those of the preceding period, whether "realized" or not. The issue, I might mention, is not one of conservatism, for under historical cost accounting acceptance of unrealized losses as well as unrealized gains may be postponed.

Although current value accounting and general pur-

---

* However, the rise or fall in value of a non-monetary asset that is neither sold nor depreciated periodically, such as land or an investment in common stocks, will never appear on the books or be taken into the financial statements unless explicitly revalued.

chasing power accounting deal with rather different questions, the distinction between them is not always drawn
sharply. Most of the published estimates of what corporate
profits, or such items as depreciation charges, would look
like when adjusted for inflation (including those I have
mentioned earlier) combine the adjustment to current value
and the adjustment for change in general purchasing power
without drawing any special attention to that fact. One
reason has already been mentioned. When inflation is substantial, it does not matter much whether conversion to
current value is made before or after correction for change
in the general price level, considering the rough character
of the published estimates. There is another reason. Most
of the estimates mentioned are prepared by economists who
generally favor current value accounting, and are often
impatient with those, particularly accountants, who prefer
the precision (and verifiability) of historical cost to the
relevance of current value, which must necssarily be estimated.

It is possible that readers of financial statements expressed in units of general purchasing power, when these
become available, will not always understand that the adjusted values shown are not current values, despite explanations to the contrary. Indeed, I expect some considerable
confusion. Should it arise, it will strengthen the hands of
the advocates of current value accounting. They will insist
that the only way out of the confusion is for accountants to
go all the way towards recognizing changes in prices—
not only changes in the average level of prices but also
changes in relative prices. My own view is that adjustment
for the general price level alone in effect puts financial officers and accountants in an uncomfortable and untenable

halfway house, from which they will have to advance or retreat. Given the inflation we have already had, and the prospect of more inflation, retreat is out of the question.

VIII

I have not yet addressed directly another question, one important enough to be raised and considered explicitly. This question bears on the extent to which users of conventional financial statements may actually be misled by them.

The users in mind when this qustion is put are present and potential stockholders, creditors, and the like. It is hardly conceivable that all these users of the unadjusted accounts, or the financial analysts who serve some of them, would take the conventional accounts at their face value. On the other hand, it is equally doubtful that all users of the unadjusted accounts could entirely avoid being misled by them. Some degree of error is inevitable. That this is so may be seen if we consider the extreme assumptions that must be made to conclude otherwise.

To suppose that the unadjusted accounts would be taken at their full face value is to suppose that our economy is suffering from universal and persistent "money illusion" despite continuing and substantial changes in the general price level. Accountants may fail to adjust their reports for inflation, but their reports are not the only source of information on what is happening. Nor is everybody unable to pay for and use additional information. Nor, to pursue the question further, is it reasonable to suppose that users of this information would fail—in the very act of using it—to convey to others the implications of what is happening. In one way or another, and sooner or later, people do learn from experience. To assume complete money illusion is quite inconsistent with all we know about the world.

To suppose that all users of the unadjusted accounts could entirely avoid being misled by them is equally untenable. It would be to suppose that the users of the reports know all that is going on—that they know the past and current rate of inflation, that they can and will anticipate with confidence what the rate will be in the future, and have at their disposal the detailed information about individual companies necessary to determine the effects of inflation, past and prospective, on these companies—and that they will be accustomed to taking all this into account in all their calculations and decisions.

These make up an obviously extreme set of assumptions. To be valid, the assumptions require, at least, an economy in which all changes in prices are open, none are suppressed; and in which the general price level is changing at a constant rate and has been doing so for a long time.*

The users we have been discussing are not the only users, and not the only important users. There are also the "users" to whom I referred at the the start. These are the great bulk of our citizens, the majority of the electorate. They worry not about investments in corporation shares and bonds, but about their rising cost of living. They hear about record profit levels and feel they are suffering an in-

---

* A constant rate of inflation is not necessary. It would be sufficient if the rate of change in the general price level were to follow some reasonably clear pattern of fluctuation. Fairly adequate adjustment to inflation could then take place, as it does in the case of seasonal fluctuations in prices, production and employment. But, for various reasons, inflation is a highly erratic phenomenon.

justice. They demand to know what governmental authorities intend to do about those who are profiteering from the
price rises. They, and many of their representatives also,
are misled by the conventional profit reports—if not by
reading the reports themselves, then by reading the newspaper accounts of them, or the government statistics in
which they are summarized without adequate allowance
for inflation. The sense of injustice thus engendered is not
mitigated by those who take advantage of the political possibilities opened up by these widely publicized reports.

IX

The variety of ways in which inflation disturbs the calculations and affairs of business is enormous. It is enough to
say that inflation acts on prices and costs, and on profits
and taxes. It undermines the basis on which past commit-
ments were made, creates current and urgent pressures,
and it clouds expectations about the future. It disturbs relations with customers, labor, suppliers, financial institutions,
and governmental agencies, and internal relations within
business firms. And the particular impact of inflation in
each of these respects, whether favorable or not, differs
widely among firms, depending as it does on the nature of
a firm's business; the age, size and form of its organization;
its location; and the way it customarily does its business.
But in every company, when inflation is as rapid—and as
variable—as it is now, its impact can be serious and must
be dealt with. And this in turn requires a variety of adjustments, the efficacy of which must always be in some doubt
because so many of the adjustments must be new. The fact
that inflation obscures and makes dubious the financial

accounting data with which every business executive must work when making his plans and decisions, is only one source of the problem posed for rational calculation by inflation.

True, a private enterprise system will adjust to change— if left to itself—including change in the purchasing power of money. But flexible as it is, it can do so only at a cost and only with a lag. We may presume that the costs in such a system will generally be lower, and the lags shorter, than in any other. But while the costs may even be at a minimum, in some sense, they will not necessarily be low. And the lags may be shorter but not necessarily short.

Nor will the costs be distributed evenly, nor the lags uniformly throughout the economy. Inequities of all sorts will be discovered. Private enterprise may therefore not be "left to itself." Incomes policies, price fixing in this or that particular industry, quotas on imports and exports, formal or informal rationing, foreign-exchange controls, taxes on excess (or "windfall") profit in selected industries or even across the board—these and other actions, or threats to take action, by government will abound. The cumulation of changes of this sort forced on the economy is bound to alter its character and efficiency. Taking them into account in business calculations when they happen— and before they happen—cannot be easy or their consequences costless to economic efficiency.

The difficult problems of financial management caused by inflation and its variability are exacerbated also by the innumerable and wide-ranging laws and regulations, both federal and state, already in existence which restrict, or slow down, or even prevent, adjustment to the situation. Built into these rules are assumptions that simply are not valid in a period of inflation—assumptions that the dollar is a stable unit, for example, and that anything over six percent is a usurious rate of interest. Alterations in these are sometimes made, but then only grudgingly and not everywhere they are needed. Regulatory agencies permit price increases, but not quickly, and when they do they may limit the increases to certain cost "pass-throughs." Banking authorities are slow to permit competitive interest rates.

Not only business firms but also individuals and families encounter these difficulties in adjusting. Even if they were as well equipped as business firms to deal with inflation, which they are not, individuals would not find it easy, or even possible, to care properly for their savings, for example. If nothing else, the variety of governmental and other restrictions on the directions in which they can channel their funds must hamper their adjustment to rising price levels and disparate interest rates.

Governmental units also have their difficulties, caused by constitutional, legislative, bureaucratic, and political limitations on their ability to deal with inflation. Not all state and local governments have yet shifted from property taxes to income and sales taxes as the major source of their revenue. To cite another example, salaries in the higher ranks of the federal civil service are still lagging, as are the salaries of many judges at all levels of government. The consequences for the quality of service provided, and even for the discouragement of corruption, may not be trivial.

Nor is this all. To see the ramifications of the effects of inflation on the calculations of governments (and of those they deal with), consider the fact that in much penal legislation on the statute books, fines are still at prewar dollar levels. Since the fines were designed to impose costs on criminal behavior, this lag means that the real costs have been lowered. Research in the area of law and economics supports the presumption that these costs do enter the economic calculations of potential and active criminals. The implications for the crime rate are not far-fetched. Further, where fines are set as alternatives to jail sentences, as they often are, the "trade-off" between the two has been shifted radically by inflation. The real cost of confinement in jail has risen with the average level of real wages, but the real cost of a fine has declined because of inflation. This has serious implications for the equity as well as efficiency of our penal system.

Examples of the effects of inflation on the economic calculations that influence behavior are easily found in still other areas of government regulation and taxation. A "trade-off" shift similar to the one that has occurred in our penal system has taken place also in tariff schedules. In this case it is the relation between ad valorem and specific tariff rates that has been altered by inflation. The result is a change in the costs confronting importers and in the relative degree of protection offered producers of different commodities.

X

Adjustments to inflation in economic transactions and arrangements do take place, of course, despite the difficulties. The adjustments provide some hints of the character and content of the underlying calculations. They appear in abundant variety: escalator clauses of all sorts—in wage contracts and in contracts for materials, components, construction, and rents; variable-rate mortgages and bonds; "equity kickers" in loan contracts; variable-annuity type pensions; the shortening of the term of contracts; renegotiation of long-term contracts already in force; the introduction of different first-, second-, and sometimes also third-year wages, in labor-management contracts; the use of alternatives to price, wage, or interest rate increases (especially when the option to make such increases is foreclosed) such as changes in other terms—credit, delivery, compensating balances, tied sales, fringe benefits; the postponement of payment when the conventional discount for prompt payment or the penalty for delay becomes obsolete; the speed-up in money velocity. The list is endless, reflecting as it does the ingenuity and enterprise of people anxious to protect themselves from the ravages of inflation or to profit from the opportunities they see inflation opening up for them. But we know little about the present extent of these forms of adjustment and how quickly they have spread.

It would be particularly interesting to survey the different efforts to use escalator clauses and determine how these have changed in character and extent as inflation has continued and accelerated. We know something about the number of labor-management contracts that include cost of living escalators. Concerning other contracts, such as materials and construction, however, we know little more than that they exist, and that the particular price indices used vary widely. The question—why escalator clauses have been so few, even in wage contracts, and even today, in this country —is puzzling.

"Escalation," as a general policy now being rather widely discussed, deserves a word here. One question concerns the relation between the proposal to make financial reports in units of general purchasing power, and the proposal for general income and debt escalation. The two are not quite the same, but the difference is not clear to many people and it needs to be spelled out. There are other questions about escalation that would be interesting to pursue in a thorough discussion of economic calculation under inflation. For example, there is a question about the risks of escalation—in the case of wage contracts, the risk to the wage-earner if stability of real wages comes to be regarded as desirable even when productivity is rising; the risk to the employer and consumer if the stability of real wages comes to be tolerated even when national productivity declines.* And one can only speculate on what the distribution of national income would look like—during the period of adjustment and afterward—if escalator clauses were introduced on a comprehensive scale, as some economists have been proposing.

XI

Recently the Financial Accounting Standards Board published its Discussion Memorandum presenting and analyzing the issues related to "Reporting the Effects of General Price-Level Changes in Financial Statements." The issues I have listed, and more I have not, are all covered in the Board's comprehensive review. The only exceptions are those issues in my list that would be raised by economists viewing the

---

* I say "national" productivity advisedly. The relation between wages in an industry, on the one hand, and the industry's productivity and national productivity, on the other, is not well understood. The subject is not entirely outside our area of concern. It is important in incomes policies and therefore enters wage calculations and negotiations when incomes policies are being followed and even when they only appear in the offing.

problem of inflation accounting strictly from a social stand-point.

A public hearing by the Board was held on the subject in April 1974, and at year-end 1974 the Board published an Exposure Draft of its proposed statement of financial accounting standards, "Financial Reporting in Units of General Purchasing Power." With this Exposure Draft the Board revealed its decisions on the accounting issues— subject only to its second thoughts in the light of further discussion. The Board proposed to require financial reports in units of general purchasing power as supplements to con-ventional reports. Change in general purchasing power is to be measured by change in the GNP Implicit Price De-flator on the ground that it is the most comprehensive index available. Current income, measured in units of general purchasing power, is to include the gains (or losses)—also in terms of general purchasing power—from the holding of monetary assets (or liabilities). Gains or losses on non-monetary assets and liabilities are to be reflected (implic-itly) in the determination of income only when the non-monetary items are charged or credited to income—for example, when plant is depreciated or sold. Current value accounting, then, is put aside; it is to be considered at a later date in another project now on the Board's agenda.

The issues will not be closed, of course, by the decisions set forth by the Board. We may expect many differences of opinion to be conveyed to the Board before the period for public comment on the Exposure Draft ends—comments on the choice of deflator, the postponement of a decision on current value accounting, the cut-off date selected (one of the issues I did not mention), the decision to update

("roll forward") successive annual statements, the incon-
sistencies that will arise between successive annual statements because of revision by the Department of Commerce
of its GNP Deflator, and still others of large or small moment. Later, experience with the application of the new
principles will undoubtedly stimulate still other discussion
and controversy.

This conference of ours, coming as it does at a propitious
moment in the move to modernize "generally accepted
accounting principles," can contribute to the discussion of
the technical issues involved.

Perhaps we can do more. The problem of business accounting and business financial statements under inflation
is important. However, business is not the only sector of the
economy in which accounting problems arise under inflation. Nor is accounting the only kind of economic calculation. We may serve also if we set the problem in an
economic, social, and political context wider than is usual.
This, at any rate, has been my objective.

To conclude: The problem of rational economic calculation in an era of inflation raises many issues. Some of the
issues involved are of very real substance, and also complicated; research is needed for their resolution or clarification.
Some are of real substance but not important, although
what is "material" depends on the circumstances and one's
point of view.* Some are only the result of misunderstanding
or ignorance of what the experts agree on. All, however,

---

* During World War II there was widespread complaint about the accuracy
of the Consumer Price Index, which was being used under the "Little Steel
Formula" to adjust money wages for the wartime inflation. An estimate
was therefore made by a government committee of the bias in the index.
The published estimate of the correction factor had subsequently to be

require education of the public. On the people's understanding or misunderstanding of the issues depends, in significant degree, the kind of society in which all of us will be working and living in the years ahead.

---

revised, however, when a "rounding error" in it was discovered under the close scrutiny to which the estimate was subjected by all parties concerned. Had not the "trivial" error been corrected, something on the order of a hundred million dollars more per year would have gone into the pay envelopes of workers, and a corresponding amount would have been taken out of the income of employers.

Bibliography

References in the text are to the following publications:

Accounting Principles Board. Statement No. 4. "Basic Concepts and Accounting Principles Underlying Financial Statements of Business Enterprises," October 1970.

Burns, Arthur F. "The Menace of Inflation," Address at the 141st Commencement Exercises, Illinois College, May 26, 1974.

Financial Accounting Standards Board. FASB Discussion Memorandum, "Reporting the Effects of General Price-Level Changes in Financial Statements," February 15, 1974.

Financial Accounting Standards Board. Exposure Draft, "Proposed Statement of Financial Accounting Standards, Financial Reporting in Units of General Purchasing Powers," December 31, 1974.

Hayek, F. A. "The Use of Knowledge in Society," *American Economic Review,* September 1945. Reprinted in A. Klaasen (ed.), *The Invisible Hand,* 1965.

Hobson, John A. *The Evolution of Modern Capitalism,* rev. ed., 1926.

Keynes, J. M. *The Economic Consequences of the Peace,*

1920, pp. 235–7. Reprinted in *Essays in Persuasion,* 1931.

Lent, George E. "Adjustment of Taxable Profits for Price Changes," International Monetary Fund, Fiscal Affairs Department, multigraph, December 31, 1974.

Mises, Ludwig von. "Die Wirtschaftsrechnung im sozialistischen Gemeinwesen," *Archiv für Sozialwissenschaften,* 1920; translated by S. Adler and reprinted as "Economic Calculation in the Socialist Commonwealth," in F. A. Hayek (ed.), *Collectivist Economic Planning,* 1935.

Mitchell, W. C., S. Kuznets, and M. G. Reid. "Report of the Technical Committee Appointed by the Chairman of the President's Committee on the Cost of Living, June 15, 1944," in Office of Economic Stabilization, *Report of the President's Committee on the Cost of Living,* 1945. Reference is to p. 295, footnote 17.

Mitchell, Wesley C. "The Role of Money in Economic History," *Journal of Economic History,* 1944, Supplement. Reprinted in F. C. Lane and J. C. Riemersma (eds.), *Enterprise and Secular Change,* 1953.

Moore, Geoffrey H. "Slowdowns, Recessions and Inflation: Some Issues and Answers," National Bureau of Economic Research, Xerox, January 20, 1975, to be published in *Explorations in Economic Research.*

Price Waterhouse International. *Accounting Principles and Reporting Practices, A Survey in 38 Countries,* 1973.

Schwartz, Anna J. "Secular Price Change in Historical Perspective," *Journal of Money, Credit and Banking,* February 1973.

Sombart, Werner. *Der Moderne Kapitalismus,* 2nd ed.,

1916, translated and reprinted in part in Lane and Riemersma.

Weber, Max. *General Economic History,* translated by F. H. Knight, 1927.

A few portions of the text have been drawn from the following writings of the author:

"Inflation and the Lag in Accounting Practice," in R. R. Sterling and W.F. Bentz (eds.), *Accounting in Perspective,* 1971.

"Inflation Accounting: Issues for Research," in National Bureau of Economic Research, *54th Annual Report,* September 1974.

"The Problem of Controlling Inflation," paper at the November 11, 1974, meeting of the Academy of Political Science and the Lehrman Institute, Columbia University, New York City. [To be published in the proceedings of the meeting.]

Response

My interest in the measurement problems resulting from continuing devaluation of our monetary unit, the dollar, has long been centered in the area of business accounting and financial reporting. In this field the impact of inflation has been almost entirely ignored in actual practice, despite pretensions by the American Institute of Certified Public Accountants, and other organizations, as to the progress being made by the profession in recent decades. There has been much discussion of the subject, especially in academic circles, but to date no substantial steps have been taken to improve accounting measurements and procedures. Accountants continue to "certify" that the conventional financial statements of corporations and other business concerns are valid, without even mentioning their serious limitations. The financial press, as well as newspapers generally, accepts the findings of the accountants as gospel, and gives them wide publicity, often with considerable exaggeration added. And government regulatory agencies, usually not noted for a friendly attitude toward corporate managements and stockholders, as well as groups openly hostile to private business enterprise, go along with the parade of misrepresentation. Without doubt, moreover, many executives and investors are themselves confused and misled by the diet of data fed to them by the accountants, including the professional CPAs.

This situation in accounting is nothing short of a statistical scandal. In no other major area of economic measurement, I might add, do we find such complete neglect of the impact of inflation.

In any examination of this matter there are a few elementary truths that should be recognized, in laying a foundation for systematic study.

1. A summation of unlike monetary units, even of the same name, is a misrepresentation. It's the same kind of error as would result from regarding centimeters and inches as like units of linear measure. Thus one 1960 dollar plus one 1975 dollar is not two of anything. In a record of dollars entered into the accounts over a period of years, the *dates* must be taken into consideration as well as the money numbers or amounts. Advocates of adherence to the "cost basis" generally overlook this plain truth. Determination of "actual cost," where such information is desired, obviously requires the conversion of a series of dated dollars into like units before combining. As a practical matter, in such determinations, use of the current dollar is usually preferable as the common denominator.

2. Costs of resources incurred over a period of time, even when properly computed, should be regarded as primary, basic measurements in business accounting. It is *values* with which we are dealing. A cost figure is important only because—and when—it is a reasonable expression of mar-

ket value when incurred. As time passes the recorded amount loses significance in the face of change in the market value of the particular item, or its equivalent (after taking into consideration any loss in value through the passage of time since acquisition). This point is of great importance in resource utilization. It should be plain that in the field of planning it is the present *value* of a piece of property, not what it cost, that is significant. Right here we find an outstanding weakness in property management, fostered by the stone wall of prejudice in accounting circles against any form of recognition of current values, except in the case of decreases. The accountant is eager to subtract but he abhors adding. In my own experience I have encountered many situations where the corporate officers, and directors, were tied in their thinking to recorded figures and had no information whatever regarding the current values of such important assets as land holdings, standing timber, and other natural resources. Some accountants balk at including current market values of securities owned in financial statements, if higher than the recorded cost, even when the "appreciation" of the holdings is a major factor in financial position. We find the same stubborn opposition to economic reality in the ignoring of increases in value of goods due to aging—and there are many other examples.

3. In an inflationary period the strict adherence to recorded dollars tends to result in a pattern of overstated net earnings (profits) and understated resources employed. This is particularly true of enterprises that require large investments in long-lived plant and equipment, as in the case of a producer and distributor of electric power, or a telephone company.

4. The most significant general measurement in judging

the progress of an enterprise is *earning power,* not dollars of sales, or changes in the dollar amount of net income. Earning power, of course, is represented by the earning *rate,* namely, the percentage of net income, properly computed, to the *current value* of the employed resources. Under present-day accounting procedure and financial reporting this basic measurement is almost never determined or even mentioned. (One important company that did include a careful finding of the rate of return, as just defined, year after year in its annual reports has abandoned the practice —the board of directors didn't like it and finally overruled the chief executive.) The CPAs who certify to the soundness of corporate statements almost never refer to this basic test of progress or decline. Nowadays management crows about an increase in reported dollar profits as a percentage of total sales, and complains about a decrease in this rate, although this test, ignoring the change in employed resources and stockholder equity, properly measured, is often worse than meaningless.

5. One of the persistent and serious fallacies almost universally accepted by accountants is the view that a dollar of cash in the bank (or on hand) is a resource that doesn't change in value. Actually in a period of inflation, being heavily loaded with cash can be a very bad situation. I was on the board of directors of a large company for a dozen years, and this was before dollar devaluation had achieved the current momentum. It took me six years to get the treasurer— raised as a banker—to stop bragging at our monthly meetings about increases in holdings of cash or equivalent. Undoubtedly many billions in purchasing power have been lost by American corporations in recent decades because of the fetish that a very high current ratio is a great blessing.

They should remember that in the "Great Depression" cash increases were common among companies that weren't earning a dime. A factor in this development was the stopping of construction programs and reduction in maintenance expenditures. In a time of serious inflation the ideal position to strive for—in general—is a holding of cash and equivalent not in excess of short-term liabilities, as in this position the loss in the purchasing power of cash is offset at the expense of current creditors.

Almost never, in published statements, do we find even a mention of the actual loss (or gain) incurred on the monetary holdings and offsetting debts. Most accountants have never even heard of the problem, and most managements have a blind spot here. Long since the practice should have been started of presenting a systematic schedule dealing with this important financial factor, as an attachment to the income statement. Here, of course, use of a general index, reflecting the overall change in the purchasing power of the dollar, should be employed.

Is a net monetary loss or gain, soundly computed, realized? There has been some argument on this point among the handful who have given any attention to the matter. I'll only say here that I regard a loss in buying power for a period, resulting from holdings of cash resources in excess of short-term debt, as fully realized, regardless of future developments.

6. Closely related to the problem outlined in (5) is the impact of inflation on long-term debt. In these days, with gold clauses in bond contracts a thing of the past, and liabilities in general payable in current dollars, lenders are subject to heavy losses. Should the borrower, in this situation, recognize the gain achieved at the creditor's expense?

This is an interesting question. One thing is certain: the sure losers in a sustained inflationary era are those with claims payable in dollars, and borrowing is one of the best hedges against loss that is available. In the case of interest payments, an actual gain from period to period is realized by the debtor as the dollar is debased, and ideally this should be recognized, especially in setting up complete comparative financial data, in common dollars. The accrued gain on the maturity amount should also be disclosed in such statements but should be treated as a favorable but unrealized improvement in financial position.

With the sharp advance in interest rates in recent years the current lender is in an improved position relative to the effect of inflation, but the effect upon creditors in the case of long-term liabilities issued before the upward surge in rates, with due dates far in the future, has been disastrous. As we all know, "high-grade" bond and note issues, with distant maturities, are quoted every day at prices as low or even lower than half the number of dollars invested by the lender, and he suffers an additional accrued loss in that the currently quoted prices are in dollars of much less purchasing power than the dollars loaned. The borrower, in such cases, is in a happy position as to periodic interest payments, and is presented with an opportunity, if he has funds to spare, to retire the debt by "purchase" on the market. At least a partial deterrent to such action is found in the very factor that gives rise to the opportunity—the current high level of interest rates to be earned on available funds.

7. I hardly need to add that failure to take the fall in the value of the dollar into account is particularly objectionable where comparisons are made in financial reports,

either as issued by business concerns, or as copied in financial journals or elsewhere, covering several years, including
cases where the data cover a decade or more. Comparative
columnar presentations and charts showing such data as
sales, operating expenses, net earnings, cash holdings,
dividends, retained earnings, and so on, in recorded dollars, without conversion to a common denominator, are
sheer misstatements, not worth the paper they are printed
on.

In conclusion, I want to emphasize my view that accountants have failed miserably to do the job that has been lying
right in their laps. Long since the accountant should have
added the role of "measurement man" in financial reporting
to his other chores. Instead he has been moving more and
more in the direction of a regimented clerk, pushed that way
by professional officialdom and government regulatory
agencies, notably the Securities and Exchange Commission.
Queries: Is the accountant going to continue downhill until
he is stripped of all hallmarks of the true professional, including judgment, initiative, and ability to cope with complex and difficult problems? And is the Financial Accounting
Standards Board going to go along with this trend, or try
to save him from complete subservience to a detailed book
of directives and rules?

I have taken the liberty of outlining my views before
commenting directly upon Professor Fabricant's excellent
paper. This I will now do, briefly.

Solomon Fabricant is almost alone among American
economists in his thoroughgoing understanding of business
accounting and reporting. Wesley Clair Mitchell explicitly
recognized the importance of accounting, as did my mentor
Fred M. Taylor—and Irving Fisher had a glimmer. But

in my judgment Fabricant is outstanding in this respect, among prominent academic economists in this country, past or present.

His paper covers the seminar topic broadly, interestingly, clearly, and I have little to offer by way of critical comment. In my field of special interest he at least touches on almost every phase of importance, excepting perhaps the measurement of *earning power*. To me the ratio of investor net earnings, carefully computed, to the *current value* of employed resources is the most important financial measurement in business accounting. He discusses the impact of inflation on liabilities such as bonds very briefly, from the standpoint of the lender's accounting, and only mentions the related problems of the debtor. The determination and interpretation of gain by the debtor on long-term borrowings resulting from dollar devaluation present difficulties, and this fact deserves emphasis.

Professor Fabricant brings out very clearly the distinction between adjustment of accounts and reports through application of a general price level index and "current value accounting." Basically, as I understand it, Professor Fabricant favors going all the way. I heartily agree with this position. I also agree that taking the first step is worthwhile (and especially appropriate when dealing with the monetary assets and current liabilities).

Although the subject should perhaps be viewed as outside the scope of Professor Fabricant's topic, I still wish he had touched on causes and culprits—at least to the extent of placing the major responsibility for the devaluation of the dollar squarely on the shoulders of our central government, and set in motion by the abandonment of the gold standard.

Response

Paul Grady

A few years back I was asked to review for an audience in Florida, the developments in accountancy over the past fifty years. I told them the record hadn't been as bad as they might think from reports by the media, and that the greatest failure, in my view, was the failure to require presentation of supplemental financial statements in units of stable purchasing power. Doctor Fabricant has referred to some of the efforts which fell short of that goal, such as the "Study Group on Business Income" (1952), "Accounting Research Studies 1, 3 and 6" (early 1960s), and the Accounting Principles Board "Statement No. 3" (1969), recommending but not requiring supplementary statements disclosing the effect of changes in the general price level on published financial statements.

A look at the selected bibliography to the "Accounting Research Study No. 6" identifies the following accountants as proponents of price level adjustments (as gleaned from memory and the subjects of their articles): Baxter, Bedford, Blackie, Bows, Broad, Brundage, Chambers, Corbin, Davidson, Dohr, Grady, Graham, Higgins, Jones, McAny, Mac-Neill, Mason, May, Moonitz, Paton, Peloubet, Saunders, Spacek, Sprouse, Stans, and Sweeney. I do not want the history of the price level problem to conclude that the preceding team was lacking in persuasiveness. Therefore, I should like to remind you of some of the factors which caused the accounting profession's reluctance and tardiness to deal with price level changes.

You will recall that the boom and speculative excesses of the 1920s were followed by a worldwide depression in the 1930s. In every "bust" resulting from political and economic mistakes, politicians must find villains and whipping boys to blame. In the United States, with the advent of FDR and the New Deal, Herbert Hoover was the political villain and the bankers and public utility holding company systems were the whipping boys. Pecora and other investigators put on circuses tuned to the media of radio and newspapers. Naturally some abuses were disclosed and the securities acts and Securities Exchange Commission came into existence to protect the investing public. Revaluations of fixed assets to reflect present values by utilities and some industrial companies received intensive criticism in these proceedings. The critics ignored the fact that "fair value" of properties devoted to public service, based on cost of reproduction, less observed depreciation, was the rate base established in U.S. Supreme Court decisions of that time. Later, as the depression hung on, some industrial companies got the bright idea of writing off all investment in fixed assets and thus putting an end to depreciation charges. The criticism arising from these two developments caused the accounting profession to become firmly wedded to historical cost as the safest bomb shelter available. (Actually, in my opinion, appraisals were no more a causative factor in the boom and bust of the securities market of 1929 than was pooling accounting to the more recent boom and bust in securities of conglomerates. Both became handy whipping boys.)

Historical cost of fixed assets of utilities was not a sufficiently low figure to satisfy the New Deal regulatory agencies. So, original cost to the first owner was invented in the code of accounts of the Federal Power Commission and other regulatory agencies. The wording of the codes and stipulations of witnesses for the commission should have preserved all elements of true corporate cost. However, in the actual implementation, upward adjustments, for the same company, were disallowed as "re-accounting" and downward adjustments were insisted upon as essential corrections of errors. Thus we had "original cost" resulting from "original cost or recorded cost, whichever is lower."

The "Income Study Group" report recommended dealing only with income adjustments for depreciation and inventories. This was regarded as a simplified way of reserving from earning sufficient charges to measure erosion of purchasing power invested in these items. George O. May, the director of the study, believed it was not politically feasible to expect a government to accept or permit full price level adjustment information and thus reveal the swindle involved in the sale and taxation of interest on monetary bonds issued in a period of inflation. It may be significant that the principal dissenters to the study group's recommendations were economists for labor unions and accountants then or previously identified with government agencies.

Other reasons for the reluctance of most practicing accountants to promote price level adjustments were:

1. The view that inflation was not sufficiently material at that time.

2. The natural inertia toward undertaking complicated computations necessary to translate price level changes.

3. The reluctance to meet and overcome objections of clients to the expense involved in price level adjustments and to the reporting of less favorable operating results.

The arrival and continuance of double digit inflation in the 1970s have outmoded the belief expressed by the Accounting Principles Board in 1969 that "general price level information is not required for fair presentation of financial position and results of operation in conformity with generally accepted accounting principles in the United States." It seems clear that the majority of accountants now support the mandatory position proposed by the Financial Accounting Standards Board. It remains to be seen whether there will be serious objections from labor unions, government agencies and Congress.

Dr. Fabricant has given a very broad perspective of the problem of economic calculation under inflation. Since I can add little to the technical aspects of such calculations, the broad approach encourages me to make a few remarks in exploring what must be done to get us out of this squirrel cage of spiraling inflation. The public identifies the problem as one of rising prices caused by the avarice or incompetence of business, whereas we know it is the age-old process of "clipping the coins," or the erosion in the purchasing power of money due to the fiscal irresponsibility of the government. Picket lines of protest have surrounded the supermarkets, whereas they should surround the Congress, the White House, and the Federal Reserve Board— with the clear message that integrity and reasonable stability in purchasing power of money must be restored.

The critical question is whether a government such as ours can return to fiscal responsibility after forty years of uncontrolled spending in catering to voting groups seeking greater rewards than their needs or willingness to work justifies. President Kennedy coined a catchy phrase to say that the government is supported by its people and not the reverse. However, the actions and legislative policies of the government have led too many of the population to the opposite conclusion. The headlines and commentators in the media make it loud, if not clear, that quick solutions are expected of Congress and the President to end both the recession and the concurrent inflation.

I can well remember conversations with George O. May at the time of the passage of the federal "Full Employment Act." It was our conclusion then that implementation of the concepts contained in that legislation necessarily created the machinery for continuous inflation. Leadership must be found in the Congress and the presidency with the political courage to bring the spending programs within the limits that can be supported by the productive capacity of our country.

The government must be willing to review and curtail the regulation of industry. The annual cost and burden on productivity of the harassment and red tape imposed by hundreds of government agencies on business would total billions of dollars. The ICC has practically strangled the railroads, the utilities are not far behind, and in recent years the zealots of regulation have disrupted automobile production with required changes and gadgets so that a large part of the public now has more confidence in their older cars and will not buy the new ones. This is a major cause of the current depression in the United States.

The trend to overregulation and extension of government

spending programs in all directions has resulted in building entrenched bureaucracies of tremendous size. It is estimated that one in five of employed persons in the United States works for the federal, state or local government. A very high percentage of the bureaucrats are protected by Civil Service, and this body constitutes a most powerful political lobby, second only to the national labor unions. Presidents, cabinet members and members of Congress may come and go and the bureaucrats know they can outlast them. Therefore, they can and do ignore their wishes and even their commands if they do not agree with them.

Over the years, programs of "grants in aid" and "sharing of revenues" have grown in popularity and magnitude so that federal, state and local governments participate in joint programs for spending the taxpayers' tributes. This entire procedure should be investigated from stem to stern and curtailed or eliminated as a fiscal procedure. The scheme destroys the fixing of responsibilities for the justification of a project and for the way the money is spent. It also causes the proliferation of bureaucracies and red tape at all three levels of government. The merit and cost of domestic water and sewer projects, for example, can be better judged by government officials, taxpayers and voters in the local community if they see the physical development and pay the entire cost rather than have the money of their citizens disguised and recycled through the federal and state governments.

In the sunshine and blue skies of Florida, I wish I could tell you that there is discernible evidence that we have or can produce the leadership in government to reconsider and make the hard and courageous decisions to deal with the matters mentioned, the energy problem and many more. Perhaps a ray of hope can be seen in a remark by Senator Hubert Humphrey at a seminar held last month at Georgetown University. He stated that anyone who expects Congress to step in and run the government is going to be disappointed. "Congress," he said, "can't even run the Senate restaurant." If we knew the deficit of that restaurant, we would undoubtedly agree but, at the same time, it is probably no worse, relatively, than the operating results of the entire government. If other members of the Congress and the administration were equally frank, perhaps the people would shrink their expectations and reliance on government to realistic levels. If this could happen, accompanied with a better public and governmental understanding and renewal of faith in the strength and vigor of our competitive private enterprise system, then we might say with confidence that "the sky isn't falling" and that we can get back on the track of fiscal responsibility and solvency. Wouldn't that be a pleasant dream?

Participation in the two price level seminars in recent months has caused me to question the usefulness of the fully translated supplemental financial statements as contemplated by the FASB Exposure Draft.

Investment analysts and securities dealers present at the seminars stated that investors would not attempt to read or understand the statements; they will continue to rely on simplified data such as the historical earnings per share and market tips and forecasts by brokers.

Unfortunately, the public reaction to inflation confuses cause and effect. The blame is placed on rising prices, the symptom of the disease, rather than on destruction of monetary purchasing power, which is the disease. Picket lines of protest at the supermarkets are at the wrong places; they should be at Congress, the White House, and the Federal Reserve Board.

In the Inventory of Generally Accepted Accounting Principles published ten years ago, the first basic concept was said to be "a society and government structure honoring private property rights." The discussion in that section deals briefly with the extension of government activities and regulation of business and the possible serious impact on the so-called free enterprise system. If this section were being written today, I think I would have to say that the U. S. federal government has a de facto program of continuous reduction in the purchasing power of money. The program is evidenced by the magnitude of the continuous budgetary deficits, the increasing volume of transfer payments to large segments of the population under welfare and medicaid, and the promotion of lavish public works and other less useful programs by state and local governments through grants-in-aid and so-called revenue sharing. The complexity of this subsidy system destroys any possibility of internal control and identification of responsibility at any level of government. The entire scheme has caused government bureaucracy to become our primary growth industry, employing one fifth of the working population.

Historical accounting is based on the premise of reasonable integrity of the monetary system. In the hundred years when we enjoyed the benefits of the gold standard and the British Navy, such a premise was valid, but it is no longer tenable in the prevailing circumstances. Under historical dollar accounting, business managements and the accounting profession adopted procedures to reasonably assure the identification of the dollar capital invested in the enterprise by equity stockholders, consisting of funds or property paid in as well as retained earnings. Such procedures applied to asset and liability accounts and especially to the determination of periodic revenues, expenses and net earnings.

Under current circumstances, the monetary premise must be changed to recognize the program of continuous and planned reduction of the purchasing power of the dollar. Under this premise, business managements and the accounting profession should reorient accounting procedures, within the historical framework, in order to assure the identification of the purchasing power of the capital invested in the enterprise by equity stockholders. It is obvious that losses in the purchasing power of invested equity capital should be restored by charges to income prior to determination of net earnings and "earnings per share" for any given year. The portion of the capitalization represented by fixed dollar debt or redemption values requires no similar provisions and, in effect, represents a hedge against the inflation losses for that part of the invested capital.

Modification of historical accounting in this fashion will make it unnecessary to perform and present the complicated translations contemplated in the supplemental price-level adjusted statements. In my opinion, it is a much more direct and simple method of dealing with inflation. I would suggest the following captions for dealing with the annual charge and with the capital restoration account:

Last item in income statement before determination of net earnings for period.

"Federal Inflation Tax" (representing loss in purchasing power of equity capital invested in the business, which occurred during year)

The balance sheet should show the following cumulative item in the equity capital section.

"Purchasing-power losses of equity capital, restored by charges against income for periods since————*."

I believe it is safe to speculate that the accounting treatment and presentation suggested above *will* attract the attention of the investing public. It might also penetrate the ever spreading government bureaucracy and even the Congress, and, I feel certain, it would aid the Federal Reserve Board in its struggle for independence in keeping the growth of money supply to single digit rather than double digit inflation.

An argument may be made that in the case of capital invested in depreciable assets, the inflation loss should be spread over the lives of the assets. My own strong preference is to recognize the losses in purchasing power as they occur and leave depreciation to amortize the historical dollar investment. This viewpoint causes a minimum change in the basic concepts and procedures of accounting and leaves it really "historical accounting," because the steady erosion of equity capital through inflation is a painful part of the history of the past 35 years. In the case of senior capital, the impact of inflation losses rests on individual investors rather than on the business accounting entity.

Method of Determining Inflation Tax

This computation is a very simple matter, especially when compared with the numerous translations required

---

* This date is assumed to be a selected starting point such as 1945, 1955 or 1965.

by the FASB Exposure Draft. The selected inflation index should be applied to the invested equity capital base after reductions for the investments in LIFO inventories and land. This assumes that circumstances will support the proposition that these items are reasonably immune to the erosion of inflation. Depreciable plant assets are excluded from this category because they are on the way to the "scrap heap" and there is no good reason to postpone recognition of the inflation loss.

A pragmatic selection of a starting date has to be made for any system of purchasing power accounting or measurements. It seems to me, as a minimum, the date should be early enough to cover the inflation associated with the Vietnam war, which suggests 1960.

Present Value

Support seems to be building for present value accounting as an alternative to cost based accounting. It is, of course, feasible to determine present values, at least quoted values, for marketable securities, the current values of inventories and even the estimated current values of land. However, I cannot see any useful purpose in attempting to determine the current values for the depreciable structures and equipment of industrial enterprises.

Such subjective valuations, however defined, would be a return to the appraisal era of the 1920s which brought down so much criticism of industry and the accounting profession in the New Deal reform era of the 1930s.

At a recent price level seminar, an officer of U.S. Steel Corporation said that studies showed it would cost, at today's construction prices, an amount equal to the total market value of the company's common stock to increase its productive plant capacity 10 percent. Does this suggest that present value of the existing plant facilities might be five to ten times the total market value of the common stock? This question is posed as a brief way to illustrate the reason for my distrust of anyone's ability to determine a useful or dependable present value of complex industrial plant facilities.

Relationship of Accelerated Depreciation Investment Credits and Income Tax Allocation to the Federal Inflation Tax

During the 1950s, certain industry associations retained Maurice Peloubet, Leslie Mills and me to assist them in presenting before the appropriate committees of Congress the serious impact of inflation on their ability to maintain productive plant capacities. This problem arose, of course, due to the wide gap between the funds provided, if earned, from cost depreciation allowances and the cost of replacement of facilities. It soon became evident that the committees were unfavorable to allowances of depreciation adjusted for price level changes. They were somewhat more interested but would not support a form of LIFO adjustment at the time plant facilities were replaced. The presentations did cause committee members to realize the seriousness of the matter and resulted in allowance of accelerated depreciation and ultimately investment credits. In this fashion, the Congress has recognized a relation between the corporation income tax, which in itself is a double tax on stockholders, and the unrecorded federal inflation tax.

In the event that the suggestions on restoration of purchasing power losses of equity capital should be adopted, income tax allocations related to long-term plant amortization differences should be terminated, and the substantial credit balances arising from this source in prior periods should be used to offset, to that extent, the purchasing power losses of equity capital subsequent to the selected starting point. As a matter of fact, the pragmatic and political nature of legislation establishing income tax allowances probably invalidates the reasoning behind the requirement for allocation between periods in regard to these long-term differences.

If a concluding thought is in order to this essay, it is an observation that it is very late in the time scale of inflation for the accounting profession to find an adequate method of dealing with the problem. In my opinion, it is too late for the footnote and supplemental statements outlined in the FASB Exposure Draft to have any effectiveness. The approach suggested herein is a simple short-cut method of measuring in the historical accounts, on a timely basis, the unhedged erosion of inflation suffered by the business entity due to the inherent time lags involved in the turnover of assets. Let us hope that in FASB we have found the proper organization for meeting this most difficult problem with wisdom, independence and courage.

Response

George Terborgh

I find myself in cordial agreement with the general thrust of Dr. Fabricant's paper, since both of us have been preaching the same gospel for years. This means that my comments will be limited to the amplification of some points on which we are in agreement, and to dissent on a few others where we disagree.

I agree heartily with the contention that the federal government is remiss in the reporting of corporate profits. It makes no adjustment whatever for underdepreciation, and it applies the inventory valuation adjustment only to *pre-tax* profits, leaving *after-tax* profits on retained earnings uncorrected. As a result, the publicly quoted figures for the latter are grossly overstated.

For 1974, my preliminary estimate for corporate underdepreciation and inventory revaluation combined comes to $47.5 billion. If we correct reported pre-tax profits by this figure, we reduce them by 34 percent. But the same correction reduces after-tax profits by 62 percent, and retained earnings by 90 percent. Obviously, the reported figures for these series are worthless. Yet they are solemnly published quarter by quarter, without a word of warning.

It is eminently desirable that the Department of Commerce add an estimate of underdepreciation to the inventory valuation adjustment, and that both be carried through to after-tax profits and retained earnings. But even if it does not adjust depreciation, it should certainly carry through the IVA. Both the economic and the accounting professions should join in vigorous representations to this end.

I should like next to comment on Dr. Fabricant's statements about accelerated depreciation. He believes that the acceleration of the depreciation write-off now allowed by the Internal Revenue Code yields an accrual in excess of a realistic historical cost recovery, and that this excess constitutes a partial offset for the missing inflation adjustment.

There are two components of the present acceleration: faster write-off methods, and shortened service lives. Since it is not clear which one is referred to, or whether both are included, I shall say a few words on each.

I have long supported the view that straight-line depreciation yields in general a grievously retarded write-off of the investment, and that the accelerated methods now permitted for tax purposes, double-declining-balance and sum-of-digits, are broadly realistic. This is no place to argue the case, but I should like to express the hope that Dr. Fabricant's observations do not imply a commitment to the straight-line method.

In saying that the accelerated write-offs are broadly realistic, I assume their application over the full service lives of depreciating assets. This brings me to the second factor mentioned. With the guideline life system, introduced in

1962, as supplemented in 1971 by asset depreciation ranges, it is true that in general tax depreciation lives are substantially shorter than actual lives. It is this fact, not the use of accelerated write-off methods, that yields the overstatement of historical cost depreciation.

It constitutes, however, a relatively small offset to the missing inflation adjustment. On the basis of Department of Commerce estimates, the current-cost depreciation of non-financial corporations, computed by the full-life application of the double-declining-balance write-off, is currently exceeding their historical cost tax depreciation by about $15 billion a year. This is a tremendous shortfall, dwarfing the offset under discussion.

While this offset to underdepreciation is good as far as it goes, I am unable to accept what Dr. Fabricant describes as "a more subtle and perhaps more powerful offset" arising from technological advances in productive equipment. "This serves," he says, "to make current depreciation charges higher than the amount needed to maintain current capacity."

While he apparently takes no position on the issue, describing it as "one that merits more attention than it has received," what he finds involved is a difference between two points of view, the "social" and the "private." The implication is that from the social viewpoint the test of the adequacy of depreciation is whether its reinvestment will maintain a constant quantum of physical capacity.

This conference is concerned, of course, with the *private* viewpoint. What is the proper measure of depreciation for an individual firm? I submit that it is *the recovery of the investment in real terms*. This means, of course, the maintenance of the real capital if the funds recovered are reinvested. But the proper charge does not turn on the reinvestment. It is the same if the funds are withdrawn for consumption. In no case does it turn on the maintenance of a constant physical capacity.

Suppose a company puts $1 million into productive facilities subject to rapid technological obsolescence. It buys an annual capacity for 100,000 units of output. Five years later, $1 million will buy capacity for 300,000 units. Does this mean that the company's depreciation should be limited to one-third of its original investment? By no means. If it wants to know whether it has made a profit or a loss over the economic life of the facilities, it must charge the full amount.

Since we are not concerned here with "social" depreciation, I shall not go into it except to reject the implication that, unlike private depreciation, it can properly be determined by the maintenance-of-physical-capacity test. In my opinion this would result in gross underdepreciation even from a macroeconomic standpoint.

A word of comment on Dr. Fabricant's discussion of deflators to adjust corporate accounts for inflation. As he points out, all sorts of *specific* price indices have been suggested for different lines of business and for different uses of the corporate cash flow. The alternative is to use the same *general* index for all industries and for all purposes. He finds this "another issue that would warrant careful analysis."

I would not thus dignify it. In principle, the inflation adjustment should reflect what has happened, not to specific prices, but *to the dollar itself,* in terms of its general purchasing power over finished goods and services. *In practice,* moreover, this is almost a necessity. The adjustment of corporate accounts for inflation is complicated enough, in all conscience, without the use of a multiplicity of specific price indices. I agree wholly with the decision of the Financial Accounting Standards Board to employ a single general index for all adjustments. There are of course alternative general indices available, but at least we know what we are aiming at.

Dr. Fabricant's discussion of accrual versus realization accounting in inflation adjustments is both interesting and suggestive, especially his comments on the accounting for long-term monetary assets and liabilities proposed in the FASB Exposure Draft. The draft does not deal with the "inflation interest premium" and therefore does not integrate it into the calculation of "general purchasing power gains and losses." I agree with Dr. Fabricant that it should be taken into account.

Floor Discussion

Fabricant: I greatly appreciate George Terborgh's comments. I do not think there is as much difference between us as you may believe. One reason I think you interpreted me a little differently than I had in mind is that I was trying to avoid stating my own position. I was trying to present the issues as objectively as possible and it is only perhaps by implication or by emphasis that my own position, in fact, got in. But that, of course, means I wasn't as clear as I could have been, so let me be a little more explicit.

On accelerated depreciation, I do not mean that the straight-line method is good. I agree that it is not an efficient thing at all. As to the extent of the offset by accelerated depreciation, I did not mean to imply that there was a large offset. I was merely trying to report that some economists, and I think a lot more economists than accountants, take the position that accelerated depreciation has done the job, so why worry about inflation accounting?

I agree with you on the need for information on what

actually does happen by way of wear and tear and depreciation to different capital goods.

In the 1930s I wrote a book on capital consumption in which I tried to find as much as I could about that. Not much was available then and not much has been added since on the question.

As for the technological offset, some economists have taken the position that because of the changes in technology, etc., capacity is replaced at a much lower price. They are looking at the whole thing from the social point of view —that may not be the best word to use in that connection —they are looking at the entire economy as economists. They are not concerned with private accounting.

On the question of deflators, I was presenting various arguments that are found in discussions these days. I agree it would be a mess if we had more than one deflator. There is still a question as to which one it should be and there are some issues which are not resolved by saying it has to be general purchasing power over goods and services.

Terborgh: I am inclined to go for private GNP Deflator.

Fabricant: I tend to prefer that and I would prefer particularly the one with fixed weights to the Implicit Price Deflator. The trouble is it is not available all the way back and is not as well known. It becomes a practical problem. But there would be minor differences. I would therefore go along with the FASB on the Implicit Price Deflator.

Rogge: What is the difference between the private and the total GNP Deflator?

Fabricant: The total GNP includes an estimate for government operations and, therefore, when they get at the Implicit

Price Deflator, they are dealing with the total economy and that rather arbitrary accounting for government. It is arbitrary particularly in that the implicit price for government is way off the beam. It is assumed, for example, that there is absolutely no change in productivity in government workers. We may agree productivity in government has not grown as it might have but it would be foolish to say it has not grown at all. The Post Office uses motor cars and not horses and buggies. Delivery is not faster but you have to assess output in terms of obsolescence that has to be overcome. The government uses computer equipment, etc. It is foolish to say there has been no increase in productivity and, therefore, the assumption made in the national accounts is not valid.

Davidson: The English recommendation urges the private deflator rather than the GNP.

Baxter: That is right. The effective cost-of-living index rather than GNP. I think there is a justification for this in that it stresses the fact that you are trying to find out whether the human beings who own the enterprise are better off or not. But one could criticize the cost-of-living index on the grounds that it reflects all classes rather than the typical investor; maybe the accounting profession should be trying out a typical investor's index. One should find what a dollar means to a person and not some more arid statistical measure.

Rogge: I am sorry Paul Grady could not be here. Grady has a discussion of some of the reasons that allowed the accounting profession to turn to original cost in the 1930s and stick with it. That is extremely interesting, particularly his reference to the fact that because of the atmosphere of the day which was antagonistic to the entire utility industry and to the business community generally. It came to be interpreted that the rate base was to be original cost or reproduction cost, whichever was lower—whichever would permit them to have maximum leverage against the investors' interest. The accounting community and the business community that it serves were reluctant to move away from original cost in depreciation and elsewhere because of the fear it would lead to reporting of less favorable operating results. It is very difficult for officers of a corporation to announce to the general public that, in fact, their profits were much less than they might otherwise have reported them to be.

I want to ask Bill Paton for some of his early efforts to persuade business firms to make adjustments of this kind and the reasons they gave for rejecting.

Paton: I had an interesting experience while doing some work for Republic Steel in connection with two labor arbitration hearings. I sold Tom Patton, chief counsel at the time, and Charlie White, the president, who worked his way from a foundry hand to the top, on the idea that some attention should be given to the impact of the debasement of the dollar in their financial reporting. Joining forces we sold the officers of the company, and I concocted some illustrative supplementary statements. We did not propose that the conventional accounting followed should be revamped. We went to the Board of Directors and were turned down cold, largely because my calculations showed that in some recent years dividends had been declared and paid in excess of revised current net. Whether such payments impaired capital or not was a moot question, depending on how "capital" is defined. But the Board was afraid that their actions might be viewed as illegal, if our revised comparative figures were released.

This experience is illustrative of several experiences I've had.

George, you raised a lot of interesting questions. Nobody knows more than you about the weaknesses of government statistics. I was mad in 1963 when I read the first page of an issue of *The Survey of Current Business*. In presenting aggregate "profits" data in this summary page no mention was made of the fact that the figures used were "before taxes." Earlier the qualification was always attached. Now you have to do quite a bit of looking to find figures of "profits after taxes," in the detailed tables, in very small type.

Terborgh: We need a semantic improvement. It should be called taxable income instead of pre-tax profits and profits should be limited to what they are after taxes.

Paton: Drop the word profits. It is confusing.

Fabricant: Profit by definition, in the minds of many people, is something you should not get.

George, you did not mean to imply that when a fellow goes into an enterprise, he is guaranteed he will recover his investment?

Terborgh: I said if the company wants to know if it made a profit or loss, it has to charge the full cost and not the cost of its replacement.

Paton: In the private economy, there is a risk when you go into business and there has to be a general lure or you will not do it. But there is no guarantee. None of us would be in favor of that if we were private-enterprise people.

Fabricant: There is another point. When the price level rises, a person who owns his own home is making some kind of gain because the value of the house is going up. This income is confined, generally, to the cash income received. It will not include increments in the value of that house. If we follow some of the ideas that are being booted about to include capital gains realized or unrealized on assets, there will be a capital gain. And if it is included even when it isn't realized, the income of the older people who own their homes will be higher than we think it is.

You can't really decide what is happening to the economic position of anybody or any family or company if you look only at what they spend. You also have to look at what is happening to their assets and income and to their imputed income. For example, food stamps are an important source of income for many people in the United States and a growing source as you know from reading in the newspapers. That does not get into the conventional income figures because it is not in cash. You would have to impute an income there—make an estimate of the value of the contribution by government, that is, by all the other people in the population—to those who are benefiting from the food stamps. This will, I think, change the picture we get of the impact of inflation, which is our initial problem, on different income groups. Medical services would be another example.

Paton, Jr.: In other words, you are imputing to the consumer the rent in terms of current prices, but if you do not impute an equal amount of rental income to the owner of the house there will be a difference in the income.

Fabricant: That's beginning to get the idea. Incidentally, this prompts a general observation on my paper. One of the other objectives I had was to indicate problems, issues that deserve some further attention. This is one of the things that one can write a book on. A certain amount of discussion has already taken place in the economic literature, but not in the literature of accounting or public affairs. It is a mystery reserved to economists.

Sprouse: Ben, may I follow that up?

Rogge: Yes, please do, we have a number here who want to get in on this discussion, so let's go right ahead.

Sprouse: Sol, one of the important parts of your paper is the identification of issues that you have made, but there is one here that escapes me. I refer to the cut-off date, selected as being an issue.

Fabricant: You are talking about the Exposure Draft of the FASB. There is a cut-off date—I forget whether they used that term itself—you said, "Let's not go back in 1943." Do you remember that?

Sprouse: Yes.

Fabricant: Now, one can say, should it be 1946 or 1939, or should it be 1956, you know. I don't really know how important that issue is, but it would deserve a little attention.

Sprouse: Well, I don't want to miss any of the pearls in this paper. Thank you.

Rogge: Bill Fletcher and Sid Davidson want to get back in.

Fletcher: As the little old married couple pass beyond 65 and on into 70 and their house becomes worth more dollars but indeed the doors start sagging, the windows don't fit so well and things like that—do they, indeed, have a capital gain—do they, indeed, have income?

Fabricant: Well, probably with the example that you set, it isn't warranted, and I think we all agree that in assessing the capital gains you do have to take account of the condition of the home and the degree to which it has been maintained, what has happened to the neighborhood and so on.

Fletcher: Only if it is worth more dollars.

Fabricant: Well, I took for granted a reasonable amount of maintenance and I have already in my own implicit calculations allowed for obsolescence. I sold a house in which we lived for 25 or 30 years only a few years ago and it was obsolete in many ways, but had been reasonably well maintained and there was a considerable capital gain. Incidentally, I had to pay a hell of a whopping tax from which I haven't yet recovered. There were a lot of taxes on it from pure price level changes.

Fletcher: I think that is my point. Pure price level change does not equal income.

Terborgh: But suppose it is real appreciation—appreciation in excess of the price level change. Suppose it is well maintained.

Real capital appreciation unrealized isn't current income. It's an enhancement of the asset position of the couple, but doesn't do anything to their current income.

Carsberg: I was interested in George Terborgh's comments. I think the comments bring out the point that you have problems in accounting for the use of fixed assets even in a situation in which there is no general inflation.

If there is no general inflation, one ought to have a user cost depreciation charge combined with interest charge which would move more or less in step with the current cost of new assets of the type concerned. If you have assets which are increasing in real cost over time, then the imputed user cost would also increase over time. On the other hand, if the real cost of the assets is falling, then the computed user costs would also fall. The user charge might be more or less than the conventional accounting depreciation. I entirely agree with George Terborgh in saying that he should index the thing by the General Price Index which you can do either by increasing the depreciation charge or by increasing the money rate of interest charge in the new calculations.

Sprouse: Bryan, I understand your comment was for pricing purposes and not for income measurement necessarily.

Carsberg: Right, I think that should be emphasized here.

Sprouse: George was talking about income measurement, which is rather a different question.

Carsberg: It depends on why you want to measure income.

Rogge: That is one of the areas of confusion where many of us are hoping you'll set us straight as the session continues here. Is this a return of capital in terms of general purchasing power, or a return of capital in terms of dollars of some very specific kind of purchasing power, for example, to purchase telephone equipment. Is there one answer or a variety of answers to that kind of question? Again, Professor

Fabricant, your paper, excellent in so many ways, raises so many fundamental questions. How do you treat these differences between original cost, historical cost, and current value? How do you treat them, if at all, on the income statement, in terms of timing, in terms of quantity?

Fabricant: Let me make one comment—we can clarify our thinking on this question of general price level or purchasing power in terms of telephone equipment, by asking ourselves how we would handle the problem of changes in the price of the telephone equipment relative to other prices if there were no inflation? You still have that problem. No inflation. How would you handle it? I think if you think in those terms, on that assumption, you can begin to clarify the question and begin to get an answer to the question. I would agree with George and the others that when we are talking about general price level purchasing power, it is a single index for everybody. The question of telephone equipment or other individual kinds of price changes is an entirely different question, and is tied up with the question of obsolescence and technological change. Obviously, there are all kinds of tax and public utility regulation questions which involve various assumptions. But to clarify our thinking with regard to the question I started with, think of how you should be handling it, apart from regulations, utility regulations, if there were no inflation, and then I think we can begin to get the answer.

* * *

Fabricant: What is an appropriate fiscal period? Many years ago when I had juvenile notions about the regularity of the business cycle, I argued that the appropriate fiscal period for accounting, at least for national accounting, maybe also private accounting, was a business cycle—because it took account of fluctuations presumed to be fairly regular. Just as the calendar year is a reasonable fiscal period because it allows for the seasonal swing.

Well, the business cycle, which is still with us despite some people's thinking it had gone, I have come to learn isn't quite that regular. But there are problems about the length of the fiscal period which are very difficult and which it might be worthwhile talking about some time. There are related problems, of course—the treatment of what we used to call capital adjustments or surplus adjustments. Not much has been done, you know, statistically to find out the magnitudes of these adjustments.

Paton: Not expecting to attend even this opening session of the seminar, I submitted a statement outlining my views on the general subject, to which I added, after receiving and reading a copy of Professor Fabricant's excellent paper, a one-page commentary. In making a few observations off the cuff after hearing Professor Fabricant's oral presentation I'll try not to be unduly garrulous.

I have little but praise to offer. Our speaker has covered the waterfront, so to speak. This is commendable, as our subject has a lot of ramifications, some of which are widely overlooked.

I became interested in this problem in 1913, after, somewhat accidentally, drifting from economic theory toward accounting. I have long tended to approach the problem of inflation in terms of what's happening to the monetary unit, a measuring rod that is never stable even under the gold standard. The value of any monetary unit is affected by many factors, including the fluctuating attitudes and desires of human beings. Thus the problem of economic measurement is quite different from the measuring of physical volume, distances, and so on.

In my written statement I mentioned my work for the National Bureau of Economic Research forty years back, and the help I received from Professor Fabricant at that time. Perhaps you folks won't mind if I refer again to Wesley Clair Mitchell in this connection. He was one of the early economists who had some perception of the possibilities of accounting. In the 1918 edition of Paton and Stevenson's *Principles of Accounting* is included a statement from Mitchell. In discussing the price system he notes that the system "renders possible the rational direction of economic activity by accounting, for accounting is based upon the principle of representing all the heterogeneous commodities, services, and rights with which a business enterprise is concerned in terms of money price."

I might also mention that Mitchell's monumental study of business cycles was the true gospel to me, and the first piece I ever had in print, in 1914, appeared in a book of readings on *Current Economic Problems,* collected and edited by Walton H. Hamilton. My callow effort, under the title "The Severity of the Trade Cycle in America," is in a section in which there are five selections from Mitchell. I was surely in fast company.

Professor Fabricant, as I understand, favors recognition of the impact of inflation in terms of indices of purchasing power in measuring recorded costs in common dollars, where such measurements are needed, and I think he would agree that a general index is useful in dealing with loss or gain associated with current monetary resources and short-term liabilities. But it seems clear from this presentation that he also favors disclosure of *specific current values of resources* in financial reporting where such measurable values differ markedly from recorded data. I go along heartily. Values, not costs, are the basic data we are after. Recording costs, initially, are justified only when assets— including services—are acquired by purchase or equivalent action, and are the best available evidence of actual worth at the time. And I hope the FASB will too. Accounting practice to date, in this country, has failed miserably to seize opportunities to put its house in order. One such opportunity appeared right after World War II. Congress was interested. Several major companies started to adjust depreciation charges. But the movement died on the vine, largely because the American Institute of Accountants (the name at that time) was completely stagnant, and made no recommendations. Perhaps we are going to be given one last chance.

I agree that current value is less difficult to determine than is often alleged. Marketable securities held provide a clear case, and values of land, timber, and other natural resources can generally be approximated without undue difficulty. Values of all sorts of assets are being estimated every day in market transactions, estate settlements (including finding applicable taxes), and in other connections.

In the statement which I submitted earlier I note the need for emphasis on the measurement of *earning power* (relation of income, properly computed, to current value of employed resources). Professor Fabricant deals with the problem of the impact of changing dollar value on long-term debt very briefly. I find this problem very puzzling. He forbears attacking the chief culprit in the erosion of the value of our dollar, and he also ignores the Pollyannas who have been accepting and even supporting "creeping inflation," following in the tracks of Sumner Slichter, after that gentleman lost his way.

Fabricant: I was reminded by Dr. Paton mentioning the National Bureau and Wesley Mitchell of a very interesting fact. Irving Fisher wrote a book, *Purchasing Power of Money,* which goes back before World War I. When Wesley Mitchell died, many of his books were given to the National Bureau. I happened to look a few years ago at a copy of Fisher's *Purchasing Power of Money* which Mitchell had owned. Mitchell read a book with a pencil, underlining, questioning and writing in comments. He wrote a little comment next to Fisher's proposal for a tabular standard, which is, in fact, indexing, "What would this mean for business accounting?" You see what was in his mind—how widely it ranged and the implication.

Paton: He was a better man than Fisher.

Fabricant: I won't quarrel with anybody who calls Mitchell a great man—a remarkable man.

Rogge: There have been those who have been aware of this problem for a very long time and have attempted to direct society's attention to this problem, including my department chairman and good friend of Pierre Goodrich, John Van Sickle. John handed me a copy of some material by a man named George Terborgh and said, "Read it and you will know more than you now do." I did and I did. I would like to recognize that debt I owe to George Terborgh.

II

Inflation, Accounting Principles, and the Accounting Profession

Robert T. Sprouse

The increased rate of inflation experienced in the United States has been accompanied by increased concern and active discussion about the effect of inflation on all facets of the economy. One of the many concerns subjected to active discussion has been the interpretation of financial information derived from the so-called "conventional historical cost model." Because the equal dollar amounts in conventional financial statements can represent varying amounts of purchasing power, a particularly serious question has been raised concerning the meaning of an income figure derived by deducting past dollars of expenses—particularly costs of goods sold and depreciation—from current dollars of revenue.

As a result of the increased concern about the effects of

The Financial Accounting Standards Board, as a matter of policy, disclaims responsibility for any publication or speech by any of its members or staff. Accordingly, the views of the author do not necessarily reflect the views of the Standards Board.

The author is grateful for the assistance of George E. McClammy, Jr., Technical Assistant, in the preparation of this paper.

inflation on the information presented in the financial reports of individual enterprises, the Financial Accounting
Standards Board (FASB) was urged by its Advisory Council, at the Council's December 1973 meeting, to place the
topic of "Reporting the Effects of General Price-Level
Changes in Financial Statements" on its technical agenda.

The Board placed the subject on its agenda in January
1974 and a Discussion Memorandum on the topic was
issued on February 15, 1974.[1] The FASB's discussion
memoranda are neutral documents in which financial reporting issues, alternative solutions, and related arguments
and implications are put forth for public comment; the
FASB does not attempt to reach any conclusions before
issuing of such discussion memoranda. The basic question
addressed in this Discussion Memorandum was whether
reporting the effects of general price level changes should
be required as *supplemental* information in the conventional historical dollar financial statements.

The word *supplemental* deserves emphasis. Financial information derived from statements that have been restated
in terms of units of general purchasing power would be
required in addition to the conventional historical units of
money statements; replacing the conventional units of
money financial statements with statements that have been
restated in terms of units of general purchasing power has
not been under consideration.

Over 130 position papers containing a wide spectrum
of responses to the Discussion Memorandum were received
by the FASB. The sources of the position papers included
industry, public accounting, academe, government, and

---

[1] Financial Accounting Standards Board, Discussion Memorandum, "Reporting the Effects of General Price-Level Changes in Financial Statements"
(Stamford, Ct.: FASB, February 1974).

the financial community. These included papers from several professional organizations so the representation was much broader than the mere number of position papers might indicate.

On April 23 and 24, 1974, a public hearing on the question was held in New York City. This hearing provided an opportunity for 23 interested parties to present their views orally and enabled the Board members to question them.

After the public hearing, the Board spent some time weighing a number of technical issues outlined in the Discussion Memorandum that were subsidiary to the basic question whether reporting the effects of general price level changes should be required as supplemental information. In the process, the close relationship between the general price level issue and another extremely complex issue that was under consideration at the same time—that of accounting for foreign currency translations—became increasingly evident. Both of these projects involve the translation of one unit of measurement into another unit of measurement —that is, units of money into units of general purchasing power and units of foreign money into units of U.S. money. Although admittedly the timing was coincidental, dealing with these two projects concurrently proved to be beneficial to the understanding and tentative resolution of each.

In December 1974 the Board issued an Exposure Draft of a proposed statement of financial accounting standards entitled "Financial Reporting in Units of General Purchasing Power."[2] Ultimately, if this proposed statement is

---

[2] Financial Accounting Standards Board, Exposure Draft, "Financial Reporting in Units of General Purchasing Power" (Stamford, Ct.: FASB, December 31, 1974).

adopted, it will require that, "when financial statements are issued that present financial position at the end of an enterprise's fiscal year or results of operations or changes in financial position for that fiscal year, they shall include certain information that is stated in terms of units of the general purchasing power of the U.S. dollar."[3]

Basically, the Exposure Draft calls for the method of restatement recommended in the Accounting Principles Board "Statement No. 3."[4] The Gross National Product Implicit Price Deflator (GNP Deflator) is designated as the index to be used to measure the change in the general purchasing power of the dollar. Using percentage changes in the index as multipliers, dollars of varying purchasing power at different dates in the past are restated in terms of the number of current dollars having an equivalent amount of general purchasing power. For example, the GNP Implicit Price Deflator increased from 135.2 in 1970 to 158.36 for the last quarter of 1973; this represents approximately a 17 percent increase. Thus, a machine bought in 1970 for $10,000 would be restated by multiplying its historical cost by 1.17. The historical cost of the machine restated in terms of dollars of December 31, 1973, purchasing power would be $(73)11,700. It is purely a mechanical arithmetic process; no new subjective judgments are involved. The supplemental general purchasing power information would reflect the $(73)11,700 cost and depreciation based on the $(73)11,700 cost.

Although the APB "Statement No. 3" was issued in 1969,

---

[3] *Ibid.*, para. 31.

[4] Accounting Principles Board, "Statement No. 3: Financial Statements Restated for General Price-Level Changes" (New York: American Institute of Certified Public Accountants, June 1969).

general purchasing power accounting is still relatively untried in this country. For this reason the Exposure Draft was offered for public comment for an extended period. The response deadline was September 30, 1975; if adopted, the proposed statement would become effective for fiscal years beginning on or after January 1, 1976. The Board is interested in learning about any problems encountered in applying the proposed techniques and about the development of any reasonable shortcuts that would reduce the effort required for the initial restatement. "The extended exposure period will also allow opportunity for financial statement users and other persons involved or interested in financial accounting and reporting to react to this proposal for providing general purchasing power information."[5]

In the area of experimentation, the Financial Executives Institute (FEI) has enlisted approximately 100 companies to field test the Exposure Draft by applying it to their 1972, 1973, and 1974 financial statements. Well over 100 volunteered, including smaller and medium size companies as well as some of the larger corporations, and representing a wide variety of industries.

THE ISSUE

In conventional financial statements, amounts are generally stated on the basis of the actual number of units of money expended or received, regardless of the purchasing power of those units. Whether this has been done because purchasing power changes have been regarded as immaterial

---

[5] Financial Accounting Standards Board, Exposure Draft, "Financial Reporting in Units of General Purchasing Power" (Stamford, Ct.: FASB, December 31, 1974), Preface.

or simply because accounting has never proposed to measure purchasing power is a debatable question. In any event, changes in the purchasing power of the dollar have not been recognized in conventional financial statements.

If income implies an increase in wellbeing, and wellbeing is measured in terms of command over economic resources, it can be argued that a meaningful measurement of income cannot ignore changes in the purchasing power of the dollar. Ignoring the changing value of the dollar in the measurement of wealth and income and pretending that 1942 and 1952 and 1962 and 1974 dollars are homogeneous and can properly be added together and subtracted from one another will inevitably produce some distortions and, in the case of taxes, may produce inequitable results. I should think we would all agree about that. I am reasonably confident, however, that we all do *not* agree we should attempt to change the present method of measuring wealth and income. And I am absolutely certain that all those who do favor a change do *not* agree on the kind of change that is appropriate.

The noted economist J. R. Hicks defined income as "the maximum value he [a man] can consume during a week, and still expect to be as well off at the end of the week as he was at the beginning."[6] This concept of income can easily be modified to apply to an enterprise. For example, a definition of the income of a business enterprise could be stated as that amount which, if there were no additional investment or withdrawals by the stockholders during the period, could be distributed by the enterprise to its stockholders, while the amount of stockholders' equity at the end

---

[6] J. R. Hicks, *Value and Capital* (London: Oxford Press, 1939), p. 172.

of the period was unchanged from the beginning of the period. Of course, the maintenance of stockholders' equity can be viewed in several ways. For example, it can be viewed as having the same *number of dollars* in stockholders' equity at the beginning and end of the period, it can mean having the same *amount of general purchasing power* in stockholders' equity at the beginning and end of the period, and it can mean having the same *operating capacity* reflected in stockholders' equity at the beginning and end of the period.[7]

Some of those who favor a change in the method of measuring wealth and income advocate only that conventional financial statements be restated in terms of units of general purchasing power. This restatement is based on historical cost. It merely converts historical cost in terms of numbers of dollars to historical cost in terms of units of general purchasing power. This point is emphasized because some have the false impression that general purchasing-power financial statements would report items at their replacement costs or some other form of "current value." General purchasing-power restatements do *not* measure any form of "current value." It would be sheer coincidence if the historical cost of an asset restated for changes in the general purchasing power of the dollar, resulted in a quantity that was equivalent, in any sense, to the asset's "current value."

In the example used earlier, the machine bought in 1970

---

[7] An especially lucid treatment of these distinctions will be found in Jean St. G. Kerr, "Three Concepts of Business Income," *The Australian Accountant* (April 1956), pp. 139–46. The article has been reprinted in Sidney Davidson, *et al., An Income Approach to Accounting Theory: Readings and Questions* (Englewood Cliffs, N.J.: Prentice-Hall, 1964), pp. 40–48.

for $10,000 would be accounted for in the conventional statements at December 31, 1973, at the historical cost of $10,000. In the general purchasing power financial statements, the machine would be accounted for in December 31, 1973, dollars at $(73)11,700. From this it cannot be inferred that at December 31, 1973, the asset could be sold or replaced for $11,700. All that can be inferred is that the amount of general purchasing power invested in the asset when it was acquired in 1970 was the equivalent of 11,700 December 31, 1973, dollars.

There are some who favor changing the conventional accounting for historical cost to some type of current value accounting. That alternative calls for a change in the attribute being measured; instead of using historical cost as the attribute to be measured, some form of "current value" such as present value of future cash flows, replacement cost, or market value would be measured.

Others support a change which would include both general purchasing power restatement and current value accounting. They suggest that both a stable measuring unit and a change in the attribute being measured are necessary in order to supply users of financial statements with useful information.

A simple illustration may help clarify this last proposal. Assume a company has an investment in marketable securities on January 1, with a current value of $100,000. During the year the current value increases to $120,000. Most advocates of the use of current values would recognize a holding gain of $20,000. If during the same year the general price level index increased 12 percent, however, those who insist that information is needed that reflects both current values and changes in purchasing power would recognize a holding gain of only 8,000 end-of-year dollars.

The beginning current value would be restated to 112,000 end-of-year dollars and only the additional 8,000-dollar write-up to 120,000 end-of-year dollars would be recognized in the measurement of income as a "real" holding gain.

Supporters of changing both the attribute being measured and the unit of measure argue that the $20,000 holding gain that would be recognized through the use of current values alone (i.e., without restatement) does not represent a meaningful indication of economic gain. They argue that although the attribute being measured may be more meaningful, the unit of measure is still unstable and therefore deficient. The $20,000 gain is calculated by deducting 100,000 January dollars from 120,000 December dollars; but, as indicated by the 12 percent increase in the general price level index, the unit of measure used at the beginning of the year does not have the same economic significance as the unit of measure used at the end of the year. Accordingly, it is inappropriate to compare the two amounts and it is difficult, if not impossible, to interpret the economic significance of the difference between the two—the $20,000 "gain." By restating the January current value in terms of December dollars, a more meaningful measure of the economic gain from holding the marketable securities during the past year is obtained.

On the other hand, some feel that the restatement is an unnecessary exercise. They claim that, if current value is the attribute to be measured, the marketable securities in this illustration would be displayed in the balance sheet at $120,000 whether or not the units of measurement were restated. They argue that everyone knows the "value" of the dollar has declined over time and can take that into consideration in their own analysis of financial information.

They have asserted that by issuing a standard calling for general purchasing-power restatements, the FASB will focus attention on an inadequate and illusory solution and divert resources from tackling the only effective and useful solution—the recognition of "current value."

As a private inducted into the Army in 1942, I was either sufficiently patriotic or sufficiently naive—I am not sure which—to sign up for a payroll deduction to buy Series E savings bonds. Each payday $6.25 was deducted from my $50 per month pay and at the end of one year I was the proud and properous possessor of a $100 bond that had cost a total of $75. Held to maturity at the end of ten years, the bond had an effective rate of interest of 2.9 percent compounded semiannually. Army service did not do much for my level of sophistication; I actually held some of those hard-earned Series E savings bonds until they matured. At that time, I found it was necessary to report to the Internal Revenue Service $25 income on each $100 bond. That is, based on the unadjusted historical cost of $75, I had income of $25 during the 10-year period; I had 25 more dollars at the end of the 10-year period than I had at the beginning. According to the Consumer Price Index, however, anyone who invested $75 in such bonds during 1942 would have to receive about $122 in 1952 merely to recover the amount of purchasing power he had originally invested. Based on the historical cost adjusted for changes in the general price level (as measured by the CPI), there was a loss of twenty-two 1952 dollars during the 10-year period; I actually had $(52)22 less purchasing power at the end of the 10-year period than I had at the beginning. To make a bad matter worse, I was required to pay federal income taxes on the $25 "income." As I recall, my income tax rate was about 20 percent; so I was required to pay five 1952 dollars in federal income taxes. The $5 tax brought the total loss of purchasing power to twenty-seven 1952 dollars.

Please note that the recognition of "current values" would not have alleviated this distorted measure of "income" in any way whatsoever. The current values were readily and objectively determinable; indeed, a schedule of "current values" was printed right on the savings bond itself. After the first couple of years a new and higher current value was attained each six months. As a matter of fact, in this case selling price and replacement cost and the present value of future cash flows were identical; presumably, all "current value" advocates would be satisfied, regardless of the variation they prefer.

Perhaps in recognition that the use of current values alone does not cope with the effects of inflation on monetary items—such as Series E savings bond—in a recently published study Morton Backer recommended recognition of general price level gains and losses on monetary assets and liabilities "in a non-operating section of the income statement." At the same time he recommended the use of current values only (i.e., no restatement) in connection with non-monetary items, but he rejected the notion of a holding gain resulting from increases in replacement cost of operating assets on the grounds it was a "mythical gain" that must be set aside for replacement of assets.[8]

Whether a holding gain is "mythical" or "real" necessarily depends on the underlying concept of income that is

---

[8] Morton Backer, *Current Value Accounting* (New York: Financial Executives Research Foundation, 1973), pp. 41–42.

being measured. The income concept underlying Backer's analysis deserves careful scrutiny, but I do not propose to undertake that here. Let me merely acknowledge my difficulty in reconciling (1) the recognition of a gain in purchasing power as a result of having outstanding long-term debt and (2) the rejection of a gain in purchasing power as a result of holding property, plant, and equipment whose specific prices increase more rapidly than the general price level.

Lest my discussion and examples obscure my point, let me recapitulate. Because general purchasing-power restatement is concerned with the measuring unit and current value accounting is concerned with the attribute being measured, the merits of each can and should be evaluated independently. They cannot be viewed as alternatives. It would be more constructive to analyze the merits and deficiencies of one without confusing the issue with the pros and cons of the other.[9] The FASB has followed this approach. The December 1974 Exposure Draft relates only to the proposal for general purchasing power accounting;

---

[9] An example of such confusion appears in a recent article in which it is asserted that "the current cost approach is conceptually superior" to "the general price-level approach." (Sidney Davidson and Roman L. Weil, "Inflation Accounting: What Will General Price Level Adjusted Income Statements Show?" *Financial Analysts Journal* [January–February 1975], p. 27.) This is akin to asserting that a cow is superior to a horse. Each is superior for the very different purpose for which it is intended. Because the two "approaches" deal with entirely different objectives, their conceptual merits simply cannot be compared. The conceptual merits of accounting in terms of units of general purchasing power can only be compared with the conceptual merits of accounting in terms of units of money regardless of the general purchasing power they represent, or in terms of some other measuring unit.

its adoption would not in any way preclude FASB consideration of current value accounting.

The Board is taking action now on general purchasing power accounting because techniques for restating financial information in terms of units of general purchasing power are well developed, the feasibility of applying them has been demonstrated in a number of field tests, and the current rate of inflation has created a perceived need for a stable unit of measurement. The perceived need for reporting current values may be as great or greater, but such an action would be a significant departure from the historical cost basis of accounting and much work remains to be done in considering the concepts and implementation issues related to that proposal. Consideration of current value accounting is within the scope of another project presently on the FASB agenda: the conceptual framework for accounting and reporting.

I propose to limit the remainder of my discussion to the area of financial statements restated for changes in the general purchasing power of the dollar. This topic, as it should be, will be discussed without consideration of the issue of current value accounting.

RESISTANCE TO GENERAL PURCHASING POWER ACCOUNTING

The problem of using an unstable measuring unit in preparing financial statements has been recognized for a long time. About 25 years ago, the Study Group on Business Income, a group of more than 40 distinguished individuals with a wide variety of backgrounds and interests, discussed the defects of the monetary unit as the accounting unit and advocated general price level adjustments in their report.[10] Also in the early 1950s, the American Accounting Association sponsored a major research effort by Professor Ralph Jones of Yale University that involved implementation of restatement techniques in four companies, including the New York Telephone Company and Armstrong Cork.[11]

In 1963 the Research Division of the AICPA published the results of an Accounting Research Study[12] and in 1969 the Accounting Principles Board issued "Statement No. 3,"[13] in which it concluded that financial statements adjusted for changes in the general price level present useful information not available from basic historical dollar financial statements. Accordingly, the APB recommended—but did not require—that price-level adjusted statements or information extracted from them be presented in addition to the historical dollar statements. However, as far as I know only one company, Indiana Telephone Company, followed the APB's recommendation, and it had been publishing some restatements since 1964.[14]

The history of lack of implementation in the face of

---

[10] Report of Study Group on Business Income, *Changing Concepts of Business Income* (New York: Macmillan, 1952), pp. 53–57.

[11] Ralph Jones, *Price Level Changes and Financial Statements—Case Studies of Four Companies* (American Accounting Association, 1955).

[12] Staff of the Accounting Research Division, Accounting Research Study No. 6, "Reporting the Financial Effects of Price-Level Changes" (New York: American Institute of Certified Public Accountants, 1963).

[13] Accounting Principles Board, "Statement No. 3, Financial Statements Restated for General Price-Level Changes" (New York: American Institute of Certified Public Accountants, June 1969).

[14] T. Alan Russell, "An Application of Price Level Accounting," *Financial Executive* (February 1975), p. 21.

intensive study and vigorous urging leads one naturally to ask why no authoritative action has yet been taken to require general purchasing power restatements. I should like to offer a few possible answers.

Materiality

One possible reason for not dealing with the unstable measuring unit may be the perceived lack of materiality. This reason was implied by the Accounting Principles Board when it said:

> The Board believes that general price level information is not required at this time for fair presentation of financial position and results of operations in conformity with generally accepted accounting principles in the United States. The Board recognizes that the degree of inflation or deflation in an economy may become so great that conventional statements lose much of their significance and general price level statements clearly become more meaningful.[15]

If the crux of the question is materiality, we should focus our attention on the question, "What amount of fluctuation in the unit of measure produces a material distortion in financial information?"

Recently, John C. Burton, Chief Accountant of the Securities and Exchange Commission, suggested the following:

> At low levels—perhaps under 3 percent per annum—financial statements based on an historical monetary unit of account have been felt to provide adequate information for most users. While a number of academics, thirsting for perfection in measurement, may always be found in the act of criticizing the historical mone-

---

[15] *Ibid.*, paras. 25–26.

tary unit approach, for most people the system worked pretty well. At the other extreme, when the rate of inflation reached dramatic levels—say over 25 percent per annum—financial statements based on historical monetary units could be generally agreed to have little value outside of a ritual dance enjoyed by preparers and action to supersede such statements was necessary. In the middle range, however, practical answers are not so simple to arrive at. This can be called the discussion range, where traditional approaches must be reconsidered but where precipitous action to cope with crisis need not be taken. It is this stage which has given rise to most of the published work on inflation accounting and it is this stage that we are in today.[16]

I submit that anyone who suggests that a 6 percent or 10 percent or 25 percent annual rate of inflation would call for general purchasing power restatements but that a lower rate does not, must defend his position on something other than a conceptual basis.

Money Illusion

Another possible reason for ignoring changes in the measuring unit is the notion that a dollar is a dollar is a dollar is a dollar is firmly entrenched in the minds of businessmen, financial statement users, and most of the people of America. Maurice Moonitz has noted that this same idea was stated in a different manner by Irving Fisher. In a book entitled *The Money Illusion,* Fisher said that the financial community in general believes that during a period of inflation prices rise but that the dollar remains stable. It was this belief that Fisher referred to as the "money illu-

---

[16] John C. Burton, "Financial Reporting in an Age of Inflation," a speech given at the Accounting Day of the University of California at Berkeley, May 30, 1974, pp. 1–2.

sion."[17] One can understand how this illusion has become ingrained in our thinking. During a period of inflation we always hear about how much prices have risen. In recent months, newspapers and television have continuously reported price increases of specific items such as fuel and sugar. The Consumer Price Index is published monthly, and the GNP Deflator is published quarterly to keep us well informed about the rise of prices. The reports are always made in terms of prices rising, seldom in terms of the dollar shrinking. People tend to think in those terms; we begin to believe that the dollar is stable, that only the prices fluctuate.[18]

Perhaps the need for a change in the unit of measure used in financial statements would be more readily accepted if the shrinkage of the dollar's value were given more emphasis. A current GNP Deflator of 170 indicates that the current general level of prices is 70 percent greater than the general level of prices in the base year (1958) of the GNP Deflator. The index of 170 also means that the general purchasing power of the dollar has declined by approximately 41 percent since 1958. Both statements say the same thing, but the latter calls attention to the distortions inherent in using the dollar as a unit of measure.

In a modest effort to deal with this problem, the FASB Exposure Draft focuses on "units of general purchasing power" rather than "general price level changes." It is also noteworthy that the recent United Kingdom pronouncement

---

[17] Maurice Moonitz, *Changing Prices and Financial Reporting* (Champaign, Ill.: Stipes Publishing Company, 1974), p. 1.

[18] *Ibid.*, p. 11.

on this subject centers on "changes in the purchasing power of money."[19] Careful attention to terminology may enhance recognition and understanding of the limited but important problem with which general purchasing power accounting is designed to deal—namely, the instability of the conventional unit of measurement.

Status Quo

Status quo may be another reason for not dealing with the instability of the measuring unit in financial reporting. All of us have a tendency to resist change. This is true in many facets of our lives—from how we think about business decisions to what time we get up in the morning.

As a professor, I was terribly upset a few years ago when at the Stanford University Business School the pattern for each course was changed, eliminating three 70-minute classes per week and substituting two 110-minute classes per week. No amount of rational explanation of the need for change was about to make it acceptable to me. After twenty years of teaching, it meant I had to reorganize my notes!

If people resist change in the normal routines in their lives, it is not surprising that preparers and users of financial statements have a tendency to resist a fundamental change in the measuring unit used in financial statements. Preparers would have to change both their methods of processing data for financial statements and their methods of interpreting those financial statements, once prepared.

---

[19] The Institute of Chartered Accountants in England and Wales, Provisional Statement of Standard Accounting Practice No. 7, "Accounting for Changes in the Purchasing Power of Money," May 1974.

Users would receive "strange" figures which, at the outset, they might not understand. This assumes, of course, that it is possible for them to "understand" the figures they have been receiving. Their standard ratios and trends would change; like me, with my class notes, they would probably have to reorganize their methods of analysis. It is human nature to resist a fundamental change of this kind, even if the change might provide useful information. The FASB proposal that the general purchasing power information be provided *in addition* to conventional unit of money financial statements permits making use of such information in financial analysis on a gradual basis, or even not at all.

Usefulness

A reason given by some for not adjusting the unstable measuring unit is that general purchasing power information would not be useful. One argument against its usefulness is based on the assumption that investors are basically interested in forecasting future dividend payments and common stock prices. It is argued that it can be shown that over the years a close direct relationship has existed between conventional earnings and dividends and that the growth rates of conventional earnings and dividends increase as inflation becomes more rapid. Thus, it is argued that users are given adequate information to predict dividend payments from conventional statements. The proponents of this view believe that the earnings figures in the adjusted statements would be of no additional aid to statement users. Furthermore, they believe that the restated earnings would not have a direct relationship with dividend payments and could easily confuse professional and individual investors.[20] This argument assumes, of course, that future dividend policies would be unaffected by general purchasing power information. Perhaps, however, dividends might prove to be more highly correlated with general purchasing power income.

Others argue that general purchasing-power financial statements would not be useful because statement users would not understand either how to interpret them or how to apply them to the decision-making process. This argument has been supported with examples of financial executives who say they have prepared current value financial statements when actually they have prepared general purchasing-power statements. If financial executives do not understand what they are preparing, how can users understand what has been prepared?

The logical consequences of this objection need careful consideration. Should progress in the development of financial reporting be restricted to what is already generally familiar or readily understandable? If general purchasing power accounting information is indeed useful, education and experience will surely be necessary in order to reap the benefits. Ultimate usefulness of such information is not likely to be determined without several years' exposure to it.

Occasionally, seemingly insignificant incidents provide profound insights. For example, the matter of usefulness of general purchasing power accounting information reminds me of a friend who when asked, "How's your wife?" responded, "Compared to what?"

The usefulness of general purchasing power information

---

[20] For a more thorough exposition of this general view, including some empirical testing, see C. Reed Parker, "The Trueblood Report: An Analyst's View," *Financial Analysts Journal* (January–February 1975), p. 32.

must be compared with alternatives. As a practical matter, the most obvious starting place is the conventional historical cost unit of money statements. One might reasonably argue that, if the conventional historical cost unit of money statements are useful, restatements of those financial statements in terms of units of general purchasing power should be even more useful. The basic difference between the two statements is that the unstable unit of measure in the former is restated in terms of a stable unit of measure in the latter; the historical cost basis is retained. If the change results in an improvement in the measuring unit, can the conventional statement be useful and the restated statement not be useful? Or, does the true question of usefulness lie with the conventional historical cost statements and not with the process of changing the measuring unit of those statements?

The matter of usefulness of restatements in terms of a stable unit of general purchasing power is equally relevant with respect to the use of "current values" in financial statements. Presumably a current value balance sheet is automatically completely stated in a single unit of measure —specifically, dollars as of the balance sheet date. In the absence of restatements to adjust for changes in the general purchasing power of the dollar, however, comparative balance sheets and income statements may be said not to be comparable, thereby thwarting trend analyses. Also, even the most recent income statements would continue to reflect an unsegregated mixture of "real" gains and losses and the results of changes in the general purchasing power of units of money. The fundamental question about usefulness remains: Does the use of a stable unit of measurement enhance financial information or detract from it?

Costs versus Benefits

Another reason for not correcting for the unstable measuring unit centers on a cost-benefit analysis. That is, even if it is assumed that information based on general purchasing power restatements is useful, do the benefits to statement users exceed the incremental costs of preparing and providing such information? The most significant cost of preparation probably would be the man hours required at the outset to determine the dates of acquisition for property, plant, and equipment. For companies which have maintained detailed records that include acquisition dates of property, plant, and equipment this may be a relatively simple task. However, for firms which have not maintained such records the accumulation of these data may be difficult. Indeed, some firms have indicated that it would be impossible to gather accurate data. In any event, it is important to understand that the cost of determining past acquisition data would be incurred only in the first year of implementation. In subsequent years, applying the general price level index to data from the current and past years should be a relatively simple task. Some evidence about costs of implementation is already available; the extensive field tests now under way should permit a reasonable appraisal of the cost side of the question; reliable assessments of the benefits are much more elusive.

An indirect cost of implementing the presentation of general purchasing power information is the aforementioned cost of educating statement users. If it is true that some sophisticated and most average statement users would not understand what general purchasing power financial statements represent, the "cost" of educating such statement users could be significant.

SUMMARY AND CONCLUSIONS

The Exposure Draft issued by the FASB on "Financial Reporting in Units of General Purchasing Power" is unusual in one important respect. The primary issue is not whether the proposed standard embodies an appropriate solution to the unit of measurement problem but rather whether there *is* a unit of measurement problem.

Among those who feel that units of money do not constitute a satisfactory unit of measurement, there is little controversy about the appropriate remedy. Some differences of opinion exist but those differences tend to center on relatively minor matters, such as the classification of a particular balance sheet item as monetary or non-monetary. Indeed, there is substantial worldwide agreement on the technical aspects of implementing the use of units of general purchasing power. The recent pronouncements of the Accounting Standards Steering Committee of the United Kingdom, the Steering Committee of the Accounting Research Committee of the Canadian Institute of Chartered Accountants, and the Australian Accounting Standards Committee are substantially in agreement with the FASB Exposure Draft.

The fundamental question remains. Do the benefits of making general purchasing power financial information available outweigh the costs involved? One can predict with some confidence that the FASB will learn a good deal about "the costs involved." Obtaining meaningful information about the benefits of having the information available, however, is much more difficult. One hopes a number of corporations will publish general purchasing power financial information in connection with their 1974 financial statements, as they have in the U.K. If so, at least some information about usefulness may be elicited from users before a final decision is made.

Some "current value" advocates have predicted that the FASB Exposure Draft, and especially the ultimate adoption of the FASB statement of financial accounting standards requiring the presentation of general purchasing power information would retard, if not preclude, consideration of reporting current values. Others have predicted that acceptance of a change as revolutionary as a different unit of measurement—even if reflected only as additional information—may create widespread receptivity to consideration of other fundamental changes and hence facilitate the consideration of reporting current values. In any event, it should be clearly understood that adoption of general purchasing power accounting will not obviate consideration of the use of current values.

A number of important studies has been made of the problem of using an unstable unit of measure in financial reports. Typically, these studies have noted the deficiencies of the unit of money serving as the unit of measurement and have *recommended* the use of units of general purchasing power. Yet thus far no authoritative group in the U.S. has required that general purchasing power information be included in financial reports. Several possible reasons why general purchasing power information has not been required are:

1. Lack of materiality.
2. Focus on rising prices rather than changing value of the dollar.
3. Preservation of the status quo.
4. Reservations about usefulness of the information.

5. Fear that incremental costs (in the broadest sense) would exceed the incremental benefits.

Unfortunately, these kinds of reasons are not likely to be convincingly corroborated or compellingly overcome by concrete evidence. In the final analysis, the basic issue of whether reporting certain general purchasing power financial information should be required in addition to the conventional historical dollar financial statements must be resolved on the basis of informed judgment. The decision will be made only after careful examination of all the evidence, but ultimately it will be a policy decision, not a decision susceptible to scientific proof or rejection.

Response

Stephen A. Zeff

I

It may be instructive to examine the reaction of the accounting profession to the inflationary phenomenon in the 10 countries in which tentative or final positions have been taken. The record is curious indeed.

In the United States, the profession issued a pronouncement devoid of obligatory character (Accounting Principles Board "Statement No. 3," June 1969), recommending that companies issue supplementary financial statements restated for the change in the general price level. No evidence is available to indicate that the APB or other agents of the accounting profession actively and aggressively sought to persuade companies to follow the statement or to convince the Securities and Exchange Commission, which appears to have been an indifferent bystander, to become allied in the project. In fact, only one company, Indiana Telephone Corporation, which had already been applying a price level adjustment to depreciable assets and depreciation expense in a complementary set of financial statements, adhered in large measure to the statement.[1]

Early in 1974, the Financial Accounting Standards Board hastily addressed the general price level question, and issued a Discussion Memorandum which, in this writer's opinion, fell considerably short of a critical and thoughtful conspectus. Ten months later, the Board issued an Exposure Draft which did no more than reaffirm the contents of the well-known APB "Statement No. 3" and announced an unprecedented nine-month exposure period. It is not known whether the FASB has actively sought the understanding or allegiance of the Departments of Treasury and Commerce, the Council of Economic Advisers, pertinent committees of the Congress, the SEC, or other federal regulatory agencies—for it is well known that these units of the government had, on various occasions between 1962 and 1973, used their influence and political might to thwart proposed opinions of the Accounting Principles Board.[2] If the FASB believes that it will gain converts to general price level accounting merely by holding a public hearing and inviting comments on an Exposure Draft, it misjudges its environment. More on this later.

Even before the FASB issued its Exposure Draft in December 1974, the SEC Chief Accountant had, in speech and article, made known his antipathy to a solution such as that

---

[1] It is necessary to remark that Indiana Telephone Corporation does not include in income the purchasing power gain on long-term debt, contrary to the recommendation in APB "Statement No. 3."

[2] See Stephen A. Zeff, *Forging Accounting Principles in Five Countries: A History and an Analysis of Trends* (Champaign, Ill.: Stipes Publishing Co., 1972), pp. 155–59, 178–80, 201–04, 212–16, and 219–21.

contained in "Statement No. 3."[3] Finally, in August 1975, the SEC promulgated a draft of proposed amendments to the footnote disclosures required of all registrants by Regulation S–X. Departing from its more than 40-year-coolness to the inclusion of current value data in SEC filings, the Commission recommended extensive disclosure of replacement cost data, for both assets and expenses, in footnotes to the financial statements. The exposure period closes on January 31, 1976, and it is now understood that the Commission aimed for a May 1976 publication date for a final ruling along the lines of the Exposure Draft.

In the United States, therefore, the FASB and SEC are working on opposite sides of the tracks. The FASB, which recently announced that a decision on general price level accounting has been "deferred" until sometime in 1976, has repeatedly stated that its position on current value accounting must await a resolution of its major project on the "conceptual framework" of accounting. This project, which represents the Board's response to the Trueblood Committee report on the objectives of financial statements, is still in the Discussion Memorandum stage more than two years after the publication of the Trueblood Committee report. While the SEC proposal deals with footnote disclosure, not the measurement of the amounts contained in the body of the financial statements, it would seem that the SEC believes that the Board has moved too slowly on current value accounting.

---

[3] John C. Burton, "Accounting That Allows for Inflation," *Business Week*, November 30, 1974, pp. 12, 14; "Financial Reporting in an Age of Inflation," *The Journal of Accountancy*, February 1975, pp. 68–71. (The latter was a speech given on May 30, 1974.)

In Britain, the Accounting Standards Steering Committee decided in 1971, a time when the annual inflation rate was approaching 10 percent, that a full-scale program of professional diplomacy would be required to implement a general price level proposal. Its chairman, Sir Ronald Leach, correctly observed: "The real problem is not the conversion of financial accounts but the conversion of financial attitudes."[4]

The ASSC began by issuing a discussion paper and proceeded to launch a dialogue with powerful entities in government, industry, and the City of London financial community. Through quiet but persistent discussions, the ASSC succeeded in persuading the influential Confederation of British Industry to lend public support to current purchasing power accounting (as it is known in Britain).[5] In January 1973, the ASSC issued its exposure draft in favor of required supplementary general price level disclosures, and all appeared to be running smoothly[6] until, with but a few

---

[4] Quoted in *The Accountant,* July 22, 1971, p. 115.

[5] See the interim and final reports: *Inflation and Company Accounts* (January 1973) and *Accounting for Inflation* (September 1973). The interim report was published during the same month in which the ASSC's exposure draft on current purchasing power accounting appeared.

[6] More than 40 companies voluntarily published supplementary price level disclosures in accordance with the proposal contained in the ASSC's exposure draft. C. A. Westwick and N. J. Ballanger, "How Companies Account for Inflation: I," *The Accountant,* April 10, 1975, p. 455. In this regard, it may be noted that the British accounting profession is potentially in a better position than is its American counterpart to secure the cooperation of industry. Many top-level British company executives are members, not infrequently active members, of the five leading accountancy bodies. In the United States, by contrast, very few top-level executives (it is believed) are members of the American Institute of Certified Public Accountants or of the National Association of Accountants. So far, only one corporation (Shell Oil Company) has voluntarily implemented the FASB Exposure Draft in its annual report to shareholders.

days left in the six-month exposure period, the government, which had until then declined to commit itself on the subject, announced that it would appoint a committee to study the entire matter of inflation accounting. There was no way of anticipating this belated move by the government. A somewhat embarrassed ASSC nonetheless proposed that the Councils of its five constituent bodies issue a provisional pronouncement, subject, of course, to the final decision by the government. "Provisional Statement of Standard Accounting Practice 7" was issued in May 1974.

In August and September 1975, two important reports were published in Great Britain. In August, an ASSC working party on the scope and aims of published accounts concluded, in a booklet entitled *The Corporate Report,* that "the thrust of development [in financial reporting] should now be towards the adoption of current value systems." The kind of accounting recommended in "PSSAP 7" was said to be only a stop-gap measure, until a proper current value system were devised and ready for implementation. The working party did not, however, express a preference for any particular kind of current value. Three weeks later, the report of the Sandilands Committee, the short title given to the government's Inflation Accounting Committee, was published. It eschewed the general price level approach and instead advocated a replacement cost system which it dubbed "current cost accounting." In reply to Sandilands, a committee representing the accounting profession suggested that current cost accounting should be complemented by current purchasing power accounting.[7] The same accountancy bodies are now constituting a steering group which

---

[7] " 'Qualified' Support for Sandilands—The CCAB Response," *The Accountant,* November 6, 1975, pp. 520–21.

will be charged with making specific proposals for carrying forward and implementing the Sandilands recommendations. That current purchasing power accounting is not a dead issue in Britain may perhaps be inferred by the selection of the deputy chairman of the ASSC as chairman of the steering group.

In Canada, Australia, New Zealand, Mexico, West Germany, and South Africa, where, one supposes, the recent actions by the American and British bodies inexplicably caught the profession by surprise, the accountancy bodies responded, at first, with hastily prepared papers. The initial papers issued by the three countries in the Northern Hemisphere were all published in the last month of 1974, evidently in order to get something out that might be applied to December 31 closings.

In Canada, the paper was called a "guideline," a new kind of pre-exposure draft which is issued on the authority of the steering committee of the Accounting Research Committee.[8] Such guidelines, we are told, allow the committee to publish advice in much less time than is required by the use of the full committee's lengthy procedures,[9] but one wonders why the need to adapt financial statements to inflationary times revealed itself so tardily to the Canadians. The Canadian Institute of Chartered Accountants' research study on price level accounting had been published a full 30 months earlier. In July 1975, the CICA Accounting Research Committee issued an exposure draft elaborating upon the contents of

---

[8] Although it was the first guideline on accounting, a guideline on auditing was issued a month earlier. The guideline series was only recently authorized. See R. D. Thomas, "Accounting/ Auditing Guidelines," *CA Magazine,* November 1974, p. 61.

[9] *Ibid.*

the guideline. Both pronouncements closely follow the American and British approaches to general price level accounting.

In Mexico, the paper was an article written by the *Comisión de Principios de Contabilidad* (Accounting Principles Committee) in the monthly journal of the *Instituto Mexicano de Contadores Públicos*. The committee points out that the definition of "original historical cost" which appears in one of its earlier bulletins provides that the comprehensive application of a general price index to the accounts is not a violation of the historical cost principle, and, in its article, the committee recommends that companies issue general price-level-adjusted supplementary statements. The article in *Contaduría Pública* is unlike anything hitherto issued by the committee. It seems to have been produced as a kind of progress report, since it refers to a more detailed study which was then in process in the committee. It is more a pre-exposure draft than an exposure draft, for it implies that the more detailed study will fill in the broad terms of the article. With an annual inflation rate of about 20 percent in Mexico, it is surprising that the Institute's committee had not seen the need for action much earlier—especially with the precedents available in Britain, the United States, and Argentina. The Committee's more detailed study was published in the form of an exposure draft in the September 1975 issue of *Contaduría Pública*. The exposure period extends to December 31, 1976, establishing a new world's record for accounting exposure drafts, 16 months. The terms of the draft follow the American and British precedents in all important respects.

In West Germany, an exposure draft calling for replacement cost accounting was published during the last month of 1974 in the semi-monthly journal, *Die Wirtschaft-spruefung*. In principle, replacement costs are to be used only for non-monetary assets that are matched by the amount of the shareholders' equity. Any upward replacement cost adjustment of the amount of non-monetary assets in excess of the amount of shareholders' equity is presumed to be offset by a purchasing power gain on debt. Thus, the replacement cost of fixed assets (and the depreciation expense thereon) is recognized in the supplementary accounts only to the extent the fixed assets are covered by the balance in shareholders' equity. If the balance in shareholders' equity exceeds the amount of fixed assets and also covers a significant portion of the merchandise inventories, the covered fraction of the merchandise inventories is also adjusted to its replacement cost. The exposure period expired on April 15, 1975.

In Australia, South Africa, and New Zealand, exposure drafts were issued between December 1974 and June 1975. Like West Germany's, the draft in South Africa and one of the two drafts in Australia deal with current value accounting.

In Australia, the first of two "preliminary exposure drafts" was issued in December 1974 and is a virtual carbon copy of the British "PSSAP 7." In its preface to the draft, the Australian Accounting Standards Committee seems to disclaim its very contents, making the somewhat remarkable assertion (for the preface to an exposure draft) that "the AASC is not yet convinced that CPP accounting should be recommended as the preferred solution to the problems associated with accounting for changes in prices and/or the general price level. . . ." Of what is it an exposure draft? Six months later, however, the same committee boldly issued another draft proposing a system of replacement cost accounting, but without the prefatory disclaimer found in its predecessor. This second draft, which represents a dramatic departure from the Australian profession's traditional inclination to follow either British or American recommended practices, is especially well written and illustrated. The exposure period ended on December 31, 1975, and while the Australian profession is closely watching the current value initiatives in Britain and the United States, it seems possible that AASC might become the first major accountancy body to take decisive action on the subject.

The South African discussion paper was published in the January 1975 issue of *The South African Chartered Accountant*. It appears to have been hastily prepared, and recommends replacement cost accounting coupled with a general purchasing power restatement. Like all general price level recommendations thus far issued by accountancy bodies, the South African version would include in income the purchasing power gain on long-term debt. In line with the Sandilands, West German, and Australian recommendations, holding gains on non-monetary assets would be excluded from income. The exposure period terminated on May 23, 1975.

The New Zealand exposure was published in the March 1975 issue of the *Accountants' Journal*. The draft is a virtual copy of British "PSSAP 7," including appendices. The exposure period ended on September 30, 1975.

Less precipitate and more decisive action has been taken in two South American countries where inflation has been endemic. In 1965, following 10 years of severe inflation, the Argentine accounting profession began a determined campaign to gain acceptance of general price level accounting. More than any other country, Argentina is responsible for the supportive actions taken on the subject at the 1965, 1967, 1970, and 1972 conferences of the Inter-American

Accounting Association. In 1965, the *Bolsa de Comercio de Buenos Aires* (Buenos Aires Stock Exchange) offered to sponsor a major study on the most appropriate means by which to adapt financial statements to inflationary conditions. The 10-man committee, composed principally of *contadores públicos* (CPAs), reported in 1967 that a comprehensive restatement by the use of a general price index should be used, similar in result to the conclusions of the U.S. "Accounting Research Study No. 6." When, in 1969, the Argentine profession established a mechanism for drafting and approving pronouncements on accounting principles, one of the first subjects to be considered was general price level accounting. A "Recommendation" (equivalent to an exposure draft) was approved in 1971, followed by a formal Opinion in late 1972. Both the Recommendation and the Opinion advocated the comprehensive, general index approach, and the obligatory pronouncement was to take effect on July 1, 1973. But the expected support of the Buenos Aires Stock Exchange never materialized, and there apeared to be no interest on the part of the government department charged with enforcing the companies' law. In the absence of formal support by these powerful agencies, the force of the Opinion was nil, obliging the accountancy body to postpone the effective date of its pronouncement. A reduction in the Argentine inflation rate to a more modest 30 percent per year seems to explain the absence of extra-professional support. In recent months, however, the Argentine inflation rate is reported to have soared to more than 300 percent annually, a factor that will probably have a noticeable impact on attitudes toward some kind of inflation accounting.

In Chile, where the annual rates of inflation during 1973 and 1974 were 508 and 376 percent, respectively, the government has recently acted. In May 1974 the Chilean accountancy body approved an accounting bulletin which called for complementary financial statements in the style of the proposal contained in the APB "Statement No. 3." The profession knew that the bulletin was unenforceable until the government acted to prescribe the same kind of accounting for federal income tax purposes and, as a corollary, for inclusion in published financial statements. In its intensive discussions with the government, the representatives of the accountancy body cited its own pronouncement as well as the resolutions of the Inter-American Accounting Association. Precedents in the United States and Britain were also invoked. In the end, the debilitating rate of inflation overcame any remaining objections, and on December 31, 1974, Chile became the first country to require comprehensive inflation accounting, by use of a general index, for income tax purposes. Inventories, moreover, are to be stated at current replacement cost, the annual unrealized increment therein being subject to tax. The government agency in charge of enforcing the companies' law has not yet prescribed the same form of accounting for published financial statements, but a new regulation is expected at any time. The government's hand has already been tipped, as the new tax law requires that taxpayer-companies introduce the adjustments in their books of account.[10]

II

This 10-country survey suggests the lack of an effective early-warning system within the accounting profession, at

---

[10] See Stephen A. Zeff and Hugo Ovando Z., "Inflation Accounting and the Development of Accounting Principles in Chile," *The Accountant's Magazine*, June 1975, pp. 212–13.

least in regard to price level accounting. Only Britain commenced to deal with the question in advance of its becoming a critical problem. Furthermore, on a problem as common to all the countries as the impact of inflation on accounting, pride of authorship and the usual nationalistic drives seem to have obliged the United States and Britain to behave as if each were propounding a novel solution. Neither the FASB Discussion Memorandum nor the resulting Exposure Draft makes reference to the earlier British initiatives, and neither the ASSC exposure draft nor the five bodies' "PSSAP 7" cites the APB "Statement No. 3." The ASSC discussion paper, however, does reproduce some empirical data drawn from American sources. On the whole, the Americans and the British give no official credence or credit in their own published utterances on general price level accounting to the arguments, conclusions, and even to much of the data developed by their overseas colleagues. Whether their trans-Atlantic counterpart's writings were actually used in the drafts and debate is not known. Such insularity hardly conduces to the international image which these two countries, and others, are attempting to bestow on the accounting profession. Characteristically, the Canadian guideline refers to both the American and British pronouncements. By long tradition, Australia and New Zealand have paid close attention to British pronouncements.

More important still is the excessively narrow conception which most of the accountancy bodies have of their role. Were a proposed pronouncement to deal with a topic of little import to industry, government, and the financial community, the accountancy body might conceivably confine itself to the purely accounting questions. But on such subjects as inflation accounting, business combinations, leases, and full costing, it is not enough for an accountancy body to issue discussion memoranda, hold public hearings, and solicit comments on an exposure draft. As has been demonstrated (not always, it may be added, with success) in Britain, Argentina, and Chile, an accounting proposal which portends such profound shock waves as does general price level accounting must be *sold* to sectors of the economy likely to be affected the most seriously. Moonitz has ably argued that the profession must acquire allies,[11] a task which, if done properly, will place heavy demands on the diplomatic and persuasive powers of the leaders of the profession. Call it lobbying if you will, for the process is essentially political, whether the society is a republican democracy or a military dictatorship.

In carrying its argument to those who have the political power to assure implementation, the profession must not confine itself to the technical accounting questions. A study should be commissioned on the likely economic impact of the proposal so that economic policy makers, businessmen, and financial analysts can translate the proposed pronouncement into macro-economic, industry-wide, and microeconomic terms. In the case of general price level accounting, experimentation by individual companies is but a part of the economic impact analysis—it is only the micro consideration. Government and industry will not stand mute in the face of proposals carrying potentially great economic implications for their spheres of activity, particularly when no economic studies are at hand which analyze the probable

---

[11] See Maurice Moonitz, *Obtaining Agreement on Standards in the Accounting Profession,* Studies in Accounting Research No. 8 (Sarasota, Fla.: American Accounting Association, 1974), Chapters 8 and 9.

consequences of the accountants' handiwork. Even in the presence of such studies, political opposition may be expected. If the accounting profession lacks political power, it can at least raise the likelihood that the ensuing struggle will have some basis in rational economic analysis.

Floor Discussion

Sprouse: I'd like to take just a minute to go back about 25 years. Around 1950, there was a very prestigious group of about 40 individuals engaged in, so-called, a study group on business income. Very much concerned with the problem we're concerned with today—25 years later. I mention this in particular because that group engaged some consultants and among those consultants was Solomon Fabricant, and Solomon Fabricant 25 years ago prepared, I think, its two monographs. Here is Solomon 25 years later still trying to get to know something about this problem. About that same time, it was, I think, a very important group of studies that haven't got the recognition, not half, that they deserve, at least not outside the academic circles.

From the user's point of view, you think of three groups —preparer, financial executor, financial analyst—who can use financial statements. I am increasingly convinced it's a matter of status quo; they don't want to have to learn all over again what financial information means. Now, you see that immediately assumes that they understand what they're getting now and you know what that means. They are worse than any of us, that's a total mystery also, but they feel they completely understand what they are getting today and they don't want that changed. I think the biggest hurdle for users is the status quo thing—inertia. It's really a serious problem and it's the sort of problem that I don't know what to do about. The general notion of usefulness is coming from all directions, but certainly from preparers as well as from users and understandably so. I don't think any of us know how useful this information is.

Moonitz: Bob, I found your paper to be an excellent presentation of the position taken by the FASB, at least in the Exposure Draft. For our purposes here today, I propose to accept the constraints and limitations of the paper and to resist the temptation to argue the case afresh except with respect to one or two points. My general comments are in two main parts. First I'll take care of a few of these specific points in your paper; in the second part, however, I want to extend the discussion to look into some of the results which would obtain if the financial community should, in fact, follow the lead of the FASB and its reporting practices.

Now for the first part, the FASB Exposure Draft refers to supplementary financial statements restated in, and I quote, "units of general purchasing power of the U.S. dollars." This language unfortunately is ambiguous, because the U.S. dollar at any and all dates has general purchasing power. The problem, of course, is that the magnitude of its general purchasing power varies from time to time. I would prefer language that refers to financial magnitude that's expressed in terms of exchange value of U.S. dollars at one date.

Second point. Bob, you note that the accounting profession has never used purchasing power as a unit of measure. And I simply want to point out that accounting for centuries has been and still is a method of accounting for cash receipts and disbursements. It's true that under accrual accounting we lead and lag these cash receipts and disbursements in the form of receivables, payables, prepayments and the like. But in every case, these accruals—those are the ones that are actually received in accounts in financial statements—refer to cash movement from the past to the present or the future. Events not linked to actual or prospective cash movements are foreign to such a system and are admitted to the account sparingly and haltingly, invariably labeled as "exceptions."

Now, my third point was to compliment you on the distinction between price level accounting and current value accounting. There is no need to comment further than that I obviously agree thoroughly with the necessity of keeping a distinction clearly in mind. When I was in England in 1973, I talked to the head of one moderate-sized manufacturing company. He knew about the proposal by the British accounting bodies to recommend price level accounting. He told me he would go along with the recommendation on two conditions, and of course, it is sensible in that his competitors also issue financial statements restated for the price level effect. In other words, he wasn't going to go it alone, but he would if all the rest did. And second, that the taxing authority accept the restated figures for assessment of income tax. As a second condition, that's more than sufficient to explain its reluctance. If FASB wants a spectacular victory in getting one of its major standards adopted overnight, let us persuade the U.S. Treasury to accept the restated income figures for tax purposes. All the difficulties that you catalog will diminish in size or disappear altogether. One final comment in this first section—this has to do with the question of the usefulness of general purchasing power information. My reading in the literature of the subject convinces me that the price level accounting will be useful precisely where the strength of conventional accounting lies; namely, in an accounting report on what did happen. For example, what rate of return did that company enjoy during fiscal year 1974? What was its dividend payout ratio? Was it equal to, greater than, or less than the apparent ratio calculated from the conventional basis? What was the effective rate of income tax? To answer these questions more precisely you need as accurate a measuring unit as possible, and price level accounting offers us a more accurate unit than we now have. Whether or not price level accounting will possess predictive ability, for example, is debatable, just as it is debatable whether or not historical costs financial statements possess predictive ability.

Now to shift to the second part. What would be the impact on the story told by the financial statements if FASB adopts in substantially present form the Exposure Draft? I hope that FASB will release the data it receives from most companies that have actually restated their financial statements in accordance with the recommendations of the Exposure Draft. I for one would like to see the differential impact on firms in aerospace, construction, steel, coal mining, petroleum, etc. Another line of cleavage that will be of interest is the relative effect on regulated and unregulated enterprise. In regulated enterprises the accounting procedures employed are much more important than in non-regulated. An unregulated company is relatively free to ignore its accounts in adapting to inflation. The regulated company has no such option. If it cannot convince its regulators to approve new policies, it is frustrated and must live with the consequences of the old one. Now, cutting across both approaches suggested above is the problem of growth. Growing firms are less likely to be affected by price level accounting because more of their assets are recently acquired. Hence, inflation has less chance to affect the validity of the underlying figures reflecting the investment tied up in them. Stable and declining firms of industry will show a greater difference in restated versus conventional financial statements, but we need to know more about how much difference it will make. The way in which a business is financed and how it finances its sales to customers determines the extent to which it may have a hedge against the loss of monetary items during inflation. At present we can describe the ways in which this type of potential loss can be hedged against, but I know of no study that tells the extent to which banks, savings and loan associations, and the insurance companies have, in fact, withstood the erosive effects of inflation on their assets.

Paton, Jr.: I wish to concentrate my comments on the following: the long-standing monetary versus non-monetary classification question, and then, too, the efficient market model and its relevance in the accounting price level analysis. These two points are not independent, as I hope my subsequent comments will serve to indicate, but Professor Sprouse's statement provides a convenient starting point.

Among those who feel that units of money do not constitute a satisfactory means of measurement, there is little controversy about the appropriate remedy. Some differences of opinion exist, but those differences tend to center on relatively minor matters, such as a classification of a particular balance sheet item as monetary or non-monetary. I believe that these classification questions are not relatively minor matters, and I want to give one example to suggest this. For example, if convertible debt is monetary and so treated in APB No. 3 and the Exposure Draft, you can suggest similar treatment. The borrower reflects a gain if the price level rises, assuming reasonable price level conversion procedure is followed, but if convertible debt is deemed to be non-monetary then no such gain is recognized. Convertible debt securities may assume the status of common stock equivalent for purposes of reporting primary earnings per share amounts. Thus convertible debt may be treated as monetary in the price level conversion process and as so-called common stock equivalent in the primary earnings per share calculation. I believe that efforts designed to establish more precise monetary versus non-monetary boundaries divert our attention. If we concentrate instead on common attributes of financial statement items, the monetary versus non-monetary line fades, and what you can use may be the important element of the analysis come into focus. For if inflation is anticipated, via operation of participants in the efficient markets, nominal returns on monetary assets and nominal interest rates on liabilities may be expected to express price level expectations. It then appears that there are no general price level gains or losses, unless these are unanticipated.

There is, by the way, in the April 1974 *Accounting Review,* a very interesting article by Professor Bradford, who makes an attempt to set up a methodology to measure anticipated and unanticipated price level gains and losses. The monetary–non-monetary question is not a relatively minor matter in practice or in theory. There are no losses and gains on monetary accounts unless unanticipated and to the extent price level conversion process does not capture the unanticipated amount. FASB should not require price level converted data as supplementary information. Such requirements will place us in Dr. Fabricant's uncomfortable and untenable halfway house. I think he's already there, if not before, already.

Vancil: I'm very disturbed about the halfway house idea. I think, if I can quote Sandy Burton properly, one of his concerns is that adopting the FASB position is halfway somewhere, but that to get the rest of the way—to get halfway without a major investment not in terms of implementing the opinions but in terms of educating users to what these statements mean, and it is unlikely to undertake a second investment to get the rest of the way.

Meiselman: I don't think there are very many people, including economists, who appreciate the crucial role of information in the market system and, in fact, I think if you look at most of the studies about the effect of inflation, they tend to focus on what I feel are rather trivial aspects of it. I think there is a high *cost* and one which Americans are just starting to appreciate, the cost that is associated with destroying useful information, so that we are talking about the difficulties of decision-making by responsible management in the face of uncertain inflation. We are talking about problems that investors have, and you haven't even talked about problems that ordinary savers have in trying to make provision for the future. Effectively useful information has been wiped out. Now that has a tremendous impact on resource efficiency and I think this lesson is one that people are starting to learn. I don't think they appreciate that sufficiently.

III

Inflation Accounting:
A British View

W. T. Baxter

I t is fitting that this paper* should be presented in the United States. For it owes its main ideas to two Americans (my colleagues during a happy year at Columbia Business School), namely, Professors J. C. Bonbright and H. W. Sweeney. Bonbright must rank as patron saint of asset valuers, thanks to his *Valuation of Property*.[1] Sweeney (while still a student) wrote the first book in English explaining attempts by German accountants to cope with the huge inflation of 1923–24 by "stabilizing" the historical figures, i.e., raising them with price index factors.[2]

AILMENTS OF TRADITIONAL ACCOUNTS

By and large, accounting relies on historical figures. Such figures might work admirably in a world with stable prices.

---

* My colleagues Susan Dev and Peter Watson have greatly helped me with this article.

[1] J. C. Bonbright, *Valuation of Property* (New York: McGraw-Hill, 1937; reprinted in Charlottesville, Va.: Michie Company, 1965).

[2] H. W. Sweeney, *Stabilized Accounting* (New York: Harper & Brothers, 1936; republished by Holt, Rinehart and Winston, 1964).

But they give poor information in the real world: even in fairly stable times, current prices of at least some of a given firm's assets are apt to vary from their historical cost ("special price change"); during times of inflation or deflation ("general price change"), such variation becomes the norm. So historical accounts are always drifting away from current reality. Both the two main accounts, the balance sheet and income statement, are harmed by their antique contents. But the nature of the harm differs: the accountant commits sins of omission in the balance sheet, of commission in the income statement.

Balance Sheet

Assets, no matter how old, are usually kept in the balance sheet at not more than the prices originally paid for them. Upward change in value is rarely recognized until it is proved by the test of realization (as when sale turns goods into cash). Downward change tends to be recognized more readily, at least where the asset will be sold soon; permanent assets (e.g., land) are seldom written down, and assets with a limited life (e.g., machines) are revalued only in the sense that slices of their historical cost are written off. The old values are not even consistent with one another, since different vintages are added together (giving totals of "mixed" dollars). Further, the historical balance sheet fails to draw the important distinction between money items and non-money items—between items with a fixed dollar value, and items that reflect price change. Examples of the two types are (among the assets) cash and claims on debtors—in contrast to goods and fixed assets, and (among the credit balances) amounts due to suppliers, loans, and preference shares—in contrast to the equity ("owner's balances").

If assets are not revalued, the owners' balances cannot show any holding gain (i.e., appreciation on assets) or the corresponding loss. Still less can they distinguish nominal change (due to general price movement) from real change (net of such movement). One form of the neglected real change is *gain or loss on net money assets*—a statistic of the greatest moment during inflation.

Income Statement

In historical accounts, the charges and revenues may well be measured in dollars of many dates. General price change turns such dollars into units of differing worth; to subtract them from one another is as wrong as to subtract cats from cows. Revenue dollars for different months of the firm's year may usually for simplicity be treated as dollars of about the middle of the year. Some of the cost dollars tend to date back to earlier dates.

Cost of goods sold. Typically there is a lag between the dates when goods and stores are bought, and the dates of the resulting sales; during inflation, the cost of goods sold is measured in dollars that are worth more than the revenue dollars. Where the revenue dollars can be treated as dollars of midyear, the cost dollars can usually be treated as dollars of a date that precedes midyear by a suitable turnover period. If this period stretches back several months, and inflation is not negligible, historical cost à la FIFO is too low compared with revenue. This error gives an artificial boost to profits; it is often called "inventory profit" or "stock appreciation" in Britain, but "time-lag error on cost of goods sold" is more precise.

Depreciation cost. There may well be a much longer time-lag between the acquisition of a depreciating asset and revenue date. Then the cost dollars will during inflation be of a vintage far superior to that of the revenue dollar.

Thus cost is again understated *vis-à-vis* revenue, and profit is puffed up. The time-lag error is apt also to bias *capital gain* calculation: old costs may be set off against recent revenue, so that the gain is exaggerated.

On the other hand, *appropriation charges* are often for payments (tax and dividends) made months after midyear. During inflation, bad outgoing dollars are set off against less bad revenue dollars; here the error makes for understatement of surplus.

Consequences of Historical Cost

The outdated asset values may well be poor guides to investors (actual and potential stockholders). They may also mislead management, especially if they are put into decision budgets (e.g., for pricing). They often rob statistics such as "assets per share" of meaning, particularly when different companies are being compared.

The time-lag error in the income statement is perhaps even more pernicious. It too can deceive both investors and managers. It imposes an extra income tax (never sanctioned explicitly by the legislature) on owners of goods and machines. It provides trade unions with false but plausible grounds for pay demands. It exaggerates profits during the price upswing and understates them during the downswing; possibly therefore it has accentuated the boom and slump of the traditional trade cycle. It makes nonsense of statistics for "earnings rate on assets employed," the more so if the asset values are wrong too.

It is interesting to speculate on how far the disillusion with reported profits may be responsible for the present fall in stock markets (so bad in Britain that many investors have in a few months seen the bulk of their life savings evaporate). Other forces—oil prices, acts by governments hostile to business—seem more pertinent. But the markets might resist the uncertainties of inflation better if accounting reform helped to bring a sister reform, the indexing of bonds (tying interest payments to the price level). A new and safe kind of security is needed if saving is not to become a mug's game, and a wise government would lead the way by issuing indexed bonds.

One could spell out traditional accounting's faults, and their ill consequences, in much more detail. But I do not propose to curry a dead dog by so doing. The ailments are at least generally conceded; the proposed cures are what now excite us.

PROPOSED CURES

These vary greatly in both scope and concept.

Scope of cures. Reform can be fragmentary, as when it is confined to the revaluation of some assets, or the use of LIFO, or the updating of cost (with an index factor) in a capital gains calculation. Or it may be comprehensive, as when all the historical figures in both balance sheet and income statement are stabilized with index factors; and these revised figures may be used in the main published accounts (ousting historical costs), or merely in a supplementary statement.

Range of concepts. The reformers fall into two groups: (1) The *general index man*[3] advocates the adjustment of

---

[3] This name is used by Professor R. S. Gynther, in his vigorous presentation of the special index view—*Accounting for Price Level Changes: Theory and Procedure* (Oxford: Pergamon Press, 1966).

historical data with factors found from the general index (G.I.). (2) The *specific index man* advocates the revaluation of each asset at its own current price—or, as a shortcut, the adjustment of historical costs with a specific (or "special") index (S.I.) for each kind of asset. His balance sheet values are often at odds with those found by the general index men; and (quite another matter, to be judged separately) his income figures may also differ.

The conflict between these two schools is the most interesting and important part of our topic, and bids fair to be the center of accounting debate throughout the next decade.

BRITISH EXPERIMENTS

Events in Britain illustrate the move towards reform. Till recently, British accountants tended to view reform with incomprehension, indifference, and sometimes outright hostility. But inflation is a forceful teacher; when its rate reached some 10 percent a year (in the late 1960s), attitudes changed abruptly.

"SSAP 7"

In 1973, the Accounting Standards Steering Committee (representing the main accounting bodies) issued a proposed "standard" on "Accounting for Changes in the Purchasing Power of Money." The proposal had a mixed reception, but in 1974 became the "Provisional Statement of Standard Accounting Practice," "SSAP 7." The "Provisional" in the name is a diplomatic recognition of the setting up of a government committee—the "Sandilands Committee," after its chairman—to report on inflation accounting.

"SSAP 7" has not the force of law, but is likely to be widely accepted by the bigger British companies. Its effects will be seen in accounts issued later this year. It calls on quoted companies to add a "current purchasing power" (CPP) supplement to their published reports. This supplement consists of a stabilized income statement and a somewhat truncated balance sheet; it includes too a note reconciling the stabilized and the historical profit figures, i.e., listing the various time-lag and other errors. Stabilization is to be based on the general index.

This standard is clearly a notable step, but it is open to (and is attracting) much criticism. Particularly because of its reliance on the general index alone, its figures have limited usefulness and may sometimes be absurd. But it will be educative, and its use of a single index will make it relatively simple to introduce into the accounts. Perhaps it is best viewed as a halfway house—sooner or later to be superseded by methods that employ multiple special indices, and so give more realistic asset values.

Tax Relief on "Stock Appreciation"

In 1974, British business was beset by troubles. One of them was lack of liquid funds thanks to inflation, severe new taxes, and high interest rates. In a belated attempt to lessen the tax burden, the Chancellor in an autumn budget offered some relief for the time-lag error on cost of goods. (Earlier tax law already gave generous relief for the error on depreciation, but forbade the use of LIFO, etc.)

The Chancellor's method is tentative and arbitrary. It can best be described as a variant of LIFO. Companies may (for tax purposes) value their end stock at their opening stock figure plus (as an approximation to "normal" increase) 10 percent of the profit. For instance, suppose:

	£
Opening stock is	100
Profit (by the usual FIFO rules) is	50
and the normal value of end stock is	120
then end stock is for tax purposes revalued at:	
£ $(100 + \frac{1}{10} \times 50)$	105
so taxable profit is reduced by	15

Welcome though any relief may be, such *ad hoc* patching is objectionable. The method is too clumsy to allow for actual stock movements, in quantity or value; by what reasoning is the "normal expansion" of every firm equated with 10 percent of its profit? The method is inconsistent with the relief given for depreciation. It can hardly be fitted into stabilized accounts. And it relies on the logic of LIFO, which many critics (including me) find unconvincing.

Future Action by Government

When a tax rule is such a hurried makeshift, we may expect a later Finance Act to bring in something different. Possibly too the Sandilands Committee may recommend an integrated approach to inflation accounting (e.g., full stabilization), and may sell this view to the government. Reform could then be backed up by law. We must hope that the law will be wise. Perhaps the real danger is that it will be rigid, and so will curb the later reforms that more experience and understanding will no doubt make desirable.

AIMS AND CONCEPTS

Inflation accounting, as we have seen, is concerned with two problems: (1) How should we measure wealth (the net assets in a balance sheet, etc.)? (2) How should we measure change in wealth (the balance on the income statement for a year, etc.)?

Wealth, and Change in Wealth over Time

One can visualize these two problems with a diagram such as this:

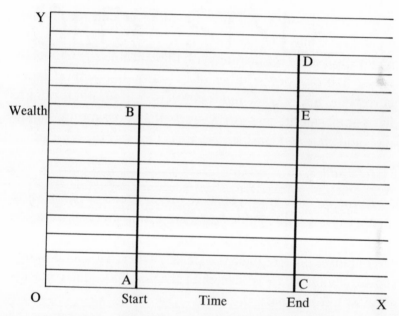

FIGURE 1   Simple Comparison of Wealth over Time

Time is measured along OX, value up OY. AB is the wealth at the start of a firm's year (in the opening balance sheet), CD at the end. ED is the income.

Now, why is this diagram too simple? First, it glosses over the problem of how to measure wealth. The height of AB and CD: should we appraise the assets one by one and add up their values—and, if so, which value concept should we use (e.g., historical cost, net realizable value, etc., etc.)? Second, it is overambitious in trying to compare the wealth of different dates. When prices keep changing, with what kind of unit can we calibrate OY? Diagrams of physical growth can safely use yards, pints, and so on, confident that such units stay the same from start to end. When, however, we are tackling value problems, we must not rely on physical analogies. (Perhaps this is the main moral of our story.) We have no fault-free unit for measuring *both* AB and CD.

The proposals for dealing with these problems can mostly be set into one or the other of two groups—general index correction, and specific index correction. Both kinds of cure have some merit, and my view is that accounting should pick and choose. Consider the areas that call for reform:

Asset Values

In the balance sheet. Special values usually are far more likely to be reliable guides than are historical costs adjusted with the general index. But "special value" can mean several things, e.g., replacement cost or net realizable value. So we shall have to ask which of the possible value concepts is most informative.

In decision budgets. Managers often have to compare the sacrifices and benefits of a proposed activity. The sacrifices may include the using up of assets already owned, e.g., raw materials. Current value is here all-important; and historical cost adjustment with the general index may be a poor surrogate. (Some may protest that businessmen have enough sense to brush aside unsound accounting data. But the latter obtrude so often in otherwise knowledgeable discussions—of costs, pricing, government controls, etc.—that

I am not wholly convinced; specific index reform would be at least a safety precaution.)

Measures of holding gain and loss. If the figures are to mean much, measurement of "surplus on revaluation," etc., demands the separate treatment of each asset (or group of like assets), as recommended by the specific index man.

But full analysis (i.e., splitting up of total gain into its nominal and real parts) demands use of *both* specific index and general index. Suppose a man invested $100 in a non-money asset, and $100 in a money asset, when both indices stood at 100; and that the specific index now stands at 130, and the general index at 120. He will deem each investment (100 of the dollars of starting date) to have maintained its real value, by the test of his purchasing power over things-in-general, if it has become worth 120 of the dollars of end date. To see whether this has happened, he needs some such analysis as:

	Non-money asset	*Money asset*
	Starting-dollars	Starting-dollars
His initial capital was	100	100
	End-dollars	End-dollars
In his eyes, the current equivalent of the initial investment is now	120	120
But the asset's actual value is now	130	100
So his real gain (loss) is . . .	10	(20)

With the non-money asset, he has not merely maintained but increased capital; with the money asset, he has failed to maintain capital. His analysis employs the specific index to revalue the asset, and the general index to revalue opening capital.

Income

When we use our chosen value concept to measure the assets at the start of an accounting period (date 1), we express our result in dollars of that date. When we again use that concept to measure the assets at the end of the period (date 2), we express our result in dollars of date 2. To compare the totals—i.e., to measure income—we must decide how to allow for the discrepancy between the two brands of dollars.

The essence of this task, it seems to me, is to provide the owner with a "translation"—to show him at date 2 what his starting total *now* means. Like language translation, this task defies complete solution. But I can think of no more helpful treatment (especially if the main use of income figures is to guide the owner's consumption and investment) than to compare his purchasing power at the two dates— i.e., to raise his opening wealth with a general index factor.

It is tempting to justify the general index translation of $x at date 1 into $y at date 2 by saying "If the owner of a firm had at date 1 invested $x in a package of things-in-general instead of in the firm, his package would at date 2 be worth $y." I must myself plead guilty to having used this glib argument. The snag is that so many of the things in his consumption package—e.g., vacations, apartment hire, electricity, repairs, bus rides, newspapers—cannot be moth-balled over long periods. We must be content with the more abstract notion that "$x at date 1" and "$y at date 2" convey the sensation of ability to buy the same quantity of what we want. The difficulty of translation is merely one of the many ills that follow money's failure as a store of value.

We must now return to the problem posed already, and ask how assets should be valued.

If we abandon the historical concept of value, we shall have to pick its successor from a longish list of contenders.

The Available Concepts

One group consists of *ex ante* measurements of the future cash flow of the whole firm. These are attractive to the theorist, but probably too subjective for everyday use. Accounts must normally rely on the more pedestrian asset-by-asset concepts. The three main ones are:

1. Sale price (or "exit value" or "net realizable value"). This has considerable appeal, in particular because it automatically answers the awkward question of what is an asset: if no one will buy your preliminary expenses or research, these are not assets. But it cannot allow for the difference between the assets of a going firm and one at death's door, and it fails dismally to give an informative picture of the fixed assets' size, particularly if they are specific to the given firm. It often fails too when asset values are used in decision budgets, or when they are integrated (as they surely should be) with income measurement.

2. Contribution to future net receipts. This is the concept used in budgets that appraise capital investments with a cost-of-capital rate. Its actuarial trappings make it impressive. But its excellence in capital budgets does not mean that it is equally good for the balance sheet. The two calculations have quite different aims. The capital budget seeks to assess the contribution that the proposed addition of an asset would bring, i.e., to find whether the asset would yield consumer's or producer's surplus after payment of the purchase price; it studies the extra asset only, and takes existing assets as given. The balance sheet must deal with all the assets. It can do this sensibly if it uses their current prices, not if it uses their future contributions. When a firm, on the strength of favorable capital budgets, buys and then continues to hold an asset, there is a presumption that its contribution is bigger than the price, perhaps by a huge surplus. To add the marginal contributions of all the assets would be meaningless, and might yield a fatuously high total. Or (looking at the matter in a slightly different way) one can say that normally the decision to own an asset puts its contribution into *all* the alternative budgets used at its valuation, so that the comparative effect of the contribution is *nil*.

However, contribution is not always irrelevant. It becomes the most informative value when the asset will not be replaced in its present form; for instance, when it will soon be scrapped, it should be valued at its cash contribution when sold as scrap.

3. Replacement cost (or "entry price"). This is a strong candidate, since it must often figure in a manager's own calculations for important decisions: if an existing asset will be used up on some proposed activity, the sacrifice is normally the resulting outflow of cash to replace the asset. But "normally" is not "always"; replacement cost fails if the firm will not replace, i.e., where replacement is not worthwhile because assets of the given type have become less useful or too dear.

Deprival value. So, to find a value formula that will fit a manager's needs in all circumstances, one must elaborate on replacement cost. Professor Bonbright's "value to the owner" seems to fit the bill better than any other proposal.[4] Perhaps, however, his phrase is nowadays a trifle ambiguous, since it may be thought to mean the contribution. As the essence of his approach is to find the worsening of the cash flows if the owner deprives himself (or is deprived) of the asset, I have suggested "deprival value." This can be defined as (1) the lower of replacement cost and (2) the higher of the two forms of contribution: (a) sale value and (b) value in use.[5]

The deprival value concept seems to have great merit. It works well for assets with well established market prices, and particularly well for depreciating assets.[6] But, like its rivals, it flounders when the asset is not the subject of frequent market dealings, e.g., work in progress; it lets us down too where "replacement" of the one machine, etc., is likely to be part of a grand scheme for renewing the whole of an obsolete plant with very different units.

Thus the deprival value of some assets will have to be computed in a rule-of-thumb way; and no doubt its present definition needs improvement if it is to fit all circumstances. Despite such faults, it seems to offer the best way forward.

INCOME MEASUREMENT

Here the problem should be thought of (I submit) in terms not of costs and revenues but of growth in wealth. The key to most of the relevant questions is the definition, mea-

---

[4] Bonbright, *op. cit.,* p. 66.

[5] The formula is amplified in my *Accounting Values and Inflation* (London: McGraw-Hill, 1975).

[6] In budgets comparing the future cash flows of a deprived and undeprived owner. See my *Depreciation* (London: Sweet and Maxwell, 1971).

surement, and comparison of net assets. Further, where arithmetical examples are helpful, a series of consecutive balance sheets can often show the issues more sharply than can an income statement.

The Subconcepts of Capital Maintenance

In terms of Figure 1, we must choose not only between concepts for appraising wealth at a given moment, i.e., for measuring AB and CD, but also between subconcepts for comparing AB with CD. To find the growth in wealth over a period (the size of the surplus after capital has been maintained), we must decide on a suitable unit for the OY axis. Traditional accounting has been content to use the dollars —to maintain *money capital;* as the dollar's value has proved fickle, this is the unit that we now may discard. The alternatives are to maintain one of the following:

1. Real capital. Here we measure with a dollar of constant purchasing power. In accounts and diagrams, we use a general index factor to make the owner's opening capital comparable with his closing net assets.

2. Physical capital. If specific index factors are chosen instead, the effect is much the same as if physical units were used to calibrate the OY axis in Figure 1. Income is earned only if physical wealth grows. LIFO comes near to reflecting this view. The loose phrase *replacement cost accounting* can be used in different ways: it may mean a system for valuing assets, or measuring income, or both; in the income context, it too seems to imply a physical maintenance concept.

The argument can be illustrated by amplifying Figure 1. Figure 2 assumes that the net assets at the start of the year are measured by the chosen value concept (historical cost, sale price, deprival value, or whatever), and their total is first expressed in opening dollars, as A_1B_1. The net assets are measured at the year end by the same concept, in end dollars—CD. If A_1B_1 is not adjusted, the growth is E_1D, i.e., this is the income by the subconcept of money capital maintenance. To show income by the two other subconcepts, one must adjust A_1B_1 (cf., the updating of opening capital in a balance sheet by stabilizing in closing dollars). The general index factor (for real capital maintenance) might produce say A_2B_2, and so cut income to E_2D. The specific index factor (for physical capital maintenance) might produce say A_3B_3, and cut income to E_3D.

Use of the three subconcepts allows us to arrange all the possible figures in a systematic mental framework: a list of x capital concepts must yield $3x$ income concepts.

Unraveling General and Specific Changes

In real life, values tend to change because both general and specific movements occur, to differing degrees, at the same time.

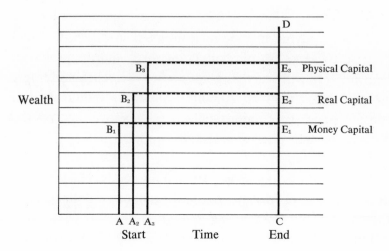

FIGURE 2   Comparison of Wealth Using Alternative Units

As an aid to understanding, however, it is useful to unravel the two types of change, and to consider each by itself. Thus one might consider a problem under three sets of circumstances, perhaps in this order:

1. Specific change takes place in a time when general prices are fairly stable. (Specific index moves, general index does not, so real change occurs.)

2. General change takes place, without further change in the given assets. (General index and specific index move in step.)

3. Both specific and general change occur, to different extents. (Specific index and general index move, but not in step, and so real change occurs.)

A further point. Reform proposals for dealing with real change under (3) should, surely, be worth adopting under (1) also: we should reject them when they are part of an inflation accounting package unless we are·willing to accept them for ordinary accounts when general prices are fairly stable.

Three Test Questions

Before studying income measurement in depth, we shall be wise to make up our minds on three simple questions. Our answers will serve as guides when we reach seemingly more complex matters. All three questions should first be considered in the circumstances of (1) above, i.e., on the assumption that *general prices are stable*.

The questions are:

1. If I make a dollar loss on selling goods, but my creditors cut their claims by an equal number of dollars, have I a zero income from selling goods?

Put this way, the question sounds frivolous. My net gain

of zero obviously covers up two equal and opposite movements of different kinds: a loss from bad trading and a gain
from the good act of my creditors. For clear thinking, I
must mix up the two movements; and clear accounts must
show them separately.

2. If I win a Rolls Royce in a raffle, am I better off (a)
only if this gain leads me to increase the number of cars in
my fleet—for example, to expand it from 0 to 1; (b) even
if I now retire a car (perhaps cheap and worn out), so that
I merely maintain my fleet at the same physical size—for
example, at 1?

This question is perhaps a trifle unfair to those who base
income on physical capital maintenance. But I suspect that
it does have a bearing on their case. Most of us would feel
that I have made an agreeable gain regardless of whether
my fleet grows; when this is conceded, the specific index view
of income seems to become shaky.

My hypothetical Rolls can be used too for a related question:

3. When I win the Rolls, should my friends congratulate
me on my gain, or commiserate with me because I shall now
bear higher depreciation costs?

Commiseration strikes us as incongruous. Why? The
higher depreciation during the Rolls' life is genuine enough.
But one must look at the whole episode. At the start of the
story, I have a given initial capital; at the date of the draw,
my wealth grows (or does anyone seriously contend that
growth occurs only if the fleet expands—that the market
value of the cars is irrelevant to wealth measurement?);
throughout the Rolls' life, I am indeed afflicted with extra
depreciation; finally, I am back where I started. The gain
and the extra depreciation cancel one another. If my ac-

counts ignore both, and yet show that I end the period as well off as I was at the start, they have measured correctly. If they charge the extra depreciation, they should also credit my gain (perhaps first to an account labeled "unrealized gain"; and then, over the years of the asset's life, to the income statement as transferred slices of "realized gain"[7]). Good statistics cannot logically record death but ignore birth. The special index man must justify accounts that recognize the exit of wealth but not its entrance.

He may seek to do so by giving the story of my Rolls another ending. Suppose that the joys of driving this car make me change my plans: I decide that henceforth I must always drive a Rolls—that reversion to my earlier situation would hurt my pride or my earnings. After the decision, certainly I must put aside extra sums to replace my first Rolls. These sums enable me to maintain my *postexpansion* capital, but are excessive for the *original* capital (which is the proper base for measuring the income of the whole period). My accounts should still record the gain, but may show that I intend to retain it as permanent saving (i.e., as an appropriation to finance expansion).

The Three Questions and General Price Change

Now let us use our answers to the three questions as guides in a more realistic setting, where inflation is superimposed on real change.

1. Gain-on-owing and the time-lag error. Question (1) dealt with creditors who voluntarily cut their claims. With inflation, the cuts are involuntary.

---

[7] Principles and bookkeeping are ably explained in E. O. Edwards and P. W. Bell, *The Theory and Measurement of Business Income* (Berkeley: University of California Press, 1960).

Opponents of accounting reform (or of tax concessions to firms with time-lag error) sometimes argue from the example of a firm whose inputs are financed entirely by loan capital. During inflation, the gain-on-owing will here equal and offset the time-lag error. Therefore (the argument runs) the reformers' case is invalid.

I find this view naive. But it has been put forward *inter alia* by economists in an article that was quoted with respect in the *London Times*.[8] So we must not brush it aside too curtly.

The *Times* quoted a numerical example in which a loan finances goods. The tale is best told in steps:

(1) *Start of year.* The firm owns goods worth £100, bought with a £100 loan.

(2) *Inflation takes place.* Prices rise 30 percent. So the goods' value becomes £130; judged, however, by the owner's purchasing power, this £30 gain is unreal, i.e., is merely a matter of changing the measurement unit (bad pounds for good pounds). But the loan's size does *not* rise; the loan can now be repaid in bad pounds; so the owner makes a £30 real gain, thanks to owing. This gain is not shown in ordinary accounts.

(3) *Goods are sold.* Goods now worth £130 are sold for £130. Real profit is *nil*. But ordinary accounts unfortunately set the £130 revenue against the £100 historical cost, and thus invent a £30 trading profit.

(4) *Goods are replaced.* The £130 of cash from sale proceeds is invested in fresh goods.

(5) *Dividend and tax are paid.* In consequence of the illusory £30 of trading profit in the ordinary accounts, the

---

[8] November 1, 1974.

firm pays out this sum in tax and dividends (borrowing a further £30 to do so).

One can retell the story in consecutive balance sheets, as in Table 1. The left-hand column gives the ordinary opening

TABLE 1   Consecutive balance sheets illustrating gain-on-owing and the time-lag

	Ordinary	*Stabilized*				
	i	i	ii	iii	iv	v
						Tax and
	Start	*Start*	*Inflation*	*Sale*	*Replacement*	*dividend*
Date	£	end-£	end-£	end-£	end-£	end-£
Goods	100	130	130	—	130	130
Cash				130		
Less Loan						
At start	(100)	(130)	(100)	(100)	(100)	(100)
Extra						(30)
	—	—	30	30	30	—
Owners' balances:						
Gain-on-owing			30	30	30	30
Tax and						(30)
dividend						

balance sheet. But only stabilized balance sheets can show change in the value of money and of money claims. The next column therefore stabilizes the opening balance sheet, in end-pounds, by raising the figures by 30 percent; at this time (which precedes the pound's loss of value) the loan is still equivalent in purchasing power to 130 of the end-pounds, and so must be shown at 130. At date (2), when inflation occurs, the burden of the loan is reduced to 100 end-pounds, and the owners' balances expand by this gain.

At date (3) (sale), the stabilized accounts rightly show no trading profit. At (4), replacement goods are substituted for cash. At (5), the gain-on-owing is wiped out by tax and dividend.

Thus the firm ends up exactly where it started. But this would not be true without the £30 gain-on-owing; but for it, the firm would end up with a negative real capital of — £30.

If one's prime purpose is to study the time-lag, to put money liabilities into one's example is to bring in a confusing extra variable (which does not in practice affect tax or dividend directly). The issues stand out more clearly in an example where the firm is financed by the owners' equity. Such an example suggests strongly that the error exaggerates profit, and that firms should be allowed to adjust their profit figures for dividend and tax purposes.

The example does serve at least one useful end. Reformed accounts will stress the reality of loss and gain on money; indeed, the accountants' recommendations in both America and Britain suggest that such figures should be combined with trading profit (which is asking for trouble). When these items become familiar, the next step may be to suggest that they should be put into tax calculations. We can picture a hungry finance minister asking why, if he taxes a gain on an asset, he should let a reduction in liabilities escape. One answer is that tax should not be levied until income is realized; and at what point in time can we treat inflation's gain on liabilities, or deflation's gain on cash, as "realized"?

2. *Economic versus physical growth.* My question about the Rolls is of course an *hors d'oeuvre* to the discussion of whether, in times of inflation, the general index or the

specific index is the better tool for correcting the time-lag error.

I have stated the problem in terms of quest for a stable measuring unit, suggesting that a reasonable substitute for the dollar is a package of all the kinds of goods and services that enable the owner of a firm to preserve his standard of life. If his assets at both the start and end of the year are equivalent to the same number of such packages, he is maintaining this standard. By using the general index (despite its admitted statistical imperfections) to cure the time-lag error, he can with fair accuracy see whether he has achieved the equivalence.

The alternative is to maintain the given set of physical assets. But wealth is not a function of physical characteristics. Reliance on physical units lands us in absurdities; my question about the Rolls illustrates the difficulty of distinguishing between the maintenance and the expansion of capital. To the specific index man, extra tons of material usually constitute expansion, regardless of the material's benefits. But does not the firm expand more convincingly, for purposes of wealth measurement, if the same number of tons reaches a higher real value because of market forces? Again, the makeup of the physical unit often varies over time, as when a machine's replacement is bigger and works faster; should not the specific index man recognize its improvement, and any consequent rise in its price? His explanations of such points seem obscure; I suspect that he must in the end seek for physical measures less crude than the number of units, and that his search will in fact be guided by economic tests. Is it not wiser to recognize from the start that the real value does not hinge on number, size, shape, etc.—that "maintenance" and "expansion" of wealth depend on economic and not physical criteria?

The specific index case has many other flaws. By the physical test, a firm dealing in commodities can never make any gain or loss (so long as it keeps on replacing); and other firms can make "current operating profit" but not "holding gain." Presumably the man who owns shares makes a profit only if their value rises more than some market index (for all companies, or ones in the same industry, or ones of the same size?).

While the real values of their assets are soaring, businessmen are naturally tempted to press for specific index accounting and tax rules. But the cat may jump the other way. When real values fall, shareholders will dislike accounts that give no warning of crisis; and tax rules that do not give relief for holding loss (no matter how disastrous) become intolerable, as LIFO's history shows. If the perhaps abnormal price change of the last few years persuades accountants to adopt the specific index view, they risk a later backlash of resentment, and may be forced to eat their words.

3. Replacement cost charges. The specific index case can be couched in terms of need to charge inputs at replacement cost.

My discussion of the Rolls agreed that it would be sensible and informative to write off inputs at their current value. But it suggested that it is irrational to write off what has never been written on; the extra sacrifice at input date is canceled by the holding gain; and income statements that put in the debit should put in the credit too.

The earlier discussion assumed stable general prices.

When inflation joins real growth, the replacement cost charge must allow for both. But, since inflation brings no real gain, the credit should be confined to real growth only. An example is given in column (3) of Table 2.

The simplest way to charge current replacement cost is usually to update historical cost with the specific index. LIFO is a poor substitute. Its initial justification (on grounds of physical sequence of material issues, etc.) is plainly a silly irrelevance. It is an incomplete cure, even by its own standards, when physical quantities are not the same at both the start and end of the year, and also if there is a peak during the year. Its fossil figures do not suit the modern balance sheet. And it cannot easily fit into accounts that are reformed by revaluation or stabilization.

If input prices rise much faster than the general index, the specific index approach may place an unwelcome burden on the income statement. And one may ask whether the pure specific index doctrine does not demand an even heavier burden. Where input will not be replaced till some future date (depreciating assets), the specific index man fails by his own standards if he charges only *current* replacement cost. He ought to guess the extent of real change between now and replacement date, and base his charges on the *future* figures.[9] But this additional burden would hardly endear him to managers and shareholders, and would be wholly unacceptable to outsiders such as tax officials. Thus the more modest aim of the general index man—maintenance of real capital, not replacement of assets—seems superior for practical as well as logical reasons.

---

[9] The discounting formula for general index and specific index forecasts has been set out by N. Carrier in "Depreciation, Replacement Price, and Cost-of-Capital," *Journal of Accounting Research,* Spring 1971.

THE FINANCIAL BURDEN OF REPLACEMENT

The specific index man will rightly complain that I have so far left out what is perhaps his most telling argument. Rising input prices bring liquidity problems, and his proposals might go a long way to ease these.

Expansion and Cash Needs

I suggest that the argument should be considered in two steps.

1. Physical expansion. Suppose a firm expands by building an extra wing on its factory, and in consequence is hard pressed for cash. To remedy the shortage, it may ask its stockholders to plow back more by accepting a dividend cut; or it may ask existing and potential stockholders to put up fresh capital. These people will then consider whether the proposed investment will be the most fruitful use of their money. The firm should give them the clearest possible data on profits, cash flows, etc.; and it will not achieve clarity if it muddles up its income statement and cash budgets, and says that income is reduced by the cash needs.

2. Value expansion. When the expansion takes the less obvious form of real appreciation on the same physical level of assets, surely stockholders should again have the right to decide on their best policy—how much to plow back, and how much to withdraw as dividend. Surely too they should again be given a clear income statement, which here means a statement that reveals the appreciation on trading assets, and is not biased by pending cash needs.

Managers however do not take kindly to the notion of

non-physical growth. They doubtless concede that, when asset values rise, it is better to own such assets than not to do so. But they are apt to argue that even such real growth is somewhat hollow, because their firms cannot raise sale prices in step with asset values, and so the extra wealth will yield no extra revenue—a singularly short-sighted belief. More important, they dislike the physical contraction (caused by inability to pay for replacement of the same number of tons, etc.) that high taxes and dividends can bring. And they may have solid grounds for this dislike: contraction sometimes causes a disproportionately big fall in economic efficiency and real profit, e.g., when machines stand idle for lack of materials; it may cause unemployment too. Therefore managers enthuse over any accounting device (such as specific index reform) that conceals economic growth and chokes off stockholders' demands. Their enthusiasm grows still warmer if the tax man is also cajoled into ignoring the growth.

The difficulty is genuine enough. General index reform would lighten it, but would not cure it completely. I do not believe that the best solution lies in debasing our figures—in mixing up the income statement with the cash budget. Bad statistics are not likely in the long run to encourage wise conduct. Directors are not inarticulate; normally they have little trouble in persuading stockholders to limit dividends when this is plainly desirable. If tax concessions are in the national interest, they should be grounded on clear appraisal of the economy's needs, not on expedient makeshifts. Taxes might be geared more closely to dividends, not to total profit; or firms might be given the option of meeting taxes on real appreciation by paying the state with interest-bearing securities (which would be written down again if the assets later suffered decline in real value).

When one looks at him closely, the specific index man turns out to be twin brothers. One is good, the other bad. The asset-brother is usually helpful; the income-brother is a black sheep who seeks to lead us all astray.

APPENDIX: SUMMARY AND ILLUSTRATION

I conclude by recapitulating my proposals and illustrating them with a short example.

Stabilization program. I think that nothing short of full stabilization will meet accounting's needs. In more detail, my program covers these points:

1. Yearly reports should include stabilized accounts.

2. The stabilized balance sheet should update the assets with special indices, and the owners' balances with general indices.

3. Income measurement should allow for the time-lag error, and should consist of separate statements for (a) unrealized real gain, (b) real gain on money liabilities and assets, and (c) profit from operations (including realized real gain).

4. The time-lag error should be corrected with the general index. But, if the assets are revalued with the special index (as real gain calculation implies), the accounts need some device to harmonize the two sets of figures. By far the neatest and most informative device is that described earlier: the income statement that charges used-up inputs at specific index levels, but credits real gain on them—leaving net profit at the level found by general index correction.

An arithmetical example may make these proposals clearer. Suppose that a firm starts with a capital of $1,200. It invests $1,000 in a store of future inputs (goods or machinery), and keeps $200 in cash. Soon after, the general index jumps 10 percent and the special index for inputs 15 percent; then prices are stable. Sales start after the price rise; 30 percent of the inputs (historical cost $300) are used up, and yield $550 sales, so uncorrected profit is $250.

Table 2 shows the firm's accounts in some of their possible versions. Column (1) has the ordinary figures, columns (2), (3), and (4) their stabilized counterparts.

Columns (2) and (3) rely on the subconcept of real capital maintenance. By this test, the time-lag error is 10 percent on $300, i.e., $30; profit falls from $250 of (1) to $220. (2) uses general index factors throughout; so its assets and costs fail to match the current market. (3) uses specific index factors for the assets and costs, which are thus more informative; it also treats the real holding gain on the year's input (300 × [115 − 110] = 15) as realized profit.

Column (4) agrees with (3) in applying the specific index to assets and costs. But it relies on the subconcept of physical capital maintenance, and therefore cannot admit that the $15 real appreciation on the year's input is gain; the only profit that it recognizes is the current operating figure of $205. Presumably it is still less likely to label the $35 appreciation on the remaining asset as gain. Specific index advocates hardly seem clear about how to name or calculate the owners' balances. I have done my best to help them, but have sprinkled this area with question marks as warnings of my limited understanding of their thoughts.

TABLE 2 Various forms of price level adjustment

Type of capital maintained	Ordinary accounts Money (1) $	Real (2) end-$	Stabilized accounts — Real (with SI asset values) (3) end-$	Stabilized accounts — Physical (4) end-$
Income statement				
Input cost	300	330	345	345
Operating revenue	550	550	550	550
Current operating profit			205	205
Realized real holding gain on input (345 − 330)			15	
Total operating profit	250	220	220	205
Balance sheet				
Cash ($200 + $550)	750	750	750	750
Non-money asset (future input)	700	770	805	805
	1450	1520	1555	1555
	1200	1320	1320	1320
Capital:				?
Original				
Real holding gain (unrealized asset)			35	?
Revaluation surplus (unrealized asset)				35
Replacement cost allowance (realized asset)				15
Profit:				
Loss on holding cash		(20)	(20)	?
Operating	250	220	220	205
	1450	1520	1555	1555

Floor Discussion

Baxter: The position in our two countries, Britain and America, is not very dissimilar. In both, we accountants are told that on such-and-such a date we must introduce supplementary statements that are based on stabilization, that is, wholesale adjustments with indices. In Britain, the adjustment is to be based entirely on a general index; and, in America, almost entirely. I think that in later years, we'll be saying the new American system is inconsistent in that there will still be a LIFO element in it. I'm pretty certain that, in retrospect, we shall see that these statements were, as Professor Fabricant has said, halfway houses. I should imagine that, in the long run, they will be amended. So I should like to look at the problem from the standpoint of not so much what they are going to do now, as what they'll have to do in the long run. What do we think they are going to reveal?

The first point, already discussed, is that these asset values will merely be updated historical costs. We've commented on the fact that we are all using words in different senses.

May I say that "current value accounting" is probably the last name to apply to costs updated with a general index. Current value should be found from the current price of the given asset; but it can also be found, as a matter of convenience and simple arithmetic, with a specific index provided the specific index is good enough. So, if I use "specific index" I am referring to current value accounting; I use that particular label as a convenient shorthand for describing the process by which it is sometimes cheap and simple to get the answer. But to be precise, current value must be narrowed down further—I believe with a formula that compares replacement cost with the higher net realizable value and value in use, and so arrives at "deprival value." This is the gospel of Professor J. C. Bonbright, who seems to me one of the two great Americans in this field. I suspect that there will be great criticism of both the American and British standards on the ground that they don't deal well with assets.

For purposes of management, assets should be valued in the way that gives the most realistic help with problems and decision making (that is, at deprival value); and, while adjusted historical costs may on occasion come near this value, obviously there will be very many exceptions, and sometimes the margin will be wide. And it seems to me that, of the various figures you could use to inform shareholders, probably the best is the one that is also the most useful to management in its decisions. The balance sheet should show current values.

This would bring unrealized appreciation into the accounts. My second point concerns its treatment. It seems to me that although such appreciation is a genuine enough gain, it is very different from ordinary trading results, and should not be displayed cheek-by-jowl with the ordinary trading operations but in some separate part of the accounts. The two gains are as different, say, as my salary and the unrealized appreciation on my house. Both are good things and, I think, constitute income. But they are very different in two senses: one of these is concerned with the test of realization; and the other with the administration chart, that is, who is responsible for making the two different kinds of gain.

My third point is about the maintenance of capital. Should we use real or physical capital as base? The Standards Board, except for its one digression for LIFO, has come out for the maintenance of real capital. I think its decision is the right one, and that the people who believe in physical concepts will run into the most enormous difficulty. One reason is that an asset's economic properties are quite different from its physical properties. If you've got the same number of cows but their market value is growing, are you not better off in a sense that should be recognized?

LIFO theory, it seems to me, comes very near to the idea that if you have the same number of tons of raw material at the beginning and the end then you haven't made any profit—that number rather than worth is the basis of wealth. To be consistent, the American Standards Board should switch over to FIFO calculation plus general index adjustment, rather than continue to allow LIFO. Of course, it may be that in these things one doesn't need consistency. Professor Bonbright suggests that what is politely called an eclectic decision by a law court (in other words, a muddled decision) is often railed as an extremely good one because the parties in the case are also in a mental muddle.

Professor Fabricant wisely pointed out that we should test these proposals in the light of how they would work when general prices are stable. I suggest we should also look at them from the standpoint of how they would work when things are going badly rather than when things are going well. The advocates of physical maintenance say little about declines in the real value of assets. Instead, they stress the need for more cash when replacement costs rise. While I admit the budgetary need for cash, it seems to me we ought not to meet it by altering something so fundamental as the method of measuring income. I think the problem should be approached much more directly and, if I may say so, honestly. After all, the presidents of companies know how to be persuasive, and surely can advise their shareholders to take a low dividend now because of a particular situation that calls for extra finance—an expansion of inventory or plant. I certainly wouldn't be adverse to a tax concession—for instance, you might get some arrangement by which a company pays the government in equity shares, and later, if the real value of the inventories declines, may cancel such shares.

Well, here we are, in a halfway house. I'm sure that the reason we find this attractive is that it has been a very painful business for the older generation to reeducate ourselves. So we like this step-by-step progression to something rather complicated and to us strange. But younger people don't feel this way about it, and can accept more complete reform. It is rather like showing children modern art, which, to me, often seems incomprehensible, but doesn't upset them in the least because to them the classical stuff is just as unfamiliar.

Carsberg: It's a difficult job to act as a discussant to Will Baxter. I should like to begin by congratulating him on his paper—I agree substantially with his conclusions though I shall qualify that remark a little later and I also enjoyed

very thoroughly his exposition of it. It has seemed to me for
a long time that Will is a model exponent of English and I
think his presentation today has underlined my view about
that. I particularly enjoy in his use of English the un-
expected phrase which is graphic in its application. I enjoyed in this paper the notion that it was quite wrong to
subtract cats from cows and, such is the perversity of the
human mind, I immediately set to trying to think of cases in
which it would be sensible. I have to be a little whimsical in
coming up with a solution. I live in a house which has a farm
field immediately behind it and that farm field is full of cows.
I own a cat which often wanders into the field in search of
unwary field mice and then becomes terrified of the mellow
monsters in the field and has to be rescued. I imagine
(perhaps this is stretching language too far) that at that
time I'm subtracting cats from cows. I think I could find
other examples in which it would be sensible.

The problem, I think, is that the sense or nonsense of
such an action depends upon the purpose for which one
is undertaking it. It does seem to me that the argument
by analogy and by simile, while suggestive and helpful, is,
at the time, dangerous because it doesn't get down to the
fundamental issues. My main plea at this time must be for
work on an agreed framework within which a logical choice
of accounting method can be made. It appears to me that
any framework must involve a number of ingredients. It
must first identify the users of the accounting statements;
secondly, it must say what the objective of the users is; and
thirdly, it must relate the information provided to the users
with their objective in a way which shows whether various
sorts of information are more or less likely to help with the
achieving of the objectives.

The paper does, indeed, touch on these considerations. At

various times it mentions use by investors, by managers and by trade unionists, but it doesn't, nor does any other writing that I'm familiar with, develop the logical process carefully within the proper framework that I have described.

The argument that accounting information which is useful in management decisions is a strong contender for inclusion in published accounts seems to me to be dangerous. The fact that information is relevant for management in one particular use doesn't necessarily indicate that it is the right thing to report in an alternative use. If one considers the problem of reporting to shareholders, it seems to me that one would reasonably arrive at the notion that shareholders are interested in making decisions which will enable them to optimize their consumption. I'm not suggesting that shareholders should expect to get information which will enable them to beat the market. The efficient-market literature suggests that publicly available information is reflected in the share price almost immediately. What I am suggesting, however, is that if shareholders are given more efficient information, they may be able to adjust their own personal positions to the market with respect to risk and patterns of consumption; moreover, there may be incidental benefits in terms of improving the efficiency of the allocation of resources in the economy.

In that context, the mixture which Will has proposed is promising. I have prepared a very simple example in which I show how things would work out. I suggest a firm, the main business of which is simply the holding of inventory. It buys a material which is held for two years before sale. The current value of material purchased for £1 is £1.25 one year after purchase and the material will be sold for £1.5625 (i.e., £1.25²) after two years. This increase in value may be thought of as due to the material's maturing in store as well as to the impact of general inflationary forces. The initial capital of the firm is £1,000 at the start of year 1 (at time 0) and will be used to buy 1,000 tons of material. Additional capital of £1,200 will be subscribed at the end of year 1 (at time 1) and used to buy an additional 1,000 tons. The price of the material is expected to increase at 20 percent per annum. Additional supplies of 1,000 tons will be purchased at yearly intervals in order to maintain a constant physical stock. Taxation is ignored and it is assumed that there are no costs of holding or selling stock. The general price index is expected to increase by 15 percent per annum. Surplus cash is paid to shareholders as a dividend. Cash flows are summarized in Table 1 and Tables 2 to 4 give profit reports and balance sheets drawn up according to conventional historical cost accounting, CPP accounting and current value accounting.

Consider the potential of our firm's activities for generating consumption. Assume that shareholders do not expect to obtain any consumption at time 1 from their

TABLE 1   Cash flows

Time	0	1	2	3	4	5
	£	£	£	£	£	£
Profit						
Capital introduced	+1000.0	+1200.0				
Sales			+1562.5	+1875.0	+2250.0	+2700.0
Purchase of materials	−1000.0	−1200.0	−1440.0	−1728.0	−2073.6	−2488.3
Net receipts and dividend	0	0	+122.5	+147.0	+176.4	+211.7

TABLE 2   Historical cost accounts

Time	0	1	2	3	4	5
	£	£	£	£	£	£
Profit						
Sales	—	—	1562.5	1875.0	2250.0	2700.0
Cost of sales	—	—	1000.0	1200.0	1440.0	1728.0
Net profit	—	—	562.5	675.0	810.0	972.0
Dividend	—	—	122.5	147.0	176.4	211.7
Retained profit	—	—	440.0	528.0	633.6	760.3
Balance sheet						
Share capital	1000.0	2200.0	2200.0	2200.0	2200.0	2200.0
Retained profits	—	—	440.0	968.0	1601.6	2361.9
Stock	1000.0	2200.0	2640.0	3128.0	3801.6	4561.9

TABLE 3   CPP accounts

Time	0	1	2	3	4	5
	£	£	£	£	£	£
Profit						
Sales	—	—	1562.5	1875.0	2250.0	2700.0
Cost of sales	—	—	1322.5	1587.0	1904.4	2285.3
Net profit	—	—	240.0	288.0	345.6	414.7
Dividend	—	—	122.5	147.0	176.4	211.7
Retained profit	—	—	117.5	141.0	169.2	203.0
Balance sheet						
Share capital	1000.0	2350.0	2702.5	3107.9	3574.1	4110.1
Retained profits	—	—	117.5	276.1	486.7	762.7
Stock	1000.0	2350.0	2820.0	3384.0	4060.8	4872.8

investment—they regard the first year as a development phase. The value of the firm at time 1, equal to the present value of the future dividends, is:

$$W = \frac{122.5}{1.25} + \frac{147}{1.25^2} + \frac{176.4}{1.25^3} + \frac{211.7}{1.25^4} + \ldots = 2{,}450$$

TABLE 4   Current value accounts

Time	0	1	2	3	4	5
	£	£	£	£	£	£
Profit						
Sales	—	—	1562.5	1875.0	2250.0	2700.0
Cost of sales	—	—	1562.5	1875.0	2250.0	2700.0
Net profit	—	—	—	—	—	—
Holding gain (realized and unrealized)	—	100.0	245.0	294.0	352.8	423.4
	—	100.0	245.0	294.0	352.8	423.4
Dividend	—	—	122.5	147.0	176.4	211.7
Retained profit	—	100.0	122.5	147.0	176.4	211.7
Balance sheet						
Share capital	1000.0	2350.0	2702.5	3107.9	3574.1	4110.1
Retained profits	—	100.0	237.5	420.1	659.5	970.2
Stock	1000.0	2450.0	2940.0	3528.0	4233.6	5080.3

Since the money rate of return on the firm's investment is 25 percent per annum, the return at time 2 will be £612.5 (i.e., £2,450 × 0.25); 15 percent, i.e., £367.5, must be reinvested to maintain purchasing power of wealth, and the remaining £245 (£612.5 − £367.5) is available for consumption. The reinvestment will produce an increase in money income of 15 percent at time 3 and both reinvestment and consumption may be increased by this amount. Hence the shareholders can enjoy consumption of £245 at time 2 and amounts having the same general purchasing power in subsequent years.

Consider the relative usefulness of the accounting information given in Tables 2 to 4. We have assumed that shareholders will require information to help with their consumption and, implicitly, investment decisions. Shareholders would wish to base their decisions on a prediction of the effect on their consumption potential of various actions they might take. They are interested in information on the real value of their wealth under the management of the firm and on the extent to which money increases in wealth (income or profits) are retained to enable the firm to pay dividends which maintain a constant purchasing power and the extent to which retentions represent an increase in real investment which will generate extra purchasing power in the future. In other words, shareholders require information to enable them to judge whether they should consume the cash paid as dividend, reinvest some of the dividend or augment the dividend by selling some shares.

It seems to me that the historical accounts in Table 1 give a poor basis for shareholders' decisions. They do not show the real wealth that is generated by the firm's activities nor do they provide a basis for predicting the effect of various decisions on the purchasing power of dividends. The CPP (general index) accounts do somewhat better because they at least give some impression of the extent to which purchasing power is being maintained. Provided that there are positive retained profits, shareholders can be assured that the purchasing power of profits will at least be maintained unless rates of return fall. However, CPP accounts do not meet fully our criterion of usefulness because they do not show the extent to which the real wealth of the firm has increased.

The current value accounts (with a general index adjustment) are best of all because they do show the extent to which real wealth is being increased. Holding gains represent increases in the current value of stock over and above the amount required to maintain the purchasing power invested in stock. Net profits, including holding gains, represent the net real increase in investment, the amount which could be consumed without impairing future purchasing power. The profit account at time 2 shows that £245 (as calculated independently above) could be consumed without impairing future purchasing power. Half of this sum is paid as a dividend and the other half is retained to finance an increase in the real investment. Shareholders could sell shares to the value of £122.50 and consume the proceeds without impairing purchasing power (provided that the share price equaled the present value of future dividends). The profit of £294 similarly represents the amount which could be consumed at time 3; it is made up of £245 × 1.15 (to maintain previous purchasing power) plus 10 percent of the increased real investment of £122.50. The entire retained profits of the firm are required for maintenance of the physical level of activities.

In conclusion, I should like to say a word about the Sandilands Committee, the Committee appointed by the British government to investigate the problems of accounting for inflation. There is a lot of interest in predictions of their conclusions. I am not privy to their discussions but I and three of my colleagues at Manchester have given evidence to them and I enjoy sniffing the breeze, guessing at the outcome. It seems to me to be likely that the Committee will favor some form of current value accounting. My illustration and Professor Baxter's analysis agree in suggesting that to be a useful form of accounting. However, neither demonstrates that form of accounting to be best generally in more complex situations, for example, situations in which resource markets are imperfect so that entry and exit prices diverge. Additional research is needed before that stage is reached. The research should concentrate on the usefulness of various types of accounting information in predicting future events which are revelant to the decisions of the information users.

Ruebeck: From May 1971 to January 1974 I resided in Brazil as director of operations for the agricultural products division of Eli Lilly and Company. Coping with inflation was at that time and still is an important part of doing business in Brazil. Since the translation of cruzeiro income statements to dollars is adversely affected by devaluations roughly six times each year, sales, costs and income are directly adjusted for Brazil's inflation in that the amount of devaluation is roughly equal to the excess of Brazil's inflation over that of the United States.

However, even after the impact of devaluations, Brazil was and is an important contributor to corporate dollar earnings. This is the case for two primary reasons. First, Brazil had developed a booming economy which averaged at that time 10 percent real growth annually. Second, Brazil had adopted a number of measures in the previous decade to minimize the distortions of inflation upon doing business while also attempting to contain the rate of inflation through government fiscal and monetary policy.

In 1964, when inflation exceeded 100 percent annual rate at some points in the year, and the economy was near collapse, the military assumed responsibility for the country. Although some are critical of certain social aspects of this military rule, the country since that time has been viewed as a model of economic progress and national economic management. The Brazilians have a system which faces up to the existence of inflation and they have accordingly developed mechanisms to allow the economy to operate in a relatively stable fashion in spite of that fact.

The basic mechanism by which inflation adjustments are made is known as "monetary correction." The National Economic Council periodically issues coefficients of monetary correction, which are used in the calculation of interest rates, for revaluation of assets (fixed and working capital), and to adjust taxable and reported earnings. They also provide a basis for approved movements in prices and wages.

Financial instruments having maturities beyond a few months are issued with two components of interest determination: a fixed portion which might be called the real interest rate, and a variable portion which is the monetary correction. (The creditor is only taxed on the fixed or real interest rate.)

Fixed assets are revalued by the monetary correction. The resulting higher depreciation reduces reported earnings and taxes. The restated assets better reflect potential replacement cost.

Working capital growth is segmented into real and inflationary growth segments, using the coefficients of monetary correction. A tax deduction may be taken for that segment of working capital growth attributed to inflation.

The system has special value to those industries which are fixed asset-intensive, such as utilities. During the period of uncontrolled, unmonetary-corrected inflation, utilities in Brazil had been crippled by the double impact of rapid real growth, which was difficult to finance in the inflationary bond market of that time, and inadequate provision for replacement of obsolete plant and equipment. For industry in general, the revaluation of fixed assets and the working capital adjustment ensure that companies report and pay taxes on real earnings rather than earnings artificially increased by inflation.

Wages are adjusted for inflation, generally, once each year on an "industry"-wide basis. The amount of increases is determined by negotiation between official representatives of industry associations (not trade unions) and the Labor Ministry.

For companies such as ours, personnel and imported raw materials are important elements of cost. Therefore, our profitability is greatly influenced by our ability to increase cruzeiro prices sufficiently to cover the increased wage costs as well as to cover the higher cruzeiro costs of raw materials resulting from frequent devaluations. A bureaucracy (Interministerial Price Council) exists for the purpose of evaluating requests for price increases taking into account the general inflation, but also the specific profitability of the item in question. The price control mechanism therefore provides some relief from inflationary cost pressure, but also provides the government with a means of control.

Since "full relief" is hardly ever obtained in price negotiations, a certain pressure for efficiency is created by the process. While this pressure is a part of the government's objective, it is palatable to the typically efficient American firm only because of the strong underlying real growth.

In conclusion, Brazil's methods of "looking inflation in the eye" and tackling it produce a stabilizing effect upon the financial, industrial and social environment, which is a major stimulus to real growth. Growth, in turn, gives tolerance to firms such as ours to accept the necessary burdens of inflation adjustments, including the real profit impact of less-than-compensatory levels of price increase.

Finally, strong central government insures that the infla-
tion-management effort is kept on a fairly steady course and
avoids most of the detours and distractions from this objective often found in countries with less government stability.

Comparing Brazil's methods of economic calculation
under conditions of inflation with some of those proposed by
the accountants and economists represented at this seminar,
I feel that the Brazilian system accomplishes the objectives
of adjusting income for inflation's effects, of avoiding taxation of inflation-generated earnings, of adjusting capital
and money markets for inflation, and of building an awareness of inflation into corporate and government planning,
which permits both to take steps to reduce the rate of
inflation.

I am not sure that current value or specific index approaches being discussed here would further enhance the
accomplishment of these objectives and the cost of so doing
could be considerable.

From the standpoint of internal corporate planning,
appraisals of current value or special indices will vary at
different points in time and with specific project applica-
tions. The amount of effort needed to generate such information in full detail, updated in each accounting period,
would be enormous. Certainly, the cost of additional staff
required must be considered one more cost of inflation. For
internal planning and analysis, special studies could be done
more effectively and inexpensively on an ad hoc basis.
Furthermore, if accounting records were maintained as they
are now, one would have a "hard-data" base to which adjustments might be made for current reality.

Concerning use of corporate data by external analysts,
I think securities analysts have now learned to adjust finan-

cial statements for inflation as they have learned to do so for the myriad of other complexities of generally accepted accounting principles. Complex inflation adjustments would only confuse the situation for some period while analysts learn to think in terms of the new methods.

Therefore, it would be my recommendation to adjust statements and balance sheets for inflation by using simple methods such as used in Brazil. Use of such an approach in the United States could minimize the cost of adjustments, and yet clearly define the impact of inflation upon earnings.

Vermeulen: When I read Baxter's paper the first time, I had some feeling of deflation because there was so much in it with which I agreed. But then I remembered a French proverb saying that for a good discussion, you have to be basically in agreement. You will hear me supporting much of it. I may also disagree at times, or try to turn his ideas around somewhat in my discussion.

Maybe from a person who has had actual practice in fighting with the problem of current value accounting (inflation accounting is perhaps the word you prefer), you would expect something about how we did it in practice. I feel inclined not to spend too much time on that, although I am willing to answer now, and also after the sessions, any concrete questions you have on that. Generally speaking, we were very much guided by Lord Keynes, who said, "It is far better to be approximately right than to be precisely wrong." With revaluations and current valuations we felt we were coming far closer to justifiable accounting and economic concepts than one would with the historical accounting concepts. It has not been a major problem to arrive at the proper current value basis for buildings, for machines, or for inventories. Partly because a lot of these assets were own manufactured, for which there are updated standard cost prices or, if purchased items are included, you can look up suppliers' price lists to find out what the current costs are.

Machine valuations constitute probably the most difficult problem; but I think this is a problem which every manager, under whatever accounting rules, has to face in order to make justified decisions. There is always the question, When do you replace a machine? The answer to that question, based on the contribution to earnings in comparison with a more modern machine, helps in solving the current value problem of a machine. This problem of evaluation of machinery is something nobody can escape, I think.

In management accounting one always has to defend the figures that are put on the table; they are figures on the basis of which a business or its people are judged. It may even be that part of a manager's pay is dependent on the profit concept used. Now, if we do not come up with a sound theory, and with concepts that are defensible, then in actual practice—it is my experience—the management accountant has no contribution to the solution of any management problem. And partly because of that, I think I disagree with both Professor Fabricant and Professor Baxter when they say "at least it's a halfway house" when they refer to the approach that is being discussed under the title of general purchasing power accounting. I don't know if that is the right point of view. It may give rise to so much misunderstanding that the just case of inflation accounting is considerably set back. Carlyle once said, if you want to have your laws obeyed (or your accounting rules followed) you have to be sure that they are part of God Almighty's law—

otherwise, he said, no artillery in the world could keep down mutiny.

A framework should, I think, give the correlation between the why and the how of a financial statement. For stewardship accounting, historical figures may be more relevant than many people say. The concepts of continuity and capital maintenance may have different meanings for the management and the shareholder. Only when some basic questions here have been answered, can we expect that lasting solutions can be developed.

It is necessary to rigidly distinguish between asset valuation and income concept. There is, as I can see it, only one way to value assets: current value, or, as Professor Baxter says, deprival value. It is my feeling that CPP "valuations" merely replace one set of meaningless figures by another set of meaningless figures. The answer to the question, What is income? depends on the maintenance concept, and is also a question of semantics. Income can be profit plus compensation for inflation (think of bonds or debentures), or income can be either the surplus over original purchasing power or the surplus after providing for *specific* replacements. On these questions the discussion should concentrate.

In Philips answers were found to the problems connected with the establishment of current values for assets. Also, ideas were developed and partly introduced with regard to the income concept. But a consistent application through good and bad times without the support of a generally accepted accounting rule, in an environment that not always understands, and where there is seldom time to study annual reports profoundly, is asking very much from a management. I subscribe very much to what has been said before: a ruling is essential.

When dealing with the income statement, Professor Baxter discusses some shortcomings of the special index approach. I submit that they will disappear when we consistently use the term current value. It does away with the idea of physical replacement and brings us close to the economic valuation. Replacement value is a misnomer insofar as it suggests physical identical replacement.

The problem of charging future replacement costs for depreciating assets is not as grave as it looks. In an ongoing business every year the current value basis depreciation is mostly sufficient for the continuous stream of investment projects, and both are on the same price level.

As far as Professor Baxter's conclusion is concerned, that the maintenance of the real capital—that is, in general purchasing power—might be the best objective for an enterprise (especially when considering the shareholders' interest), and, consequently, is basic for the profit concept, I have very much sympathy therewith and two questions.

1. When the specific price level for a firm's assets rises faster than the general level, the business will either shrink or fall more and more in the hands of third-party financiers, given a stable level of activity in volume. What is Professor Baxter's opinion regarding the thesis of some people: maintain real capital in general purchasing power terms, unless for the individual firm the specific price trends require one to maintain the higher capital required for replacement of specific assets?

2. How do we describe or treat or neutralize that surplus that will arise in a business where the real capital is maintained on general purchasing power basis, but the specific values increase only slightly or not at all?

When I read the material for this conference, and much of what is written currently in the U.S. and the U.K., I cannot but fear that CPP accounts might appear on the scene. T. S. Eliot once said that doing the right thing, for the wrong reason, is treason. I am afraid that we will perhaps see the wrong thing done for the right reason. That would be a tragedy.

But that is not the right note to end my comments with. It is a great thing that accountants, economists, and financial people all over the world are trying to come to grips with the subject matter of this conference. I am confident that, hopefully without too much mutiny in between, our profession will succeed in developing the proper laws.

Baxter: Mr. Vermeulen touched on significant points in his questions. What he said was this: that if you seek to maintain your real capital, what do you do when the real replacement value of your inputs (materials or depreciating assets or whatever) goes up? At such a time, it would be helpful if you could keep cash in the kitty to pay for replacement, and so it would be very convenient if you could use a physical maintenance basis instead of real capital. I think this is exactly the same problem as you have when a company decides that it must expand in a physical sense, for instance, when it needs to put up a new wing on its factory, without which it will no longer be able to compete. This, heaven knows, is a genuine problem. But, if you were putting up a new wing on your factory, you wouldn't try to meet the problem by issuing low profit figures. You would instead have to look facts in the face, and say we are expanding and must get money from somewhere by borrowing or restricting dividends. Facing facts is awkward, and the pressure to pay dividends is awkward. So it seems to me that there is a very real need for accountants to explain this point fully to management, the public, and government—to argue that assets are going up faster than the prices of things in general, there ought to be tax concessions and far-sighted dividend policies. I'm always in favor of doing things in the direct way, and of producing figures that are candid. It seems to me that it would be wrong to fake our income figures, instead of explaining the facts openly.

The contrary situation suggested by Mr. Vermeulen, when a firm had maintained its real capital but the replacement prices of its assets sank, brings in a legal complication. The complications are mostly artificial rather than anything else. To protect creditors, the law doesn't readily let a company pay out capital. I appeal to the economists for guidance here, but I take it their rule would be that it is a good thing to pay out such excess capital to shareholders, so that they can use it on consumption or invest it in something more to their advantage.

Fabricant: In the case of a country like Chile or Brazil and others that have triple-digit inflation, everybody thinks the times are solid. And where's the correction?

Moonitz: That was done in Central Europe after World War I, in the 20s.

Fabricant: Well, move the cigarettes.

Moonitz: They used Swiss gold francs instead of German marks.

Rogge: Comparing the currency with the dollar is like a caddy of mine who used to mark my ball by a blackbird.

Earl: Ben, I may be confused here, but it seems to me that when we mix the concepts of current value accounting with the concepts of adjustments for the loss in purchasing power of the dollar, we are doing two different things. And if we do not keep them separate, in whatever we do, we are making a grave mistake not only in what we try to do from a practical standpoint within the company, but from the standpoint of what a regulatory agency might come up with in the way of recommendations. I say this because I have really had some reservations about current value accounting, primarily from the standpoint of how you avoid manipulations and how you handle the problem of current value accounting when you are dealing with an economic situation where you have a rate of inflation like they are experiencing in Chile and Brazil. By the time you could get the appraisal or the valuation of the asset made, the price level has changed maybe two or three points. I really have some reservations about current value accounting when you rely on people to do the evaluating who are also employees of the company. I think there is some conflict of interest that enters into the situation at that point.

Moonitz: This reminds me that some years ago I heard of a large U.S. industrial company which, for internal purposes, was using current value to determine operating results in its various plants. They developed their own specific index of construction costs, for example, as the basis of depreciation charges, but they realized they were vulnerable to dissatisfaction on the part of the plant manager because the index came from New York. So the company looked for an outside index which behaved the way theirs did and they found one in one of the McGraw-Hill

Construction Indices. The correlation with theirs was very high, so they dropped their own and used the outside index. You see, for a very large company, this will work because they were constructing continuously somewhere around the country. So this is one way you can overcome this if you can get an outside measure, you see, which is not dependent upon—

Earl: Well, I think even with outside interest, if they grow to rely on a company for that business and they are also specialists for this sort of thing—

Moonitz: Obviously, there can be situations, but in general terms it doesn't necessarily follow. I don't see how the McGraw-Hill index would be influenced by what Indiana Telephone does or doesn't buy from them.

Earl: They might very well be influenced by a company the size of AT&T, which provided 75 percent of their business.

Moonitz: McGraw-Hill's business?

Earl: Well, yes.

Moonitz: Well, yes, approximately.

Vermeulen: May I comment on that. All the journal entries that you carry on the books by which you revalue machines or buildings are, of course, subject to audit control—you have to do it in a way that stands up to verification and certification by the auditors.

Vancil: I just wanted to pick up on what Mr. Vermeulen said. I was very taken with your statement that you were preparing accounting data to help managers and for the evaluation of managers. I can understand the relevance of how you revalue inventories—you can easily do it because you have standard costs, and it is desirable, it seems to me, because then your managers are looking at the costs of the product they are going to sell; it will cost that much to replace it and that is a relevant number.

I would like to separate the inventory question from the machinery and equipment because I also was very taken with your statement that you can't tell when a machine is obsolete. It is obsolete when you finally decide that you'll throw it away and build a new one. I don't understand why you go to the trouble to calculate the current value of every piece of equipment at any particular point in time when that is not used for the replacement decision. As I would understand it, you make the effort to do that, but I don't see that decision-making value of the current valuation of equipment and plant.

Vermeulen: It is because we believe that hardly anything is more essential than the standard cost price. That cost price will be an instrument in the hands of thousands of people who have to set prices on the market. If the cost price is not reliable, they will go to the market with a price that's not a real basis to start trading with.

Rogge: How do you value a piece of motorswitch equipment in the telephone industry which is in use and giving service and yet is no longer being manufactured? I may have picked the wrong example, but the kind of equipment that is no longer manufactured.

Vermeulen: You might have to go in this case as a decision maker, considering replacement of it by another product in a new technology—maybe a solid state switch system designed to increase operating efficiency—and then find out if there is still any value to be attached to the old machine.

Russell: How do you account for the cost of obsolescence in pricing when the regulatory commission setting the utility's rates refuses to recognize the obsolescence? In your example, you would recognize the obsolescence as depreciation; however, without the regulatory commission's approval, I cannot recover the capital from rate payers and the loss must be borne by the shareholder.

Vermeulen: I would like to refer to what Mr. Terborgh said. I think what you try to do (but who am I to give an opinion on that industry?) is to come to an accelerated type of depreciation.

Davidson: But the real answer to Alan's question is that the remedy lies in the commissioner appointment process rather than in the accounting process.

Rogge: Now, remember that, world! We have two men here who have been appointed chairmen of the Public Service Commission.

Fletcher: I would like to ask Mr. Vermeulen one question and that is, what do you do with cost variances?

Vermeulen: A favorable variance goes into the P & L account if you believe in your standards. You may, of course, have to review your standards, and you may find you have to correct them.

IV

Economic Calculation by Capital Intensive Industries During Periods of Inflation

William H. Fletcher

To the extent that a local government or, for that matter the federal government, seizes the property of its citizens through taxation and expends it for purposes it deems worthy rather than the citizens' using the money for their own purposes, no inflation occurs. Purchasing power has simply moved from one party to another. The same is true when the borrower takes the purchasing power of a creditor and expends it for his purposes rather than those of the creditor. The cause of inflation which is non-self-liquidating and permanent is the federal government's monetization of its own debt; that is, the expansion of the money supply to pay for goods and services without an immediate, equal, and offsetting reduction in the taxpayers' purchasing power.

It is difficult to refrain from judging the morality of the government's action, but that is not the purpose of this paper. The purpose is rather to improve the ability to calculate during a period of inflation. The timing of the actions of government in creating inflation is not easily predicted and one might be tempted to ignore governmental action in economic calculation during inflation, but this would be an extremely perilous omission. Unpredictable as the timing may be, it seems clearly predictable that the federal government will continue to inflate. In this country we have a "universal" franchise. So far as possible, everyone has the right to vote, whether he produces or only consumes. We have a great many citizens on welfare and many of them have never lived without welfare. Increasing numbers of voters do not pay taxes. Growing numbers of people are directly employed by government at all levels, or perform government contracts to live. It is hard to imagine that those who are on welfare or who are employed by the government at any level, or who rely on government contracts for their subsistence (Lockheed), will find it possible to vote for a balanced budget, because a balanced budget is against their current interest.

FINANCIAL COMMUNICATION

For a long time, accountants, economists and other financial people have consistently found it difficult and often impossible to communicate, not only with those untutored in financial skills, but even with one another. This paper is an attempt to communicate concerning the matter of inflation and its impact on "capital intensive" business. It is directed to those with some knowledge and skill in financial matters, but may also have some success with those who are laymen in this area.

This paper begins with a comment on communication because of the patent failure of past efforts, both oral and written, to enjoy any marked degree of success in causing the best minds of our day to give us tools with which to observe and understand the impact of inflation. Failure to understand inflation makes our economic calculation much more faulty than it would otherwise be.

The one attempting to communicate invariably fails in his choice of language. He may not work hard enough at it; he undoubtedly lacks knowledge in some areas; he often does not read the impact of his communication or clearly understand the reaction; and then there are those who attempt to communicate who are trying to deceive. The person who is intended to receive the communication may not, in fact, receive it because he cannot hear or cannot read. It may be that he does not wish to hear—particularly, bad news. It may be that he is incapable of understanding, but it may be that he is ignorant and does not take steps to cure his ignorance. In addition to all this, we know that one tends to hear what he wants to hear in a given message.

Extra attention has been paid to communication because it is the essence of economic calculation. If we are given incomplete, inaccurate or misunderstood information, our calculations are bound to be erroneous. Even when given reasonably complete and accurate information, our personal limitations of intellect, knowledge, and skill reduce economic calculation to "educated prophecy."

Examples of Poor Communication

Good information ignored. A recent economic analysis prepared for the administration of a large trust department began with a well reasoned, lucid commentary assessing the investment picture during the upcoming 12 to 15 months. The end of the communication listed investment directives to portfolio managers, and these directives were not consistent with the commentary. It was determined that the economist wrote the commentary and the department administrators wrote the directives. Did the economist fail to send the proper impulse, or was there a defect in its receipt? If the administrators did not believe the economist, why did they confuse matters by printing his commentary? If they did believe him, why did they direct investment as they did? What are we to conclude?

Attempts to "remake" poor information. The late Mr. Frank Chutter, of the Massachusetts Investors Trust, believed that by using only information from published statements and published indices he could demonstrate the effect of inflation on capital intensive industries with substantial accuracy. The work of Frank Chutter was desirable and valuable; and it was an honest effort to be helpful. However, because he did not have vintage information available, it is believed his findings are wide of the mark. The work in this area with Ayrshire Collieries, Indiana Telephone Corporation, Public Telephone Corporation and Peoples Loan & Trust Company shows that these calculations require detailed knowledge of the vintage of all assets in the business and a good index of the inflationary changes occurring from one period to the next. Even so, our best effort, with vintage accounting, will produce only a reasonable approximation of the trend line, and we are only mildly successful in defining the amplitudes of deviations from a trend line.

Use of historical cost. Some years ago, the United States Government issued $770 million of 3 percent bonds maturing in February 1995. A banker of some stature considered these to be an excellent investment because they are backed by the full faith and credit of the U.S. Government. Accordingly, his bank put all available funds in this issue. Those were the days when we had bond rollovers available to the banks which would permit them to convert ordinary income into capital gain. The banker considered that the rollover technique could be used to enhance the bank's earnings. As fate would have it, however, 3 percent turned out to be a very modest rate of interest and, in a rather short time, the bonds were selling at a discount larger than the entire net worth of the bank. (I note that the 3s of '95 are now selling at 75–4/32nds.) Because these bonds were the obligations of the United States Government and bound to be paid at maturity in U.S. dollars, no write-down to fair market value was recognized in the financial statements of the bank. Yet, had a fraction of the depositors demanded their money, the net worth of the bank would have been wiped out and, indeed, the depositors would not all have been paid. I lost track of the bank for a number of years, but I have often wondered whether it escaped the sword of Damocles. Historical cost in these circumstances will not permit accurate economic calculation.

PRICE-LEVELING

The economic data must be updated from time to time to be able to make economic calculations of our present circumstances, estimates of the economic changes in the past, and prognostications of economic changes in the future. While a cost of a million dollars for motorswitch communications equipment incurred in 1962 was adequate economic information at the time of installation, it is no longer adequate because of a number of subsequent events, not the least of which is inflation.

Gross National Product Implicit Price Deflator

Indiana Telephone Corporation has been using price level computations for 20 years to figure what has happened from year to year as its fixed assets have depreciated. In recent years, the price-leveling has been done by applying the Gross National Product Implicit Price Deflator to the fixed asset accounts maintained according to the year that the assets became "used and useful." The late Ludwig von Mises, modern leader of the Austrian school of economics, seems to indicate that all indices are imperfect. The preparers of indices change the basis of computation from time to time, and it is probable that indices controlled by political bodies are biased by political considerations.

Why, then, did we use the Gross National Product Implicit Price Deflator? We used it because it is broadly based, calculated by someone else, and published to the world over a long period. Further, changes in design of the index are likely to be widely known. We believe that the purpose of the accounting exercise is to show us what has happened to the purchasing power of our capital. It would be interesting to know what our capital will do in the telephone business (construction price indexing); but before we entertain ideas about reinvestment, we want to know what has happened to our purchasing power (capital). In fact, we want to see the return of the purchasing power of the expended capital before we say there has been a return on it.

Cost-of-Reproduction-New

Why did the company not use cost-of-reproduction-new or, at least, a construction index for the particular equipment involved? We would not foreclose economic calculation by the use of any means or device. It is believed, however, that cost-of-reproduction-new, in a world where technology is moving so swiftly, produces very strange results. For instance, it does not appear economically sound to make calculations on the cost-of-reproduction-new of a 402 card system or a 1401 computer, or iron telephone wire.

These devices are in use today. They are thoroughly obsolete, and it is suspected that any particular job can be done more efficiently and at less expense than it is being done by these items of equipment.

The purchasing power tied up in a particular piece of equipment should be returned to the investor during the use of the equipment and the purchasing power need not, and perhaps should not, be used to replace the deteriorating machine.

Cost-of-reproduction-new and industry construction indices would confuse the effects of obsolescene and scarcity of supply with the general change in the purchasing power of invested capital. Another seemingly fatal defect in cost-of-reproduction-new is the fact that almost nothing now in place will be replaced. Over and over again, the function of a worn-out item is taken over by a substantially different configuration. In the telephone industry, open iron or copper wire is replaced by buried cable, the capacity of which will be expanded by the use of electronic carrier. Or, it is replaced by microwave, and the company simply sends the signal through the air. The old motorswitch and all-relay central office equipment is being replaced by a mini-cross-bar supervised by a solid state computer.

In 1972, 22 ticketers were added to a telephone exchange at a cost of $74,581. When the company prepared to order 18 more in 1974, the price had become $260,000. It would not have made sense to reprice the 92 old ticketers at $14,000 each, or $1,288,000, instead of the price-leveled installation cost.

Current Value Accounting

Why have the telephone companies not attempted to determine the "current value" of the telephone exchange at the beginning and the end of the year in determining depreciation? There seem to be several answers to this.

First, even if "current value" accounting were used, it is desirable—in managing the business and reporting on it— to determine cost. The only valid cost is a price-leveled figure. Cost versus the current value figure would then tell us something important about the increase or decrease in capital and reasons could then be assigned for the increase or decrease in current value unsullied by the changing price level.

Second, the concept of "current value" is so without foundation, without standard, so subjective as to be meaningless. The telephone exchange in place is capable of producing a rather definite number of connections per year. It takes quite a while to put one together. Alone, any piece—a ticketer—will not do the job. Putting the pieces together and "balancing" the exchange is a labor intensive operation. This balance is sometimes lost without disassembling the exchange, and is certainly lost if parts of the exchange disappear. When disassembled and sold on a second-hand market, the sale of the parts, and even of the whole, will recover only a fraction of the installed cost. The high installation cost and the low alternative use make current value a very soft and flexible number.

Current value accounting reminds me of the seemingly endless controversies in which accountants participate concerning the valuation of inventories under the "cost or market, whichever is lower" rule. What is 30 years' supply of washers worth? It seems to be fairly realistic to value one, two or three years' supply of washers but, certainly, the value of the washers for the 30th year has to be very small.

I have in mind a particular part produced by a screw machine in a company which had purchased a bankrupt production line from a competitor at about 10 cents on the dollar. The production line was dismantled and research begun to improve the product so that it could be manufactured and sold at a profit. The 10 cents on the dollar, plus the research and development costs, were capitalized for several years and each year it was argued and reargued that the product and all its associated costs were worth far more than the investment. At that time, the market's appraisal of this company's stock was 40 times earnings. It became obvious after several years, however, that the appraisal of management had been unsupportable and the 10 cents on the dollar and all of the accumulated research and development had to be written off. At just about that time, investors in the stock also reappraised the 40 times earnings down to below 10. The opinions of the management and investors of the value of the inventory and the stock for the past four or five years were simply unsustainable. Current value is so illusory, in my opinion, that I can only refer you to "The Gods of the Copybook Headings" by Rudyard Kipling and suggest a case study re current value accounting and the Webb & Knapp debacle.

Cost vs. Benefit of Price Level Information

Many times the statement is made that price level accounting is too expensive and that it introduces yet another infirmity beyond those of historical cost accounting. At the telephone companies, with all the frailties of our information accepted, the information has been much better than simple historical cost information. Its value is many times the comparatively small expense in acquiring the data.

An excellent example of the value of the price level thinking done by Pierre F. Goodrich, late President of Indiana

Telephone Corporation, lies in the Series 10 First Mortgage Bonds issued by Indiana Telephone Corporation in 1972 and maturing June 1, 2008. They bear an interest rate of 7–¾ percent. The sinking fund requirement is 1 percent, with an option in the company to raise the sinking fund payments an additional 2 percent in 1978 and thereby eliminate any balloon in 2008. Almost three-fourths of these 7–¾ percent bonds replaced old bonds maturing in 1977, 1984 and 1986, which carried interest rates between 3 and 4.25 percent and had balloons at their maturities.

This issue of bonds was novel at the time and thought by some to border on the ridiculous because of the higher interest cost. As of the writing of this paper, the benefits of these bonds and related financing policies are, that the company has no maturing bonds until 1991; its interest cost at 7–¾ percent is below financing rates in the current market; and it is financing a substantial construction program without the requirement to issue more stock or bonds in today's market.

Capital intensive companies will come through the fire of inflation in much better condition if the quality of Mr. Goodrich's bond decision is found in their financing.

Note, again, that this stroke was possible because of the continuing intensive effort to calculate what had happened to the company in units of current purchasing power and to use this information with judgment in making an educated guess about future conditions.

Borrowing to Beat Inflation

As inflation has progressed, there have been a number of people who believe they should borrow so that somehow they will be able to acquire the wealth of their creditor by paying the indebtedness with "cheaper" dollars at some future time. This has a strong appeal to certain traits in the human character and it should be highly successful, provided the debtor stays out of certain pitfalls. He must service his debt! There was a time when voices were heard among the management of a particular business, recommending that it should use short-term bank borrowings to provide working capital and allow the owners to withdraw their capital. This would have permitted greater leverage and probably would have increased the return on the investors' capital considerably while the arrangement succeeded. Nonetheless, as things turned out, banks became short of capital and there was "capital rationing." Capital rationing put some of those who were using short-term borrowing as working capital out of business, and it was the good fortune of the company in question that it had not followed the advice of those who would have satisfied the need for capital by the use of short-term debt.

In addition to the unavailability of additional capital by current bank borrowings, the history of interest rates over the last six or seven years has indicated that the cost of borrowing has doubled, or tripled, during the period. In fact, the cost of borrowing has probably increased more than the capacity of investors to realize income on the capital freed up by the bank borrowings.

If we had a stable economic condition, a company would be able to obtain short-term bank borrowings on a continuing basis and to obtain them at a stable interest rate. The ravages of inflation have made that arrangement hazardous, to the point of peril, in that it has resulted in the unavailability of capital; and when capital has been available, it has been available only at an ever-increasing interest rate. Borrowing short-term and investing long-term is fundamentally an unsound process, and the unsoundness is greatly aggravated by the workings of inflation.

CAPITAL INTENSIVE INDUSTRY

This paper attempts to deal with economic calculation during periods of inflation, with particular reference to those problems connected with companies having heavy capital requirements. It would appear that the differences between capital intensive industry and other business are simply matters of degree. No attempt will be made to define *capital intensive* other than to say that a capital intensive company turns its capital over slowly. Sales divided by total assets is a relatively small number.

The Short Cycle

Some businesses sell large amounts of labor in the form of direct efforts of employees and only small amounts of what accountants call fixed assets. Indeed, a public accounting firm is such a business; so also a TV repair shop; a barber shop; yea, even a department of economics. These enterprises are distinguished by the direct application of labor to the sales transaction. This directness of relationship means a comparatively short cycle from cash to inventory to receivables to cash. In fact, the cycle may be contracted altogether as in the case of a waitress who makes her living from the tips she is paid by customers she has served for no more than 30 to 45 minutes.

In so short a cycle, the impact of inflation on the waitress must soon be offset by increases in her tips or she stops waiting tables. So, also, the accounting house reprices its product, human labor, in line with its increasing "cost" rather currently by marking up that labor above payroll to cover fringes, rent, heat, light, power, supervision, and something for profit. If the market refuses the marked-up merchandise for long, recruiting schedules shrink, personnel are placed elsewhere, and layoffs may occur. All in all, the cycle is short; and the cleansing process of the market operates rather clearly and swiftly.

On the other hand, the cycle in a labor intensive business is not really as short as at first it would appear. For the waitress the cycle is 30 minutes; for the short-order cook the cycle may be eight hours or a week; it may require two or three years to acquire and train the shop manager; and it may take five to 10 years to acquire, train and develop top executives.

It has been observed that as inflation progresses, the customers find it harder to accommodate increasing prices, and it becomes difficult for even the short-cycle operator to pass along his ever-rising costs. So, he must decide how many potentially long-term people he will keep when margins narrow or losses occur. When things become too tight, either he will jettison his expensive, long-term talent to attain a semblance of balanced structure, or he will absorb the loss. Inflation does not repeal the laws of the market.

From this running commentary there develops some grist for us in characteristics of the short-term operator:

1. Generally, he is fully exposed to supply and demand constraints.

2. Almost immediately, he feels the reflection of falling demand in both income and cash flow.

3. Always, he faces the lure of firing the future profit makers to improve present performance.

4. For a long time, he is able to ignore capital requirements because they are relatively small and must reprice currently in an inflationary atmosphere.

The need for, and the force of, the repricing can be simply demonstrated. Suppose the cycle from cash to cash normally is four months and that the working capital requirement is $1,000,000. Let us suppose, further, that the capital was accumulated over a period of 10 years under a 50 percent income tax rate.

What happens when, in a single year, (a) collections slow and the cycle moves from four to five months; or (b) starting salaries jump 12 percent and this change is recognized throughout the organization?

Historically, the company has been adding $100,000 each year to its working capital, to accommodate growth. This has required profits of $200,000 on billings of about $500,-000 per year.

Now, as the collection cycle lengthens, there is an additional capital requirement of $250,000 (25 percent of $1,000,000). If the money can be borrowed at a little above the present prime, it will cost about $30,000 a year and extra billings must now be increased to $530,000 each year.

But suppose the banks says it will not supply the required $250,000. Then, the company must increase the extra billings suddenly to $1,000,000 a year. That may not be feasible in a market with well-financed competition, and our labor intensive, short-cycle business must contract. How much? Why, 20 percent, to bring its working capital requirement in line with its working capital. If it does not contract, it will soon go out of business. If it does contract and loses its customers or its key staff people, it may later go out of business. But, since catastrophe in the future is always less worrisome than a present catastrophe, a present contraction is almost always the answer.

Instead of the collections slowing down, let's look at the second assumption. Compensation moves up 12 percent with no lengthening of the collection period. In this case, the increase is $120,000 (12 percent × $1,000,000). Where can this capital be obtained? First, it can come from the owners, be they old or new. Frankly, this is an illusion; the cost of financing must, sooner or later, come from the customers. If the increase can be borrowed at 12 percent interest and never repaid, billings must increase a mere $14,-000. This borrowing would be feasible if it were only for one year, but not when the years multiply beyond the entrepreneur's capacity to borrow. If borrowings cannot be made, then billings must increase $120,000 to cover the permanent increase in working capital. Here the increase in compensation is tax-deductible, whereas the slowing of collections generally will not decrease taxes. So, it takes twice as much in billings to compensate for a slow account as it does for an equal amount of increase in employees' compensation.

Corrections such as these in the short cycle are needed quickly and are generally out of the way before the next complicating convulsion of inflation occurs.

The Long Cycle

Accumulation. Why have we been considering the simplified examples of inflation and the short-cycle business? Because these same effects are visited upon long-cycle (capital intensive) companies. In capital intensive companies, cash-to-cash moves much more slowly. Fixed assets in capital intensive industry simply represent labor purchased in the form of fixed assets to be used for long periods. Comparatively small amounts of on-the-spot labor are used. Property taxes and insurance rates lag behind and, for a while, capital intensive companies can absorb the short-cycle problems. But, the problems are cumulative. Labor costs are treated currently; taxes and insurance rates catch up in a year or two, and fixed asset replacements come at the end of 15 or 20 or 30 years. When replacements come, the problems of eroded capital and inadequate pricing come home to roost with a vengeance. Needless to say, expansion requirements, environmental protection and fuel crises greatly aggravate the condition.

If you will examine the balance sheet published by almost any public utility, you will see that it does not readily present the information for calculating working capital or a current ratio. People working in this industry, and the accountants who examine the financial statements, will tell you that the current ratio is unimportant, probably misleading, and, at best, irrelevant. It would be interesting to survey the controllers of all companies, including utilities, which have large investments in fixed assets, to learn their present feelings about the importance of liquidity and its measurement. They are pointedly concerned with it at this time. Commercial companies having a large capital investment do report summary information concerning working capital, including the working capital ratios, but utilities persist in ignoring such "foolishness."

Open-end pricing. Indiana Telephone Corporation ordered some telephone cable in 1974, which had a lead time of three to six months. Before the cable was delivered and after orders were placed, the supplier indicated that deliveries would be priced at the time of delivery without regard to any previous arrangement. Since cable was in short supply and the labor costs and commodity costs involved in its production were escalating rapidly, the purchaser accepted delivery on this basis. The average increase in cost of the cable was 30 percent to 40 percent over the order price. On a million dollars' worth of cable, the immediate impact on the cash account was an unplanned drain of $300,000 to $400,000. This represents an overrun in the 1974 capital budget and, itself, serves immediately to require a cutback in construction during 1975.

Borrowing or additional stock investments is the only source of additional capital with which to keep 1975 construction at the level of 1974 because the recovery of the cost of the cable, and any profit from its investment, will accrue over some 20 to 30 years. Not wishing to issue additional stock or bonds, the company will reduce its 1975 construction budget and defer the excess construction to the future. And what is the effect of this? The effect is to face construction costs increasing as much as 2 percent a month. An item deferred from 1975 is likely to be accomplished in 1980 at a cost 100 percent to 120 percent over the 1975 figure. To borrow, on the other hand, is to create debt on which the interest rate will be 11 percent to 13 percent. The debt will require service beginning immediately and since neither the customer nor the Public Service Commission guarantees the debt, the increased indebtedness serves as a threat to the equity of the company. This is especially true should miscalculations by the "masters" of the economy in Washington cause us to slide into depression. In fact, there is some indication that our government may succeed in bringing to pass simultaneous depression and inflation. This appears to be an inauspicious time in which to incur debt unless it can be long-term at a low, fixed interest rate with a modest, mandatory sinking fund. This is a time to improve liquidity, to report it accurately, and to husband it carefully.

Pricing Obstacles

Declining liquidity. Once the cable has been purchased and put in place, even at a price 30 percent to 40 percent above budget, it will then generally be necessary to raise the price to the customer to absorb these cost increases. In this regard, the business faces a large number of obstacles. First and foremost is the declining liquidity of its customers who themselves are suffering from inflation. A number of them today are unemployed. If the price cannot be increased to recover price-leveled cost and some profit to equity, the company cannot stay in business.

Governmental controls. Secondly, we have overt and covert governmental controls. The overt controls are administered by the Public Service Commission, whose job it is to see that we, the prisoners of our customers, do not receive too little for the service; and, conversely, that our customers, who are our prisoners, do not pay too much. The covert controls arise because rate making or price determination in these days is a political affair. It must be done with regard to the next election; with respect to whether the legislature or the Congress is in session; with respect to the attitude toward a federal deficit. In short, it must be determined to what extent the power of the state will interfere with the operation of the marketplace. Since it is a clearly announced policy that interference will take place, knowledge of the direction, the extent, and the weight of that interference must be sought and considered at all times.

Continued inflation. In the case of the cable, we are investing money for a period up to thirty years. What is the best guess of the government's effect on the operations of the marketplace during that period? Since the government is already taking a significant share of real income, plus a large wedge of capital each year, it would seem that the ability to take more is fairly finite. Nonetheless, it is to be observed that an almost balanced national budget for fiscal 1975 has now been abandoned, and the estimates of the deficit have moved from $5 billion to $15 billion, to $35 billion, and to perhaps as much as $70 billion to $100 billion. There may be, in fact, much greater capacity to tax than I suspect, through the use of budgetary deficits that create inflation.

Now, what does this portend for the cable being put into the ground? It would seem that the price of future cable will continue to rise, and it appears that inflation will accelerate until the spiral burns itself out. When the inflation is raging, the price of cable leaps forward. When recession is waxing strong, the demand for telephone service shrinks. As the economy hits the low amplitude of the variations around the inflationary trend, we must be prepared to pull in our horns and service debt and equity from previously accumulated funds. Sooner or later, any company which is overextended in debt is very likely to find itself unable to service the debt as the economy proceeds through ever-increasing undulations around the trend line.

Best Hope

The best hope of survival will lie in first-class fixed assets, whether they are natural resources or man-made assets, which can be put into service with relatively small amounts of capital during the period of recovery from the depression into which the inflation will drive us. Accordingly, the plan best suited to capital intensive industry is to reduce debt, not expand it, to put as much first-class plant in place as possible without outside financing, and to maintain that plant productively in prime condition to allow it to coast through periods of adversity.

The steel example. While any capital intensive industry suffers from the fact that price corrections can be deferred from time to time and for some time, the need for these price corrections does pile up and must be satisfied in the marketplace. Within the last year or two, the stock of a certain steel company was selling in the marketplace for one-third of its historical, depreciated book value. This means that it was selling for less than one-third of its price-leveled book value. The loss of value seems at least partly due to the failure to raise prices to cover existing and foreseeable costs in the production of steel. Resistance to price increases in this industry has been greatly aggravated by the price controls which are supposedly no longer with us, by the new price controls effected by President Ford (but publicly not in existence), and by the activities of the Environmental Protection Agency—witness the attempt of U.S. Steel to increase its prices by 8 percent recently.

Accounting Sins—Historical Cost, Flow-Through, and Interest

In making price increases, it seems imperative that capital intensive industry acknowledge the consumption of its capital in the production process. To use historical cost in figuring depreciation simply fritters away the company's assets to the short-term benefit of customers and to their

long-term detriment. Beclouding the cost of capital intensive industry even further, business, with some help from
government, invented a concept called "flow-through" accounting. This permits decreases in current taxes resulting
from the use of accelerated depreciation methods for tax
purposes and from the benefits of the investment tax credit
to be called income in reported statements. There was a
headline in the financial section of a newspaper indicating
that the profits of Republic Steel had climbed 44 percent in
a particular year, while Union Drawn had moved only 27
percent. A reading of the article furnished figures which
showed that the difference in profit performance was entirely
attributable to the use of flow-through by Republic and the
lack of it by Union Drawn. Many companies have used
this flow-through technique, and it generally means that
future customers must pay for the benefits received by past
customers. It will be interesting to see whether regulatory
commissions, which insisted on flow-through, will now stand
up to the political fire and require future customers to pay
for benefits which the public service commissions passed
along to old customers.

Another distorting element in utility accounting which
has its parallel in start-up costs and research and development in commercial accounting, is interest during construction. Many of the new utility installations, particularly
in the electric business, require amounts of capital far
beyond those used by most industry. In the financing
climate immediately behind us, the interest costs to carry
this capital have been very large. It has been the practice
in the utility business, growing out of the unwillingness
of customers to pay currently for the costs of the utility
during the lead time necessary to produce new plant, that

the interest during the construction period is capitalized in the cost of the asset. If all goes well, it is then recovered by depreciation over the period of use of the asset. When building a large facility, there is a real question as to the time at which it becomes used and useful. Because of that very real ambiguity in the engineering determination of used and useful, there is an equal ambiguity in the time at which interest ceases to be charged to fixed assets and begins to be charged to the income statement. In order to buy more time in the hope that conditions for utilities would improve, many utility managements have deferred the recognition of "used and useful" for varying periods of time to permit the interest charges to enter the fixed assets and avoid the income statement. Failure to recognize these costs currently has allowed these companies and the regulatory commissions to defer raising utility rates to realistic levels.

As indicated, these practices—the failure to acknowledge adequate depreciation, the use of flow-through, and the capitalization of interest during construction—have brought us to a time when utility rates must catch up because they were not raised at the point when the cost was incurred, and the cash position of some utilities has finally deteriorated to the point where even though their statements show income, they are, or soon will be, unable to pay their debts as they mature. An examination of the federal bankruptcy statutes will indicate that this is one definition of bankruptcy.

Long-term Debt (Bonds)

One of the most important economic calculations involves understanding the result of long-term debt. Incurring long-

term debt produces liquidity at the time the debt is nego-
tiated, which is more or less offset as the debt is serviced
through the payment of interest and principal. This offset
process becomes catastrophe when the debtor fails to earn
sales dollars in ever-increasing amounts. It follows that a
company which is expanding its indebtedness generally becomes more liquid, and a company which is contracting its
indebtedness becomes less liquid. It is a phenomenon of
inflation that greater quantities of currency are circulating
and debt can be paid with "cheaper dollars," but it becomes
more difficult to obtain those cheap dollars to pay debt as
the inflation progresses because of the continuing miscalculations of both business and its customers.

Accounting Questions—Bonds

Accounting questions that must be solved when the value
of the monetary unit changes include the question of how
much gain or loss results from the continuing debt, whether
the gain or loss belongs to the creditor, the stockholder or
the customer, and when it should be recognized. Without
some kind of escalation in the credit contract, the creditor
will not be entitled to any gain aside from interest payments.
Who receives the gain or loss, therefore, becomes a question
of calculating the amount and the timing as between the
stockholder and the customer. As a matter of law and good
reason, the economic gain or loss resulting from the presence of debt should inure to the stockholder. He is the one
taking the risk on the debt—whether the company is a
regulated utility or not—and the customer should be paying a market price for the product.

In this day and age, whether or not the company is regulated, the customer only coincidentally pays a "market"

price. The government has been causing the inflation and, at the same time, restraining prices. Nonetheless, the prices seem to escape and, eventually, it is the customer who must pay.

On the other hand, to the extent that the government does not, or cannot, interfere with the workings of the marketplace, those companies that enjoy the benefits of long-term leverage, such as bonds or mortgages, are in a position to bargain away part of their gain. To the extent that a company is short of debt and, therefore, not enjoying enough gain from long-term debt, it is not in a position to lower its prices in order to share the benefit of the debt with the customer. A company with an insufficient amount of debt by comparison with its competitors probably will earn a lower return to its stockholders and may, indeed, even lose money at market prices. It is my rough conclusion, therefore, that any advantage created by long-term debt belongs to the stockholder but that, over a period of time, some of it will find its way to the customers through the competitive process, and that governmental action simply alters the timing of this event.

Enabling the management and stockholders to calculate how much they can retain or give away in pricing, is a very valid function of economics and accounting. The real questions with respect to gain or loss derived from the existence of long-term debt are "how much?" and "when?" "Statement No. 3" of the Accounting Principles Board of the American Institute of Certified Public Accountants and the Exposure Draft of the Financial Accounting Standards Board provide that an index be applied to the indebtedness to produce an item flowing into the income statement. In an inflationary period, this will produce "paper income" of very question-able value.

In the Peoples Loan & Trust Company, we have made no recognition of any gain or loss because of the depositors' money we hold. This may be justified because we owe dollars and we have hedged our obligation by investing in fixed-dollar securities. On the other hand, it may not be justified because the interest rates we pay to our depositors are really government controlled and do not compensate fully for inflation. The interest rates we are able to charge our loan customers, whether the loans are on U.S. bonds or municipal bonds, or on corn, beans and farm machinery, are controlled by a combination of the government and the marketplace, but such rates do not cover the inflation we are experiencing—especially after the tax man takes his toll.

Indiana Telephone Corporation has taken the position that the gain or loss resulting from price level changes affect-ing long-term debt is to be recognized only when debt is, in fact, decreased. It is believed that the refunding of debt by substituting Creditor B for Creditor A is not an event that should cause the recognition of inflation-caused gain or loss on the loan but that, in fact, no one can predict with even reasonable certainty the effect of the long-term debt until it has been reduced. Gain or loss is recognized at the time the sinking funds operate on bonds and preferred stock. The company does not recognize gain or loss on a refunding.

Let's consider for a moment the situation of a bond-holder. Who is telling him where he stands? If we are referring to the U.S. 3s of 1995, the daily sheets published by Merrill Lynch, the Continental Illinois Bank, and nu-merous other banks in the country tell him that his 3s of '95 are worth 75–4/32nds. He can partially, through a daily quote sheet, calculate the deterioration in his already bad position. He should add to the market loss the loss in the purchasing power of the capital for which he could sell the bonds.

It is interesting at this juncture to note that the 4–3/4 percent bonds of Indiana Telephone Corporation maturing in the year 2005 are priced about 50. These were issued in 1965 at par. The current yield is approximately 10 percent on these bonds. The company has not sought to buy them back because we believe inflation will continue and these bonds will be for sale at less than 50 sometime before their maturity and that, in fact, money is worth more than 10 percent to the company in its own accounts.

In analyzing an opportunity to buy one's own bonds, it must be remembered that reacquiring $1,000,000 par value at 50 would cause the company to realize $500,000 in taxable, ordinary income. Forty-eight percent of $500,000 would be payable to the federal government and the yield would fall drastically. This limits the market for the bonds held by a previously damaged investor.

It is interesting to note that the change in the market yield on these bonds from 4–3/4 percent to 10 percent has occurred during a period in which the creditworthiness of the issuer has improved. The increase in current yield must in large part be compensation for the inflation. As long as the issuer does not buy the bonds back, its interest charges are 5–1/4 percentage points under the market, and this influences both pricing policy and return on equity. If the issuer manages to raise prices because of the higher costs of its competitors, the increased income will then be recognized, taxed, and something will be left for the stockholders' equity. If no price change occurs, the customers get the benefit by buying more cheaply here than they could elsewhere. It would appear that the sales account automatically decides who receives the benefits of, or suffers loss from, inflation.

For most issuers of bonds, the effects of the inflation on the bond transaction depend upon what is done with the proceeds of the loan—the assets—and not upon the bonds themselves. Since bond issuers usually do not provide for a change in the principal value of the bonds based on a decrease or increase in purchasing power, any change in purchasing power of the proceeds of the bond issue will flow to the stockholders unless the sales contracts with customers offset the change. It is observable, and in accordance with history, that the disease of inflation produces an undulating purchasing power curve and, at a late stage, produces a depression. When, then, can it be said with reasonable certainty and safety how much the purchasing power change in the bond proceeds will be and at what time it should be recorded in income? Prior to actual payment— reduction of debt—the answer must be a speculation. If business recognizes "gain" from the bonds as purchasing power falls and bargains this away to customers, it may find itself paying the debt with very dear dollars at maturity. It does not seem wise to rely on the availability of money at reasonable cost 15 to 30 years in advance. The inflationary change in the bond proceeds should be recognized when the debt is, in fact, reduced.

Above, the text deals with the bond principal without regard to the coupon. To the extent that interest coupons are set to include an allowance for inflation during the term of the bonds, the income account of the issuer is charged currently for a slice of the lost principal each year. To this extent the bondholder keeps up. To the extent the interest rate includes too much allowance for inflation, the stockholder loses, and to the extent the interest rate is too low to compensate for the lost purchasing power, the stockholder has an advantage dealt with earlier. In short, if the interest rate has been set to include exactly the loss in purchasing power of the bonds, the issuer is paying the loss currently and the bondholder is made whole. The issuer must take his chances on whether he can recover this extra interest cost through operations.

Adjusted Earnings as a Percentage of Reported Earnings
Compiled by Sidney Davidson

	1 Adjusted net income before gain on monetary items (YO) as a % of reported net income	*2* YO+ gain or loss on current monetary position as a % of reported net income	*3* Adjusted net income (no. pp. gains deferred taxes) as a % of reported net income	*4* Adjusted net income plus pp. gains on deferred taxes as a % of re-ported net income	*5* Adjusted net to common as a % of reported net to common
Dow Jones Public Utilities					
American Electric Power	80	90	176	181	202
Cleveland Electric Illuminating	75	83	159	162	188
Columbia Gas System	63	77	162	167	162
Commonwealth Edison	71	83	167	178	197
Consolidated Edison	78	80	176	177	229
Consolidated Natural Gas	64	75	151	155	151
Detroit Edison	75	89	186	197	246
Houston Light & Power	85	99	157	160	172
Niagara Mohawk Power	62	68	196	198	256
Pacific Gas & Electric	75	78	155	156	185
Panhandle Eastern Pipe Line	64	71	142	151	148
Peoples Gas Co.	63	74	153	158	153
Philadelphia Electric Co.	80	89	169	171	218
Public Service Electric & Gas Co.	76	82	169	171	210
Southern California Edison	74	79	168	170	213

Standard and Poors Utilities not in Dow Jones					
Allegheny Power System	68	73	199	202	199
Cincinnati Gas & Electric	77	87	157	159	188
Consumer's Power	66	82	195	210	258
Dayton Power & Light	71	84	174	176	212
Indianapolis Power & Light	75	84	160	168	184
Northern Natural Gas	48	57	144	163	158
Northern States Power	75	91	176	183	220
Southern Company	68	71	225	239	225
United Gas Co.	78	82	114	116	114
AT & T	79	83	146	153	195
Indiana Telephone Corp.	74	66	111	118	112
Distributions:					
Dow Jones Companies					
1st Quartile	85–78	99–89	196–176	198–178	256–218
2nd Quartile	76–75	83–80	169–167	177–170	213–197
3rd Quartile	75–64	80–77	167–157	170–160	197–172
Bottom Quartile	64–62	75–68	155–142	158–151	162–148
Median	75	80	167	170	197
All 26 utilities in indices					
Top Quartile	85–77	99–87	225–176	239–183	258–218
2nd Quartile	76–75	84–82	176–168	181–171	213–199
3rd Quartile	74–68	82–75	167–157	170–160	197–172
Bottom Quartile	66–48	74–57	155–114	159–116	162–114
Median	m.74–75	82	m.167–168	m.170–171	m.197–199

Floor Discussion

Fletcher: As a member of Liberty Fund, I want to thank you all for coming. It is a special privilege to have each of you. We are attempting to think this thing through. We do not have the answers; we have a long failing experience with varied results. Alan Russell can attest we don't always get the answers, but we keep working and trying to improve them.

Ben, I have some complaints about the meeting. I will lay them out because I think the group will and should attack in force. First off, there has been a lot of speech making and I am engaged in that right now, so I am engaging in sin. Our technique generally is a Socratic seminar, and if you will examine the text of this meeting, you will have to conclude that this is not a Socratic seminar; it is a series of short speeches. I would think that when you get back and rub your heads with your colleagues, that maybe there you will have a little of the Socratic approach. By no means do I apologize for not being a colleague. I am the only fellow who has ventured out of the business world to write a paper for this meeting, and everyone else, as I understand, in one way or another is a professor. I do not have a Ph.D.—I'm sorry about that, but that means the rules that affect the treatment of colleagues do not apply to me. So I hope you will feel free to criticize me without inhibitions.

We do not believe, and I speak collectively for groups that I represent—that truth is relative. And that, in fact, you can tell the facts differently to different people or to different facets of the world. Frankly, there was a good deal of conversation around the table yesterday that truth is relative and that you ought to give different facts to different people. That has been advocated by the SEC. I just simply say to you we think that is wrong, that the truth exists and that we have experienced difficulty in ascertaining the truth and may not recognize it when we've got it. But I think our job is to try to find the truth and that in doing so, we will have a better hope of people being free and acting responsibly.

Calculation does not equal accounting. I have been disappointed in the seminar because economic calculation is a much, much greater subject than profit numbers or balance sheets, P & L statements or any other set of statements which we might put together. So my paper may fail to address itself to the accounting questions because in the line of business I find that I am faced with so many other things to do, that I rely on the accounting department as eyes and ears. I hope they continue to see and hear and I hope they continue to think. But they are not running business, they are eyes and ears, and it is hoped that they refrain from reporting information that is not straight, or information that I do not understand. I find I make some strange decisions. I already have enough problems once I have the facts. But the accounting people are responsible for sending messages to me which I will understand, and that are, as near as possible, the truth.

I am full of biases and one of them is I have a strong negative feeling for footnotes. I have personally been engaged with a client in helping him to design footnotes to keep information out of other parts of the statement. The information is usually down there under some kind of a guise that says that it is important information and if stockholders really understood the stuff, they would get awfully excited. If you look at modern statements and think about them a bit, you will see great gobs of footnotes. They are an interference with communication.

I would have to confess further that I am an inveterate "bear." I believe the inflation will continue; I believe it will accelerate. I believe it will finally burn out and we will have to find our way out the other end. These convictions are based on the existence of our universal franchise—all citizens can vote, even in, and especially in their own interest; but they do not have equal responsibility. We have many voters who are actually on the government payroll as welfare recipients, or as people in the government, and it is impossible for me to see that they will vote against more government; I believe they will vote for more government. As they vote for more government, we will incur greater deficit financing, which deficits will be monetized, and we will get more inflation. So, from the economic point of view, in my opinion, we are headed for the hot place in a hand basket reasonably quickly. I don't know how fast that is.

We have just come through some overt controls by

government which did not work. They created a lot of havoc and we are still seeing some havoc. Yet I then hear pleas of "Let's go back to controls," one way or another. Mr. May can tell us about some controls that are covert—not open and above board. Theoretically, we have no controls or very few of them. But the fact is, the steel companies just tried to raise steel prices. They wanted to go up 8 percent, and when it was settled they got 4.7 percent. That will produce some shortages.

Now, there is another thing about which I wish to complain in our meeting and that is that somehow these things are different in utilities from what they are elsewhere. It is my feeling that we can talk about degrees; we can talk about the special problems of utilities and they are very, very real. But the problems of inflation are universal in the business community and these problems affect different businesses differently. A special problem of a utility is that it cannot control its price structure. It cannot go out to find a fellow who will pay more, but it must seek a price increase from a Public Service Commission.

I think I have alluded in the paper to flow-through accounting, in which utilities have indulged. They liked that because it made the statements look good. Years and years and years ago, utilities introduced a concept of "interest during construction" as a regulatory device. One can't very well expect interest to enter the profit and loss statement in the year in which it's paid because the users will not yet be paying for the service. Interest during construction is a start-up cost which is capitalized in fixed assets and recovered as depreciation after the asset goes into production. What I am saying to you is that I believe capitalization of interest during construction is fundamentally unsound as a conceptual matter, but in the utility business, because of the presence of regulation, it makes sense. But the accounting practices of utilities are different from the inflation problem. The utilities are now evidencing a lot of reaction to inflation.

Someone and I talked a couple of minutes yesterday about borrowing. Utilities simply cannot do the construction we are asking of them by internally generated funds. We just don't have them! So the gentleman to whom I was talking said, "Why don't you borrow?" Well, we have an indenture that was well written at the time—1974. It says we can't issue bonds having a maturity less remote than the most remote issue now outstanding. Our most remote issue is July 1, 2008, and the next issue must be at or beyond that date. Now, inflation has caused the market to reject 35- to 40-year issues and to drop down around 15. In fact, in the conversations I've had recently with people who might be willing to make loans, they desire a 10-year term. My reply is that 10 years will not do because the company will need to invest the money in 25- to 30-year assets. It does not make sense, in the utility business or anyplace else, to take 10- or 15-year money and put it into 30-year assets. Borrowing short and investing long has always been a hazardous sport and is now, I think, even more hazardous. But there are some utilities, I am told, that are issuing *demand* obligations in order to sustain building programs. The only way to prove what will happen there is to let someone call those demand notes. Such a call would very quickly bankrupt those utilities.

So that is my list of complaints.

Now, let's go to work on my paper. There are a couple of subjects which are confusing and important, and ought to be looked at carefully.

One is the general versus specific indices. I have paid

my respects to both of them in my paper. It is always important to separate the recovery of capital from the decision of reinvestment. These are just two different animals. Getting old purchasing power back is one kind of animal, and what to do with it is another. It may be important to go out of the business you are in. It may be there is such a low return in the business in which you are engaged that you ought to change the line of business. Specific indices just do not keep these two things apart. The use of specific indices assumes that recovered capital will be put back into a particular business; whereas that may be a highly unsound decision. So my position is that general indices are, for capital recovery purposes, superior. Whether we will go into a new or different transaction, whether we will build a new factory or plant addition, involves specific costs of that particular addition, and specific cash flows from that addition, and at this point, specific indices are very helpful.

Another point: There has been favorable comment made concerning "indexing"—that somehow or other, Brazil is in great shape and a couple of other places are doing fine because of their use of indexing. Unfortunately, Mr. Ruebeck has flown the coop. I talked with him yesterday on his South American experience. I said to him, "But the indexing is never straight. They get a 22 percent inflation and they'll index 18. Let's assume for a moment, just a moment, that the indexing is absolutely perfect, then why not stop inflation?" He said, "But that won't let the government build those public buildings." They are fibbing; they are not telling the truth. The indexing system has to be administered by government, I suppose, and they set it so that the government takes a premium. When they take it, we then enjoy those social things that governments are supposed to accomplish without knowing we have been taxed. Obviously, I am against the government running a general indexing system.

Now, I think I'll take up the great plunge with you, namely, bonds. Mr. Goodrich decided when the gain on bonds would be recognized. He examined a number of possibilities and the one that was chosen is the one that you see in our report; namely, that the gain on the bonds will be recognized at the time that indebtedness is reduced; not when these bonds disappear, not when something else takes their place, but when, in fact, debt goes down.

Paton, Jr: I don't know at that point what it does, but of course, debt will never go down.

Fletcher: Well, now, I may agree with you, but wait a minute. Remember our company cannot go issue any more long-term bonds.

Paton, Jr.: I don't think you are quoting me correctly.

Fletcher: Fine.

Paton, Jr.: I think you're quoting somebody else.

Fletcher: All right—but the point is there, anyway. An assumption that the Indian rope will stay up in the air forever is, I think, an assumption that can't be sustained. In fact, in flow-through accounting, if one continued to construct, the earnings were maintained. One counted on a continuing construction program and on continued borrowing. Now what's happened here? Right now some companies have had to stop their construction programs for lack of money. If they were flow through, then the lack of investment credit would hurt earnings. Someone was talking about electrical plant going on steam yesterday and they were thinking about interest during construction. You would be surprised how much thinking goes on in the board room about when to cut that plant over. Cutover stops the capitalization of interest and puts the interest charge right into the profit and loss statement.

But to continue, what should be done with the bonds? One thing we could do is follow the FASB proposal, multiply the index change times the bonds and credit the amount to profit and loss currently. We could take the gain over the remaining life of the bond. It was suggested at one point that one offset the bonds against the plant. This would take the price level gain or loss into income over the remaining life of the plant. Another possibility is to do what Indiana Telephone is doing, that is, wait until the debt is reduced. Now, how did Indiana Telephone get there? The inflation we've been living through hasn't seemed to be a nice, clean, smooth curve, ever ascending. It flops up and down. Every time it flops down, we have a recession. At those points, we have to service the debt out of whatever we have saved back. At that time the bond "gains" do not seem so real. There is something to be said for what I'll call transaction accounting, for recognizing whatever gain there is when the transaction is completed. The transaction is not done when Bond Issue B is substituted for Bond Issue A. The transaction is done when, in fact, debt is reduced.

Ben, I think I caused enough trouble; I'll quit right there.

Davidson: I think, in a way, it is appropriate that I follow Bill, because what I am going to say will, in part, please him; in part, disappoint him. In part, I'll agree with him; in part, disagree; but not necessarily in equal proportions. I agree with you that truth is not relative. We must continue to seek it out. I guess I do agree with your pessimism, though.

While speaking of the truth, I am reminded of a motto of one of the universities with which I've been connected which says that the truth will set you free. And so I hope that we continue to seek after it in the effort to set us free.

One of the questions is: Just how will the kind of company from which the FASB is urging additional statements, the capital intensive industry, be affected? Like Ben Rogge, I must confess that I think that public utilities, the regulated public utilities, are the epitome of capital intensive industries. So what my colleagues and I have done is study the financial statements of a group of public utilities and ask how their financial reports will look if they report in compliance with the sections of the FASB.

Indiana Telephone does recognize loss on money value in their annual reporting. I think that is correct. Column 2 says, take that operating income and add to it the gain or loss on current liability and current monetary assets. Let me say here that Indiana Telephone is unique among the 26 companies analyzed here, in that it is the only company that has more monetary assets than current monetary liabilities. Put another way, it's the only company that has quick ratio, in technical accounting jargon, of more than one. I don't know how typical that is of industrials, but certainly among the 26 public utilities that are analyzed here, Indiana Telephone is the only one that has a quick ratio of more than one. For if you look at column 2 for Indiana Telephone, you'll see that Indiana Telephone Corporation decreases from 74 percent to 66 percent. And it is after that adjusted income to 66 percent reported income rather than 74 percent. For all 25 other companies analyzed here, operating income plus a gain or loss on current value items is high—not extensively, but high. I must confess that I disagree with the Exposure Draft and think deferred taxes are also a monetary item.

Sprouse: If I can interrupt . . . as I interpret it, given the column 4 results, you've been treating the deferred taxes as non-monetary. Some have suggested that to classify deferred taxes as non-monetary produces the same results as classifying them as monetary on the grounds that, if you restate upward, you have to restate down again so that the resulting amount of deferred taxes won't exceed the number of tax dollars that would have to be paid if you immediately sold all assets at book value.

Davidson: This would be included as a monetary gain?

Sprouse: Not as a monetary gain—as a write-down of a non-monetary liability.

Davidson: Yes, but would it affect reported income?

Sprouse: It would be included in general purchasing power net income in the same way that any other write-down of non-monetary items would be included.

Davidson: An additional factor is, of course, that a good many public utilities have preferred stock outstanding, and as far as the common stockholder is concerned, preferred stock is a kind of debt. So you are saying that you want to report how the common stockholder is faring. You would want to write your preferred dividends up to year-end prices, but then recognize a monetary gain on the preferred stock.

Sprouse: Did you follow the Exposure Draft to the letter?

Davidson: With regard to sinking fund?

Sprouse: With regard to preferred stock.

Davidson: Yes.

Russell: That doesn't go into net income anyway.

Davidson: No, it goes to the common stockholders.

Russell: No, it goes to earnings per share.

Davidson: No.

Russell: It does not go to net income, but goes into the computations of earnings per share in the Exposure Draft.

Davidson: I assume those errors in the Exposure Draft will be corrected before the final pronouncement.

Russell: Okay, I just read it differently than you did.

Davidson: Again, the distributions are as filled out here. So I think this is what the numbers show. (These are for 1973 operation.) What is going to be the likely result in 1974, when we are talking about a 12 percent inflation rate rather than a 7 percent inflation rate? Clearly, the effect is going to be very much more substantial on the money value gain, especially those with heavy debt. Will that always be the case? It depends upon the rate of price level change this year relative to the rate of price level change in earlier years. If, for example, we were to have a period of 12 percent inflation for six years, that with the compounded effect means the prices would double in that six-year period. If that were to be followed by a year in which we had only 6 percent inflation, then the depreciation adjustment would be greater than the bond adjustment, because plant would have had a double value, that is, a 12-year life. And take 8 percent from that double value, that would be 8 percent income increase in depreciation and only a 6 percent money value income. So what it depends upon is the rate of change through time.

Baxter: Could you also depend on the company's new bond issue? This kind of money gained during the absence of new bond issue tapers off because the money will be repaid.

Davidson: I am assuming that the debt ratio remains relatively constant, as Bill Fletcher has suggested. Concerning the question of whether the gain in column 3 should be recognized or not, I would simply say that if you believe in general price level adjustments, that is, the truth, not relative, it applies to everything. I won't comment on this last point of disagreement about the relativeness of general price level adjustment as opposed to specific ones. Bill Fletcher and I have talked about this, and I must confess that I am whole-heartedly a specific index price level man, and if all we got was to this halfway house and stayed there, I'd be very much disappointed. In fact, I'd say let's not put any effort to getting to the halfway house, but let's put all our efforts in getting to the top of the hill.

Fletcher: I agree with Robert Sprouse that current value accounting is just simply a different animal than price-level adjusted cost. Are you saying you disagree with that?

Sprouse: Davidson and Fletcher are saying different things, and I would agree with Bill. In my mind, they are totally different animals. Whether only one is desirable or both are desirable is a separate question.

Bows: I wanted the benefit of Sid's thinking on this question; it keeps going through my mind. I am not a utility man and don't understand why it came out this way. I want to see if you agree. What happens, I think, on utilities is they are issuing a lot of debt for new construction, and that new construction is mammoth in relation to old plant and you can't take depreciation on it until it's operative. Therefore, what he's got in here is depreciation on operative plant price levels. The depreciation on the new stuff is causing a lot of debt. I just wanted to ask Sid, is that part of why it comes out this way, do you think?

Davidson: That's only, I think, a relatively small contributing factor, Al. For Indiana Telephone, you have $1 million plant under construction, compared to your $41 million that is in operation.

Bows: A nuclear plant is mammoth.

Davidson: Yes, but you know I always used to talk about how big the deferred cost item was, and people would say, yes, it may be big absolutely, but you have to compare it to the total plant. And I agree. The nuclear plant for Detroit Edison is very, very large, but Detroit Edison's *got* a very large plant.

Bows: What I was trying to get at, there wouldn't be any depreciation in the pot yet on that; but there would be price level adjustment on the bill. I just wanted to get that out.

Davidson: Yes, but I must confess, I do not think that is a major factor in this reporting.

Rogge: Let's turn to a man who's had to confront these things stated head-on as a chairman of the Public Service Commission of Indiana, and now confronts them still head-on with United Telecommunications. Your official title at United Telecommunications is what?

Hill: Vice President and Rate Counsel. They had difficulty in getting a good title.

Rogge: I guess they hand out titles instead of cash.

Hill: Well, now that I realize how well we are doing in the utility industry I will go back and reopen negotiations. I don't think we would want to use Dr. Davidson as an expert witness in rate cases based on the Exposure Draft. I get the feeling the more I learn, the less I really know. For several years I've managed investments for a small life insurance company and was always curious to know whether or not the company was earning money. You never really know with life insurance companies; they report statutory earnings and there are several formulas to adjust earnings. I finally learned all of those and decided that I found some more acceptable than others, and you can professionally have been very interested in that area. And now that I am increasingly involved in the utility industry, I have discovered some similarities in that I don't know what my own company is doing. One of my minor problems is, after a rate audit is entered, trying to describe what the commission allowed us to do. And somebody will say, what rate of earning did they allow? And I'll say, according to our operating company, they allowed this, and according to the commission they allowed a different figure. And then I demonstrate they made several adjustments to the assets, they increased earnings by half a dozen different ways, and they reduced the recorded expenses of the company in a couple of dozen ways, and then I'm not sure the operating company which we own is recording accurately in the first place. But after four or five pages, I say this is what was recorded; it's not very satisfying but that's the environment in which we live.

I'm going to address my remarks to gas and water and telephone and electric companies. It may be that the fuel industry and the oil industry and in a few states even hospitals are being regulated after their rate. And there are similarities—at least it seems to me that in the long run the enterprise must operate successfully and cover all of its capital costs. You can't go into business without the approval of the state, and you can't go out of business without the approval of the state, and you can't issue long-term bonds without the approval of the state, and you can't sell your assets, maybe even a piece of equipment that another telephone company wants, without their approval. Would it make any difference to know what your assets are worth if you can't get rid of them? I agree with Bill, that the same story should be told to all audiences. I tried that in politics and it failed there. In the long run I still believe it, and I think if you don't sell it people will get suspicious enough, that the harm is even more serious than knowing exactly what the truth is, if we can ascertain it and perhaps we can get close to it. But, I'm not at all sure that the truth can be found in accounting or economics.

The obligation of a regulated utility is to serve everybody at all times, provide adequate service at reasonable rates which are not unduly discriminatory. This is reasonably typical of every state and the last state I presume, Texas, will soon have a commission, thanks in part to Southwestern Bell and thanks in part to inflation and fuel prices.

The utility, by law, is entitled to a reasonable rate of return on the assets used and useful in providing the services, or in some states they are entitled to a reasonable rate of return of the investment. The utility must have some reserve capacity. In one area there may be a complete decline and another area growing but there may be no growth to the utility at all. Or there may be rapid growth, and whether you have growth or a decline now in most regulated industries you need rate increases and they can be justified because you need them for growth or you need them because of the decline in charges to fixed cost.

Considering the large amount of capital required and the need in most instances for large amounts of capital in the future, and the obligations and rights of a utility, what economic calculation will assure that customers will be properly served and the rights of the owners protected as stated by law?

The problems for a capital intensive and non-regulated industry are similar, at least in my opinion, over a long period of time: the need to survive, to operate successfully even in a competitive environment, to cover all costs for an indefinite period of time. The states normally don't initiate an operation to go out of business in 10 years, 20 years or 30 years.

Improving the ability to calculate is relatively easy, at least as it relates to utility managements that I know. They do so little now. The difficult task is to persuade a regulatory agency to accept and apply the economic and accounting calculations in rate-making and to do so promptly. Fixing 1975 rates on the basis of 1972 assets, revenues, and expenses is still a reality in some states.

Since we don't always understand the past and do not know the future, precise calculations, nitpicking, and being "picky, picky, picky" is really unnecessary. In many cases the commission will take days and even weeks in trying to make a precise allocation on the basis of a two-year bill at a rate of inflation of 5 percent when bond costs were 8 percent and the stock was selling at 15 times earnings instead of seven. So after you have these precise calculations you would bring unknown results within a very short period of time. Almost no utility anymore earns what the rate order says the commission allows. If it does, it was a mistake in the calculation by the commission staff, a mistake made by the company *keeping* the increase. Mistakes are possible on both sides. Every now and then you have the good fortune that the rate will prove to produce more revenue than the commission expects. This is a delightful sensation.

Most states will still use original cost for depreciation. Most of the states, that by law are required to use fair value, nevertheless use original cost. Commissions conclude that fair value is original cost; it's been appealed to the court and the court generally concludes that the Commission is right, it's precise, it's understood. Well maybe it is. Now there are some exceptions—Indiana, Ohio and North Carolina. Ohio is reproduction cost new, but it takes forever. North Carolina has required that companies use fair value, so that concluded with two-thirds original cost and one-third fair value. So they come out with something in between.

The method to be applied is less important than selling the concept. As of now, regulatory commissioners do not understand the importance of the concept, and I suspect that most of them have never heard of it. I believe the same is true of newspaper editors, radio, television, and magazine editors who influence the public who influence the politicians who influence the Commission in some degree in their decision. I am not at all sure that policy-makers in the utility industry believe in economic calculation for inflation. They are preoccupied with day-to-day affairs of running the enterprise, with the problems of raising additional capital.

Any calculation which regulatory agencies can be persuaded to use which will assure adequate services at rates which will cover all costs, including the cost of capital, should be acceptable because the rate can be adjusted the next year or the year after that if the Commission is operating properly.

May: My experience in this area, in searching for the truth, you might call it, goes back at least a quarter of a century when some of us were groping for the problem of inflation related to utility regulation and at that time sought the advice and counsel of such enlightened people as George Terborgh and Bill Paton, Sr., and Paul Grady and Leonard Spacek of Arthur Andersen and others who were very vocal on the subject, and certainly they were very helpful. I spent 32 years with a regulated utility and 12 in competitive industry since, and I'm still searching for the truth. And I think really that the truth means something different to different people, depending on what they are trying to accomplish. What is their objective? What is their concept?

My original exploration into this field was on the matter of depreciation charges in rate proceedings. At that time the state commissions were clipping the utilities on original cost depreciation. The staff and public counselors were putting on experts who were claiming that the service lives of telephone poles or cables or whatever were longer than assumed in the depreciation schedules for the utility; even though those depreciation schedules had been prescribed by the Federal Communications Commission, except that isn't binding on the state commissions. So they were saying, all right, we will assume longer lives, we'll reduce the depreciation charges for rate purposes and we'll impute a higher rate of return, and therefore, we'll have to give you a smaller increase to receive what we deem to be the proper rate of return. We did manage to stop this picking away at depreciation charges that were probably a gross understatement of real costs.

It's been five years since the APB "Statement No. 3" was issued. As Dr. Fabricant points out, this has had virtually no effect on accounting practices. Now, I think that corporate managements are criticized for not taking advantage of this recognition of how to do this in their public financial statements and I think they have been, more or less, criticized on the ground that if they did, it would probably reduce their reported earnings. There may be some truth to that. I don't think any corporation in a particular line of business wants to go out and do this if none of its competitors are going to do this. They still have the problem of attracting capital in the investment market, but if they all did it, I'm sure that all corporations would follow suit. I think, however, since it's obvious to many corporate managements, that some reflection of the effect of inflation must be taken into account in financial statements— then why haven't they done it? And I think some clue to this is evident in the position papers and presentations that were made to the FASB back last year when they were considering the matter of a proposal for price level accounting.

I haven't had access to all 130 papers but I have had 110

of them and I did attend the hearings and tried to make an analysis of what the positions were. And so far as corporate managements are concerned, I think there was very little opposition to a change in principle. Most of the opposition bore on the question of what you achieve by doing this, and I think it was based primarily on the fact that the corporations did not feel that price level trending discloses, in their judgment, the true economic income and the real worth of the corporation. And again, here is a question of concept. What are you trying to achieve? The FASB proposal does give an indication of what the assets and net worth of the corporation would have to be in current dollars. But even so, I think corporations have problems with what light this would throw on the results of operations. It's certainly a very small comfort to the company to know that if it withdrew its capital from the enterprise at any particular time, it would buy the same physical volume of goods and services nationwide that it would have when this capital was first dedicated to the enterprise; while at the same time, it's having to go out, apparently, and raise capital outside just to maintain the same level of business, the same level of productive or service capacity. And I think in the case of the going business, a corporate management would say that the purchasing power of the capital in terms of the productive capacity provided by that business or service capacity has not been maintained. Now this again is a question of concept, what you are trying to measure. I think the corporate management is fearful that if it took 20 years after the original committee was set up to study this question for the accounting profession to give official recognition to the needs of doing this in putting out "Statement No. 3"—and this is a fairly simple concept, this matter of trending original cost—that it may never get around to the difficult task of providing acceptable tools for the actual, accurate determination of income and net worth of a particular going enterprise. This may be—this is the halfway house that Dr. Fabricant talks about. Basically the FASB proposal and the Indiana Telephone practice are still an historical cost concept with capital and assets expressed in a larger number of smaller monetary units. It gives no recognition to the fact that the real worth of the asset of the particular business may actually be more or less than this trend of original cost or that the degree of difference might be significantly great. It is the existence of this difference that is of vital concern to corporate management if it is to produce truly meaningful financial statements.

I think that I have to agree with Dr. Fabricant that going only this far, that is, trending historical costs, places financial officers and accountants in an uncomfortable and uninhabitable halfway house, as he calls it, from which they will have to advance further because the financial statements will be misinterpreted as reflecting important changes that they do not in fact do.

Getting back to the question of maintaining the purchasing power of capital funds or the productive service capacity of the business, Bill Fletcher has said that if you must recover in capital recovery more than the purchasing power of the capital dedicated to the business, that perhaps the question of reinvestment in the business would require a different decision; if you must invest at higher costs than trended orginal cost to maintain productive or service capacity of the business, that perhaps you should go to some other form of business, reinvest it in some other line of business rather than staying with this business. We have got to recognize that this is not a practical answer because in the last five or six years the cost of shipbuilding has almost tripled, oil tankers have tripled in cost, tankers that we built in Japan back in 1968 for $7 million cost $20 million today. We're putting a chemical plant on stream in Texas the first of March that cost $100 million. We are making engineering and financial analysis of putting up a duplicate plant right next to it and our best judgment right now is that the same plant, with no changes whatever, will cost $190 million. The cost of an oil refinery used to be about $1,000 per every barrel of daily capacity and today it's more like $2,500 per barrel. Are you going to make a decision to go into another line because the cost of maintaining the capacity is too high? Higher than, let's say, trended historical cost of the plant? Then you must stop building ships, stop building oil tankers, stop building chemical plants and oil refineries, and yet our economy needs these things.

In my judgment, accounting must not only record transactions of business enterprise but it must also provide the means of measuring the results of operation in a purely economic sense. The accounting professor must clearly define the central objectives sought in making changes in conventional accounting determinations and then find ways to make whatever valuation changes are necessary to reach those objectives. The fact that the problem is a difficult one must not be a barrier to finding a reasonable solution, even if it isn't perfect. I think it's something, a recognition that this is better than doing nothing at all, even though it isn't precise.

Warren: A while back, several years ago now, the United States Supreme Court decided the Hope Natural Gas Case. I know for a fact that Rogge likes to refer to this case; he's done it several times. One of the questions in the Hope Natural Gas Case had to do with the rate of return. The Court finally held that it did not know precisely what the rate of return should be; but one way to get at it is—find the rate of return required to preserve the integrity of the enterprise and permit the enterprise to attract capital.

It seems to me that over a period of 25 years it has been proved that original cost accounting is just plain wrong. Even accountants who apply original cost and stick to it to the end apply it differently. It's all a judgment factor that they use. Well, more power to them! Then we get into the utilities and we get another set of rulings, the uniform system of accounts, also based on original cost. Then we get into generally accepted principles of accounting. They're just generally bad. They permit the preparation of financial statements in different ways; they permit flow-through or normalization; they permit investment tax credits that differ between utilities and industrials. How come? Why? It seems to me that the idea of original cost is wrong. Original cost has not helped businesses or business managers to improve their business practices or their financial reporting. Original cost accounting provides an accepted means for reporting profits that do not in fact exist. What are we going to do about it? Accountants, professors, regulators and others have argued and debated the question for years. It is time to do something about it—even half a loaf is better than none at all. We just might save many utilities, many in-dustries, and even this country. We just might; I would hope so. Please, gentlemen, let's get to it! We lawyers can't do much about it—very little. We are going to have to have you experts get on the witness stand and explain it in a way that the judge or commissioner knows what you are talking about. I want to tell you that it is tough, really tough, but it can be done. Let's have it happen.

Let us have that halfway house, Dr. Fabricant. Let me have half of a loaf, even a quarter of a loaf—any part of it, let me have that. Tomorrow I'll get another piece. It just may be that the whole thing, as I understand Dr. Sprouse's paper, is a question of time. It may be a question of compromise, even a compromise with principles. I surrender, Ben.

May: I think that the worst possible thing that could happen would be nothing at all. Just to stay, let's say, with historical costs. I believe that if it came to a vote as between two sources, staying with that or the FASB proposal, that almost any thinking person would say, let's at least go to the FASB, then, if it's only to the halfway house. And I agree with Mr. Warren on that, but I don't think that this is going to cure some of the regulatory problems that Mr. Warren has mentioned.

One company had two reductions and then they went in for a rate increase and the commission gave them about 40 percent of what they requested, and then emphasized the fact that by reducing the balance they were saving the customers 47 cents a month, too. Now I am sure that if the customers were made to realize that if they paid an extra 47 cents, they might get the electricity they need in the future, whereas by their not paying the 47 cents they may not get it, they would willingly pay it. But this is a political question. I don't care what kind of figures they throw at that kind of a regulatory body, it is not going to help. There's got to be some other cure for that kind of regulation.

Warren: I couldn't agree with you more.

Ryan: It has been my experience that regulation is a political and not an economic or accounting process. Regulatory accounting and economics are used to back decisions which are politically devised. Those of you who have spent time in regulation know that there is little relationship between regulatory and real-world economics. The former is an encapsulated subject, a convoluted pattern of formulas in a system which really doesn't make much sense. These formulas and procedures exist for the purpose of supporting the decisions which are political.

Dub Hill's suggestion of coming up with a simple formula that regulators can understand is a good one. Regulators are simple, and need things spelled out. Anything that would make it easier for them to understand the problems of their regulated companies would be a help.

But I don't really believe that there are any such formulas, and even if there are, I don't believe that they are what regulators are really looking for.

What regulators are looking for is the same thing legislators are looking for, and that is some way to make something out of nothing, or at least appear to. They want to find some way that they can stuff these figures through a computor or through their staff so that evidence will be produced that rates are too high or need to be raised only moderately, when in fact, rates are way too low and massive increases are needed. Such is their real motivation in investigating new theories and techniques.

So, I have no real faith that any form of new or additional information can be conditioned to produce a regulatory revelation. Neither regulators nor the government in general is looking for truth or wants it demonstrated to it. Thus, this is not just true of regulation. Matters of rates and rules are getting back into the legislative arena under the guise of regulatory reform. Legislators are no more looking for real-world economic solutions than are regulators.

Such people as believe in free enterprise in this country have to quit looking on the government as a sympathetic partner. It is not. Government is now the enemy. It is the inflator, not because of ignorance, but because of greed. The whole concept of inflation is to make it look as if you are doing something generous without hurting anybody, without costing anything. Governors do not want clarification, and they do not want amelioration of the effects of inflation. Do not rely on government to help you sell indexing or inflation accounting.

Hill: There are shortages now in Pennsylvania where the labor union members came in and testified for the increase because they discovered that when construction budgets were curtailed, unemployment increased. In another area where electricity was off several days—this is unheard of, not having electric service for 10 days—there was a shortage. They were very upset. It is possible that an adequate supply of electricity and good service is so like the electric utility industry in terms of getting increases. You used to think that if you got good service you were going to get good rates. Now to demonstrate that the business isn't very good, it may be advantageous in getting rate increases. It's sad, but true.

V

Financial Planning and Management Decisions Under Uncertainty and Inflation

W. Allen Spivey
William J. Wrobleski

I. INTRODUCTION

For more than forty years it has been recognized that financial statements should be based on a stable measuring unit if they are to be used effectively for the purposes of decision making. Studies published by the American Institute of Certified Public Accountants in 1961, 1962, 1963, and 1969 emphasized this, and the 1963 study devoted much attention to this matter, including a thorough discussion of index numbers and how to apply them to adjust financial statements for price level changes.[1]

Since 1963, interest in price level adjustments has grown steadily. More recently, as inflation rates have exceeded 10 percent, the subject has become one of great practical as well as academic and theoretical interest.

Price level adjustments of financial statements remain a controversial subject, however, and an alternative that is put forth is that of current value accounting. Price level ad-

---

[1] Accounting Research Division Staff, American Institute of Certified Public Accountants, Accounting Research Study No. 6, "Reporting the Financial Effects of Price-Level Changes" (New York: AICPA, 1963).

justments restate historical costs in terms of constant purchasing power, whereas current value accounting attempts to present the current market value of all assets and liabilities as of some specified balance sheet date. Important issues raised by current value accounting have been explored in the American Accounting Association study entitled "A Statement of Basic Accounting Theory," which was published in 1966, and in other publications.

Most of the studies concerned with price level adjustments have dealt with the making of such adjustments for a current or a past year. Although this is of great importance, management is also interested in the effects that such adjustments might have in the future, when they become interwoven with the decisions that are to be made on the basis of the adjusted values and still other considerations over a period of years. This suggests the use of a corporate planning model which can simulate the balance sheet, income and cash flow statements over a future time period.

In this paper, which is exploratory, an operational financial planning model of a large public utility is used to investigate issues related to such temporal price level adjustments of financial statements. Because of the accounting and financial data available in this firm and the various features of the model, we could, if more time were available, develop a current value analysis as well over the chosen forecast period. We restricted our attention, however, to questions of price level adjustments only.

We have used the model to develop various forecasts of earnings per share for the forecast period 1974 through 1978. The model is a large and detailed one, particularly in the plant and equipment accounts. The company has given permission to reproduce the data that appear below but wishes to remain anonymous.

The model allows us to examine the effects of a variety of financial adjustments. Using accounting data that are unadjusted for price level changes, the model will simulate financial decisions reflecting these unadjusted data and the relationships of the model, producing balance sheet, income, and cash flow statements for a five-year period in units of current or unadjusted dollars rather than in terms of units of general purchasing power (price-level adjusted data).

Price-level adjusted financial statements can be developed in at least two ways. One can take the unadjusted financial statements over the forecast period as developed above, predict the future values of the annual GNP Implicit Price Deflator for the corresponding years, and then use those values to adjust the financial statements on a year by year basis. We call this "after-the-fact" adjustment because price level adjustments are not introduced into the model itself but are performed instead on the outputs of the model.

Another approach is to use price-adjusted financial data in the model initially and then let the model, through its many interrelationships, produce a "rolling adjustment" to price level changes through time. Price level adjustments now become interrelated with other features of the model and influence the decisions that are made by it. We refer to this as the "interactive adjustments" case.

Forecasts of earnings per share for each of these three cases are presented in Part III. Other sections of the paper are devoted to analyzing these forecasts, using a variety of statistical methods. In addition, the "smoothness" of earnings over time in each of the three cases—unadjusted, after-the-fact adjustment, and interactive adjustment—is analyzed in terms of assessing what we call the temporal coherence structure of earnings per share. Finally, some general comments are made about areas of future research on temporal price level adjustments of financial statements.

II. BRIEF DISCUSSION OF THE FINANCIAL PLANNING MODEL AND ASSUMPTIONS OF THE STUDY

The simulation program involves over 800 different variables and consists of 30 subroutines representing largely separate logical functions. One five-year run of the program requires approximately 1,000 computations, where a computation is defined to be an operation executed by one arithmetical statement in the program. The data in Part III below were developed from 12 different runs of the program and so were produced by approximately 12,000 calculations, exclusive of the computations required for the statistical analysis of the data. Figure 1 presents the major modules used in the simulation model; Figure 2 indicates the flow and detail of the computations required.

The following principal inputs are required by the model for each year of the forecast period, 1974 through 1978.

1. Average number of customers to be served during the year.

2. Total number of operating, maintenance, and construction employees.

3. Power pooling expenses and revenues.

4. Construction expenditures broken down by major generation projects, transmission, distribution, and general construction expenditures.

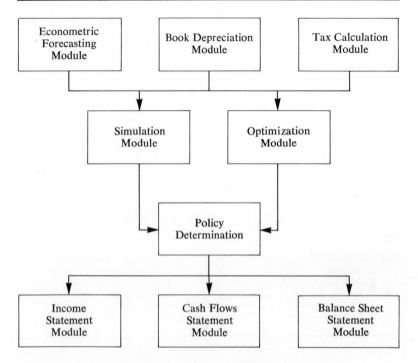

FIGURE 1   Major Modules of Financial Simulation Model

5. Kilowatt hour sales forecasts by major customer class.

6. The schedule of kilowatt hours from sources other than steam plants (interchanges, etc.).

7. Forecasts of bond interest rates and of short-term financing rates.

8. Unemployment rates for area served.

9. Values of Gross National Product Deflator.

In addition, use is made of the actual year-end blance sheet, income, and cash flow statements and other accounting data which specify the financial condition of the company at the beginning of the forecast period.

Using these inputs, the model computes the construction program budget and overhead costs for the first year of the

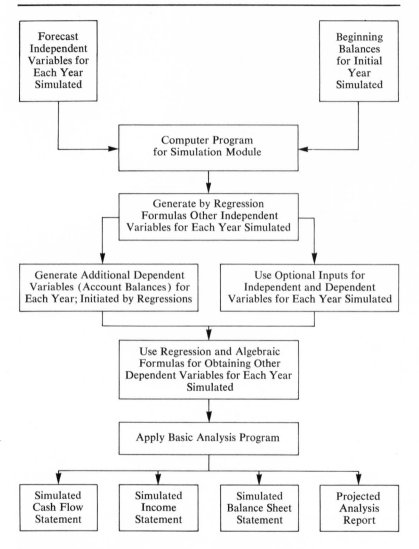

FIGURE 2   Flow Diagram of Financial Simulation Model

simulation, 1974. Given these values, the plant and tax data are determined, and using these in turn, the model obtains estimates of some of the items on the cash flow and income statements by means of multiple regression equations. When these items are forecast, the model determines the need for financing from external sources according to financial policies established by the model. Subsequently the model calculates federal, state, and other taxes and with these values determines the remaining account balances (i.e., those not determined by means of regression equations).

The final results are collected and the balance sheet, income and cash flow statements are developed. These reflect the company's operation through the year as simulated by the financial model. These financial data in turn form the beginning year or "base data" for the next year. The simulation continues year by year in this manner for each year of forecast period.

In a complete study of the effects of price level adjustments on earnings per share it is generally accepted that all elements of the financial statements should be restated in terms of units of general purchasing power by employing a single index of the general price level as of the balance sheet date.[2] Moreover, gains and losses should arise from recognizing the effects of a changing price level on the monetary items, principally the cash balance and contracts to receive or to pay money.

Executing these adjustments for a going concern, particularly a public utility, is a complex and lengthy undertaking. Because of time limitations we have found it necessary to make several simplifying assumptions. First, we

---

[2] Accounting Principles Board, American Institute of Certified Public Accountants, "Statement No. 3, Financial Statements Restated for General Price-Level Changes," *APB Accounting Principles,* Original Pronouncements as of December 1, 1971, vol. 2, pp. 9,007–55. We refer to this as "Statement No. 3."

have chosen to restate the total utility plant, depreciation, and monetary gains and losses. For a public utility, of course, these items, when adjusted for price level changes, have far more influence on net earnings and earnings per share than the remaining items, which we did not restate. Second, simplified techniques for restating total utility plant and for calculating depreciation were employed. These are set forth in detail in Appendix 1. Appendix 2 presents the calculations used to restate monetary gains and losses in units of general purchasing power.

III. SOME DESCRIPTIVE STATISTICS OF THE EFFECTS OF PRICE LEVEL ADJUSTMENTS ON EARNINGS PER SHARE

As indicated earlier, we have developed forecasts for 1974 through 1978 for three different situations: the unadjusted case, the after-the-fact case, and the interactive adjustments case.

The unadjusted case refers to the operation of the financial simulation model in its standard mode, assuming that the unit of measurement is stable and thus no price level adjustments are made of the data put into the model or of the financial statements resulting from the model simulation.

It should be emphasized that the model produces a complete set of balance sheet, income, and cash flow statements. However, we reproduce here information on earnings per share only, although many other policy analyses could be made using a variety of other financial variables of interest to management.

Among the large number of interrelationships in the

model, as previously pointed out, is a collection of regression equations. These are used to forecast account balances, which in turn help to determine the financial statements of the company. The model, like corporate financial planning models generally, treats such regression forecasts as inputs which are free from error. Actually, however, a forecast made by a regression equation is an estimate of the average or expected value of the dependent variable (more precisely an estimate of the conditional mean of the probability distribution of the dependent variable) and is thus subject to probabilistic errors of forecast. Consequently, the output forecasts of financial planning models are themselves subject to variations induced by the probabilistic structure of the input forecasts. This is the case, it should be emphasized, whether or not the unit of measurement is regarded as stable.

The forecast of earnings per share presented in Table 1 below was developed under identical model inputs and financial policy simulations, and only the regression forecasts used by the model were allowed to vary probabilistically. In other words, we inserted into the model other values besides the mean or expected value of the dependent variables specified by the regression equations. This permits us to trace the effects of such forecast errors on the model outputs in each of the three cases. For each of these cases we present six forecasts of earnings per share for each year of the forecast period. Each forecast represents a replication of the manner in which earnings per share vary under identical conditions except for the inherent uncertainty of the forecast inputs associated with the regression equations of the model.

It would be desirable to have both a larger number of

replications and a longer period of simulated financial operations, but we had to confine our study to the six replications reported on below and to the forecast period of five years because of the costs of a model run. The relatively small number of replications and forecasts mean that from the standpoint of statistical inference we must face what is called a small sample situation, and this poses difficult problems of statistical analysis which will be discussed in later sections.

Table 1 presents earnings per share forecasts for each of the six replications and for each year of the forecast period, assuming stable unit of measurement.

TABLE 1   Forecasts of Earnings Per Share, Unadjusted Case

Replication	Year	1974	1975	1976	1977	1978
1		1.51	1.73	3.79	4.29	5.63
2		1.88	2.11	4.10	5.13	6.68
3		2.25	1.92	4.68	5.86	7.71
4		2.59	2.30	5.24	6.96	9.29
5		2.99	2.68	5.82	7.74	10.38
6		3.37	3.08	6.43	8.57	11.41

To obtain the price adjusted earnings per share in the after-the-fact case, price level adjustments to plant and depreciation as well as to monetary gains and losses for a given year were made using the simulated balance sheet and income statements for the unadjusted case as described in Appendices 1 and 2. Net income was restated as a consequence of these adjustments in order to obtain the earnings per share in each year of the forecast period for the after-the-fact case. The results of these calculations, restated in terms of the six replications, are shown in Table 2.

TABLE 2   Forecasts of Earnings Per Share, After the Fact Case

Replication	Year	1974	1975	1976	1977	1978
1		4.94	4.26	5.19	5.40	6.96
2		5.27	4.55	5.67	6.28	8.03
3		5.61	4.31	6.23	7.03	9.08
4		5.00	3.71	5.95	7.49	9.77
5		6.30	4.95	7.26	8.95	11.84
6		6.65	5.28	7.80	9.69	12.74

To the best of our knowledge all previous studies of the effects of price level adjustments on financial statements have been concerned with what we call after-the-fact adjustments. Such studies have an important limitation: the temporal, interactive effects between price level adjustments and financial decisions cannot be explored satisfactorily, yet it is clear that such interaction is of critical importance in the planning process. Using our simulation methodology provides a means of making year-by-year price level adjustments to the financial statements and of simulating the effects of these interactions. Thus we changed the plant and depreciation schedules for the unadjusted case, which had been previously used as inputs to the model to obtain unadjusted earnings per share data, putting in instead price level adjusted plant and depreciation schedules, prepared as described in Appendix 1. All other inputs and the forecast values of the dependent variables in the regression equations remained the same. Runs of the financial simulation model were then made to obtain the earnings per share data for the interactive adjustments case. These were then restated to reflect price level changes in monetary gains and losses as described in Appendix 2. The resulting data are shown in Table 3 below.

Differences in earnings per share between the unadjusted

and interactive cases can be attributed to the temporal, interactive effects of price adjustments on the financial decisions made by the model, because all other factors have been held constant in the six replications. Data on earnings per share in the interactive case are shown in Table 3.

TABLE 3   Forecasts of Earnings Per Share, Interactive Case

Replication	Year	1974	1975	1976	1977	1978
1		5.66	5.04	5.93	3.40	6.54
2		5.22	4.50	5.59	4.07	7.23
3		6.31	5.13	7.09	6.01	9.44
4		6.63	5.44	7.60	7.65	11.24
5		7.00	5.75	8.13	8.93	12.40
6		7.35	6.09	8.66	10.22	13.38

It is useful to summarize these data by calculating the mean and standard deviation of earnings per share for each of the three cases. These data appear in Table 4 and the mean earnings per share are plotted in Figure 3.

TABLE 4   Mean Forecasts of Earnings Per Share, 1974–1978

Case	Year	1974	1975	1976	1977	1978
Unadjusted						
Mean		2.43	2.30	5.01	6.42	8.52
Standard Deviation		0.69	0.50	1.02	1.62	2.23
After the Fact						
Mean		5.63	4.51	6.35	7.47	9.74
Standard Deviation		0.71	0.55	0.99	1.61	2.21
Interactive						
Mean		6.36	5.33	7.17	6.73	10.04
Standard Deviation		0.81	0.56	1.21	2.70	2.78

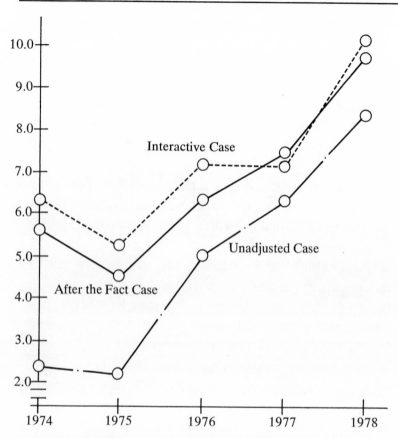

FIGURE 3   Mean Forecasts of Earnings Per Share, 1974–1978

IV. ANALYSIS OF THE EFFECTS OF
PRICE LEVEL ADJUSTMENTS ON
ANNUAL GROWTH IN EARNINGS PER SHARE

The annual growth of earnings per share can be examined conveniently within the context of the six replications for each of the years of the forecast period. This
annual growth in the unadjusted case can be represented as

(1) $\text{UAEPS}(t) = 0.0498 + 1.6292t + \varepsilon,$

where the estimated standard error of the estimated slope is
.1842 and the random error term ε associated with this regression equation has an estimated standard error of 1.4269
and $r^2 = .7364$. It is understood in (1) that t takes on the
values 1 through 5 corresponding to the years 1974
through 1978. The estimated slope in (1) of approximately
$1.63 can be interpreted as the estimated average annual
increase in earnings per share per year over the forecast
period, or the annual growth in earnings per share per unit
of time over this period.

The Durbin-Watson statistic for this case is 1.0553,
which suggests, at the 5 percent level of significance, that
the errors about this regression line may have a first order
autoregressive structure with a positive serial correlation.
This in turn suggests that it is necessary to revise the ordinary least squares estimation procedure used to obtain (1)
so as to reflect this serial correlation influence and obtain a
better statistical estimate of the annual growth of earnings
per share in the unadjusted case. We will return to a consideration of this point in the last section of the paper.

In the after-the-fact case, earnings per share can be represented as

(2) $\text{AFEPS}(t) = 3.3857 + 1.1180t + \varepsilon,$

where the estimated standard error of the estimated slope is
0.1993 and the random error term ε associated with this
equation has an estimated standard error of 1.5437 and an
$r^2 = 0.5292$.

The Durbin-Watson statistic for this case is 0.9019, again
suggesting the presence, at the .05 level of significance, of

positive serial correlation. The annual growth in this case is approximately $1.12 per unit change in time. Thus when price level adjustments are made after the fact we have a shift in the level of earnings (the intercepts changed from 0.0498 to 3.3857) while the annual change in earnings per share per unit of time (the annual growth) decreases from approximately $1.63 to approximately $1.12. This is accompanied by greater variation in the errors about the fitted regression line in the after-the-fact case as contrasted to the unadjusted case, i.e., the estimated standard deviation of these errors is approximately $1.54 for the former as contrasted to the estimated standard deviation in the latter case of approximately $1.43.

The regression equation in the interactive adjustments case is given by

(3) $\text{IAEPS}(t) = 4.4972 + 0.8755t + \varepsilon.$

The estimated standard error of the estimated slope is 0.2629, the estimated standard error of the random error term ε is 2.0367 and $r^2 = 0.2837$.

As was true for the two other cases we have considered, positive serial correlation is suggested, at the .05 level of significance, by the value of 0.8327 of the Durbin-Watson statistic in the interactive adjustments case.

The analysis of these data leads to further important observations about the effects of price level adjustments when considered interactively with financial decisions. One sees that there is a greater change in the level of earnings per share (intercept) relative to that for the previous two cases. There is a striking reduction in annual growth of earnings per unit of time (the estimated slope) to approximately $.87 per share. This is to be contrasted with the estimated annual growth in earnings per share of $1.12 and $1.63 in the other cases. At the same time, greater uncertainty is introduced in this case, as is indicated by a consideration of the estimated standard deviation of the random error term, which increases to approximately $2.04.

V. SOME INSIGHTS INTO THE TEMPORAL PROPERTIES OF EARNINGS PER SHARE

In the previous sections we were concerned with annual growth increments to earnings per share. We now turn our attention to growth rates in earnings per share under the three cases.

We have assumed a temporal growth rate model of the general form

$$(4) \qquad \text{EPS}(t) - \theta\,\text{EPS}(t-1) = e(t)$$

or alternately

$$(5) \qquad \text{EPS}(t) = \theta\,\text{EPS}(t-1) + e(t)$$

where the random errors associated with this equation are assumed to be uncorrelated and to have mean 0 and constant variance. This model is a simplified one adopted for explanatory purposes. A deeper consideration of growth rates in earnings per share would require the development of more complex models of the autoregressive moving average type, which would provide a more satisfactory treatment of the effects of price level adjustments on the temporal coherence structure of earnings per share.

For the unadjusted case we determine by ordinary least squares the equation

$$(6) \qquad \text{UAEPS}(t) = 1.3426\,\text{UAEPS}(t-1) + \varepsilon(t).$$

The estimated standard error of the estimate of the coefficient θ in (6) is 0.0524, the estimated standard deviation of the errors $\varepsilon(t)$ is 1.1573, the Durbin-Watson statistic associated with (6) is 0.6382, and the corresponding statistic for the lagged dependent variable model (LDVM) is 3.893. The latter suggests a more complicated temporal structure amongst the equation errors than is assumed for the model (4).

An estimated growth rate can be determined from (6) by replacing $\varepsilon(t)$ by 0, its expected value, and using

$$(7) \qquad \frac{\text{UAEPS}(t)}{\text{UAEPS}(t-1)} = 1.3426,$$

from which we obtain an estimated growth rate of .3426 or approximately 34 percent.

For the after-the-fact case we have the equation

$$(8) \qquad \text{AFEPS}(t) = 1.1799\,\text{AFEPS}(t-1) + \varepsilon(t),$$

with

estimated standard error of estimated θ = 0.045
estimated standard deviation of errors $\varepsilon(t)$ = 1.3747
Durbin-Watson statistic   = 0.3481
D-W Statistic for LDVM   = 4.668

The estimated growth rate in this case is approximately 18 percent, or about half the estimated growth rate for the unadjusted case.

Some interesting results emerge in considering the interactive adjustments case. Here the quotation is

$$(9) \qquad \text{LAEPS}(t) = 1.1387\,\text{LAEPS}(t-1) + \varepsilon(t),$$

where

estimated standard error of estimated θ = 0.0607
estimated standard deviation of errors $\varepsilon(t)$ = 1.960
Durbin-Watson statistic   = 0.4733
D-W statistic for **LDVM**   = 4.432

The estimated growth rate for the interactive case is approximately 14 percent, or less than half that for the unadjusted case. Also, the estimated standard deviation of the equation errors $\varepsilon(t)$ has increased over the other two cases.

This analysis reveals that insofar as the temporal coherence structure is concerned, the after-the-fact and interactive adjustments cases show similarities in terms of rates of growth and, to a lesser extent, in year-to-year movements. These two cases, however, appear to show an altogether different temporal pattern in terms of rate of growth and year-to-year movements than the unadjusted case.

Another conclusion of the exploratory analysis of this section is that ordinary least squares methods of estimation for models of the class (4) or (5) are inadequate because of the presence of serially correlated errors. Further investigation should be made by exploring the applicability of three-pass least squares, Wallis' adaptation of an iterative generalized least squares method of estimation for distributed lag models, or the more general and complete maximum likelihood methods of estimation associated with autoregressive moving average models.

VI. SUGGESTIONS FOR FUTURE RESEARCH

Corporate managers and financial executives must account for the effects of inflation when evaluating the long-lived assets of a corporation. They must also develop plans to cushion the impact of inflation in the future in order to minimize its adverse effects. Finally, they must provide investors with financial information which reflects the changing value of the dollar so that the future earning power of the corporation can be more accurately predicted.

Each of these goals requires extensive use of forecasts. For example, forecasts of the GNP Implicit Price Deflator must be made, and these must be used for the purpose of providing price-level adjusted data for use in financial models as well as for the purpose of making after-the-fact price level adjustments to the financial statements obtained as outputs of the model.

We suggest that operational financial planning models be used to study the effects of price level adjustments more thoroughly and in greater detail than has been done in this paper. This investigation could include consideration of the following problems.

1. A modular model building strategy which can be adapted to a variety of companies should be developed which would integrate the components shown in Figure 4.

2. Price level adjustments should be made to all items in the financial statements, and then forecasts developed for the three cases considered in this paper.

3. A comparative study should be made of price-level adjusted and current value accounting, so that the difference in effects upon management decision-making over time can be assessed in a more objective manner than is currently possible.

4. An investigation should be made of the effects on the three cases generated by using one or more indices other than the GNP Implicit Price Deflator to make price level adjustments.

5. Because forecasting beyond a five-to-ten-year horizon is tenuous and the cost of running a large-scale operational financial model to develop a large number of simulated replications will be considerable, research must make use of what is called small sample statistics for dependent replications. Little is known concerning such problems at the present time. New statistical methods of inference must be developed in order to study more carefully the temporal movements in earnings per share attributable to the effects of price level changes.

6. Management oftentimes regards a forecast as a "hard

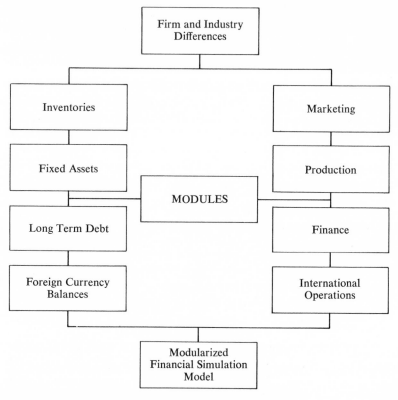

FIGURE 4   Modules for a Financial Simulation Model

number" and ignores the fact that it is subject to probabilistic variation arising from errors of forecast. For policy guidance in financial planning, one needs to study more fully the nature of the probabilistic variation of the forecast values. In statistical terminology, this means that one must develop additional stochastic simulation concepts so that distributions of forecasts can be more adequately studied and their statistical properties more fully investigated.

APPENDIX 1
CALCULATIONS FOR PRICE-LEVEL ADJUSTED
PLANT AND DEPRECIATION

The forecasts of earnings per share—unadjusted for price level effects—that were simulated by the model, were developed on the basis of inputs (unadjusted for price level changes) which included the following schedules for total utility plant and depreciation. These were provided by the company.

Following the procedures recommended in "Statement No. 3," we obtained total utility plant acquisitions expressed in units of general purchasing power according to the following formula:

$$\sum_{i=1945}^{1973} \left[\begin{array}{l} \text{Total Utility} \\ \text{Plant Acquired} \\ \text{in Year i} \end{array} \right] \left(\frac{\text{GNP Deflator at Statement Date}}{\text{GNP Deflator at Year i}} \right)$$

Total utility plant acquisitions by year from 1945 through 1968 as well as total retirements by year of acquisition for the same period were provided by the company as part of a detailed study made by members of the accounting staff for

TABLE A1.1   Plant and Depreciation Schedules in Unadjusted Dollars

Year	1974	1975	1976	1977	1978
Book Depre-ciation	84,900	88,599	94,422	103,621	117,476
Utility Plant Investment	3,788,721	4,045,644	4,535,983	5,232,300	6,083,482
Utility Plant Depreciation Reserve	658,292	728,540	799,439	872,622	954,516
Add Dep. Allow. for FIT	56,441	56,702	49,639	55,156	69,570
Depreciable Plant	3,135,586	3,237,865	3,436,774	3,707,881	4,256,857
Plant in Service	3,213,138	3,316,903	3,518,215	3,793,259	4,347,275
Salvage Income	1,172	1,190	1,470	2,003	2,485

management for policy guidance purposes. This study included plant data extending back to 1912, but we utilized data only from 1945 in accordance with "Statement No. 3." From 1969 to 1973, actual data on plant acquisitions were also used. Although total retirements by year for this period were available, they were not layered by year of acquisition, and the year of acquisition was approximated by assuming a FIFO flow-through for the plant account (i.e., oldest plant was retired first).

Thus the 1973 total utility plant in service, layered by age, was obtained by taking the actual 1968 data, adding the actual plant acquisitions from 1969 through 1973, and subtracting plant retirements for this period as approximated by the FIFO flow-through assumption.

Given the calculations for layering of age of plant from 1945 through 1973, price level adjustments were applied in accordance with "Statement No. 3" to arrive at the price-level adjusted plant for 1973.

W. Allen Spivey and William J. Wrobleski

To obtain the 1974 utility plant investment, adjusted for price level changes, which is a necessary input for the first year of the simulation, the price-level adjusted total utility plant for 1973, determined as stated immediately above, was used as follows. To this value, restated for 1974, was added a forecast of 1974 plant acquisitions, adjusted for price level changes. Then the forecast for 1974 plant retirements, adjusted for price level changes, was subtracted from this figure to arrive at a forecast of price-level adjusted utility plant for 1974. Similar calculations were made for the remaining years of the forecast period. The resulting data are shown in Table A1.2 under the designation, Utility Plant Investment.

TABLE A1.2   Plant and Depreciation Schedules in Adjusted Dollars

Year	1974	1975	1976	1977	1978
Book Depre- ciation	123,107	135,452	146,111	158,809	177,902
Utility Plant Investment	5,493,744	6,185,054	7,019,113	8,018,998	9,212,631
Utility Plant Depreciation Reserve	954,541	1,113,805	1,237,075	1,337,376	1,445,489
Add Deprecia- tion Allow- ance for FIT	81,841	86,687	76,813	84,532	105,355
Depreciable Plant	4,546,681	4,950,107	5,318,165	5,682,681	6,446,448
Plant in Service	4,659,133	5,070,942	5,444,189	5,813,531	6,583,375
Salvage Income	1,698	1,818	2,274	3,069	3,762

The price-level adjusted depreciation charges (book depreciation) appearing in Table A1.2 were also obtained by an estimation procedure. Ideally, depreciation charges should be associated with assets in terms of year of acquisition of the assets. Each layer of depreciation would then be adjusted on the basis of the index for the year in which the assets were acquired. Unfortunately, information was not available which would permit layering of depreciation in this manner. We used instead an estimation procedure which related the unadjusted depreciation charge to the price-level adjusted depreciation by means of the following computation:

$$\left[\frac{\text{Unadjusted depreciation charge}}{\text{Unadjusted plant}}\right] \times \left[\frac{\text{Price-level adjusted}}{\text{plant}}\right]$$

Given the long average life of utility plant (estimated to be 35 years) and the fact that the company uses straight-line depreciation, we believe that this procedure provides a reasonable estimate for the purposes of this paper.

The results of these calculations are shown in Table A1.2 under the designation, Book Depreciation. Similar computations were made in order to arrive at the remaining entries of the table.

APPENDIX 2
COMPUTATIONS FOR MONETARY GAINS AND LOSSES AND RESTATEMENT OF NET INCOME

Sufficient information was available from the company to permit proper identification of all monetary assets and liabilities. It was not possible, however, to analyze the changes in monetary items in the detail recommended in "Statement No. 3." We approximated the recommended procedures by assuming that changes in monetary gains and

losses took place uniformly over a given year and we therefore adjusted the data using the GNP Implicit Price Deflator
for the year. The procedure used is illustrated in the following table.

	Historical	*Conversion Factor*	*Adjusted*
Net Monetary Items 12/31/73	(1,539,638)	1.1154*	(1,717,312)
Change in Net Monetary Items 12/31/73– 12/31/74	(271,881)	1.0545**	(286,699)
Net Monetary Items Restated—if no gain	. . .	. . .	(2,004,010)
Net Monetary Items Historical—12/31/74	. . .	. . .	(1,811,519)
Monetary Gain	. . .	. . .	(192,492)

* $\dfrac{\text{GNP Deflator for 4th quarter 1974}}{\text{GNP Deflator for 4th quarter 1973}}$

** $\dfrac{\text{GNP Deflator for 4th quarter 1974}}{\text{Average GNP Deflator for 1974}}$

Price-level adjusted monetary gain as determined above
was added to unadjusted book income and the additional
depreciation resulting from restatement of the utility plant
was then subtracted from this total. The result is the restated net income for the year, which is used as a basis for
calculating earnings per share for the after-the-fact and
interactive cases.

Response

Thomas R. Dyckman

Professors Spivey and Wrobleski (S and W hereafter) have provided us with a provocative paper. Their results suggest that using alternate methods of incorporating expected inflation measures into a simulation model of a firm's financial and decision-making process will yield different output values for the financial variables—in particular, earnings per share. They further conclude that such differences will also result if inflation is not considered in the simulated decision process. Yet if we all know this, why have we not incorporated inflation measures into financial planning and decision making? This issue is the main one I wish to address.

THE S AND W MODEL

Unfortunately we are told very little about the model, what it includes, how its variables are interrelated, what assumptions it makes. Since many of the conclusions of the S and W paper are based on the crunchings of this black box, it is necessary for us to make some assumptions, inter-pretations, and leaps of faith.

S and W describe their model as "a corporate planning model" and, in another passage, as an operational financial planning model. Given these descriptions and a brief dis-cussion, we can assume that the model is what Horngren [1972, p. 122] calls a "corporate financial-planning model" (CFPM). Essentially this represents a master budget which reflects the organization's decisions and strategies for the forthcoming period. In the present case, the relationships between the operating and financial activities have been formalized into a mathematical simulation model. The out-puts are the balance sheet, income statement, and cash flow statement for the organization. The outputs plus forecasts for the exogenous variables then become the input for the second year of a five-year planning horizon.

The CFPM is used in practice to examine both the effects of management decisions which alter the input variables and the impact of factors beyond management's control. One such factor is inflation. By explicitly adjusting the data in the model, using a measure of the change in the dollar, the authors "influence the decisions that are made by it."

The assumption appears to be that the decisions on some substantive issues (including financing, at least) are made by the model. Further, we must assume that between models II (after-the-fact adjustments for price level changes) and III (interactive adjustments, where price-level adjusted data constitute inputs to the model), different management decisions are made. Certainly this can be the case if the model itself makes the decisions and if it is not properly specified. But is this so? Can we accept what appears to be such a naive view of management decision-making behavior?

Is it the case that management (of the utility in question, or of any organization) completely ignores inflationary effects? Given the feedback built into actual budget systems, would it continue over time? We are given no data that management ignores inflation, only data that EPS (and other financial output values) will differ if management makes decisions ignoring inflation. Management, in this model, does not even partially adjust overtime to the impact of inflation.

There are also reasons to question the black box simulation model. First the CFPM as used in practice does not make decisions, although it may suggest them. Rather it is used to observe the effects of management decisions. Second, various inputs to the CFPM will themselves reflect a consideration of inflation. For example, one input, the input to the CFPM from the capital budgeting decisions for the organization, will reflect consideration of the effects of inflation on those decisions. Management cannot ignore the expected effects of inflation on cash flows. Furthermore, they are also reflected in the term structure of interest rates.

The model proposed by S and W seems, then, too simplistic to address their problem. Moreover, there should be some articulation between the CFPM and other decision-relevant models.

We accept the fact that if substantive decisions are made by the model itself and if different decision-relevant input data are given the model, then different model outputs will be forthcoming. The results are what the authors built into their model. The question is not one of simulation, but of management behavior, an issue not addressed in the research at hand. Without the behavioral effect, there is no reason to assume a difference in models II and III, if management's decision behavior were properly specified. The results presented are an artifact of the simulation which assumes a naive response to inflation on management's part.

THE SIMULATION

Suppose for the moment, however, we believe in what we might call a naive management approach to inflation. Then we might wish to examine the effects on the output variables of the CFPM. Can we do so with the present model? This too is a difficult question to answer with the limited knowledge we have concerning the model. However, several observations can be advanced in a preliminary way.

First, if inputs to the CFPM involve decisions that are influenced by inflation, then we must include these inputs as they would be made both ignoring and considering inflation if the differences between models II and III are to be evaluated. But this has not been done. The capital budgeting input, for example, is separate, and appears to enter as construction expenditures. We do not know whether these data consider inflation or not, but it is a constant input for all models. Hence, the full differences between the models due to inflation is not addressed.

Second, the regression equations used "to forecast account balances" are not given. But the authors imply that the same equations are relevant whether the data are price-adjusted or not. This does not seem reasonable. Nor does it seem that management would use the same equations without regard to inflationary effects. To properly capture the output differences due to inflation, two sets of regression equations are required; one based on unadjusted historical data and another based on adjusted data. There is no indication that these differences were captured by the model.

Third, the other inputs to the CFPM involve forecasts, and hence are subject to error. While we understand that to include the uncertainty surrounding these variables in the simulation would complicate the simulation's regression analysis (a random-effects model would be required), is it reasonable to assume that only the uncertainty emanating from the regression equations is relevant to the "smoothness" and the "temporal coherence" of the model's output?

The conclusion of this subsection is that the model, as it stands, is inadequate to test the properties of the output variables in terms of the relevance of these properties to management decisions.

THE STATISTICAL ANALYSIS

The authors ran their simulation a total of 12 times. The first six runs were apparently used for models I and II and the second six runs were used for the interactive model, model III. The differences among runs were obtained by using different regression forecasts, which were "allowed to vary probabilistically." (We must assume a proper Monte Carlo simulation was used.) The variability in the final EPS figures is due entirely to the alternate account balances resulting from this segment of the CFPM.

The initial statistical analysis is based on an OLS regression equation on the EPS values for each of the three models. The authors seem to evaluate the "smoothness" of the data by looking at the standard error and the "temporal coherence" by comparing the coefficients of the three regression equations.

It is not clear why S and W elected to concentrate on EPS

(for example, why not look at return on investment?), nor is there any theory given for assuming a linear and stable relationship of EPS over time. Such expressions would seem to be resorted to because of simplicity and the small number of observations. Research on security returns suggests other models may be more descriptive. We also wonder why regression analysis was used, given that the desire is to test for differences, and the independent variable is essentially nominal. We would suggest ANOV as a more appropriate model. However, ANOV requires independent observations, and this is not the case here.

Indeed, the nature of the data-generating process suggests that autocorrelation should be expected in the absolute EPS values. An apparently large portion of the input data is identical across runs. The authors confirm this finding with the values reported for the Durbin-Watson statistic.

The Durbin-Watson statistic [1951] is given by

$$d = \frac{\sum\limits_{t=2}^{n} (e_t - e_{t-1})^2}{\sum\limits_{t=1}^{n} e_t^2}$$

where t stands for the consecutive sample

items $t = 1, \ldots, n$

and e represents the regression residual.

Since the order in which S and W obtained their runs is arbitrary, the ordering of the e values for each year as required to compute d is also arbitrary. With different run orders, different Durbin-Watson statistics result. Furthermore, as Johnston [1972, p. 252] observes, "It is important to emphasize that this test [Durbin-Watson] . . . is not applicable, for example, when lagged Y [the dependent variable] values appear among the explanatory variables." This is the case here.

The authors then go on to develop regression equations for the growth rates in EPS from year to year. This analysis is subject to the same limitations as that just discussed for the growth increments in EPS. Moreover, their growth-rate model assumes implicitly that the errors are uncorrelated, a condition the authors argue earlier is not true.

After some ten pages of analysis of the EPS data, S and W conclude "that ordinary least squares methods of estimation for models of the class (4) or (5) [and we might include (1) through (3) as well] are inadequate because of the presence of serially correlated errors." Couldn't we have expected this? The authors also tell us that small sample statistical methods of inference are not as yet adequate to investigate questions of significance in data similar to that presented. Yet that does not prevent them from making leading statements such as, "The analysis of these data leads to further important observations about the effects of price level adjustments when considered interactively with final decisions. One sees that there is a greater change in the level per share (intercept) relative to that for the previous two cases. There is a striking reduction in annual growth of earnings per unit of time (the estimated slope) to approximately $.87 per share." True, these statements don't say anything about statistical significance, but the implications are there. If the statistical analysis is not justified, why is so much attention devoted to it?

RESEARCH

The call for research appears at the end of almost all research papers. It appears here too. But I wish to call for different research from what S and W desire. Research on small statistical methods is certainly needed, but it does not go to the heart of the issue here.

First, S and W have raised what I will call the naive management hypothesis. Note that I did not say the naive manager hypothesis. Managers, singly, may ignore inflation in evaluating decisions, but this is much less likely to be the case for management. Within a given firm it may be sufficient initially for a single manager to understand the relevance of inflation in order to assure that the firm will recognize it.

But I could be wrong. Perhaps management is naive. It is an empirical question and, as such, it can be tested.

Secondly, I am not in possession of data that tell me how *well* management is able to incorporate inflation into its planning and decision-making process. For example, consider the capital budgeting model. Inflation may influence the ability of management to estimate the necessary costs and benefits of capital projects. The appropriate discount rate to use depends on whether money or real cash flows are being used. In addition, as the risk of inflation increases, the cost of debt increases relative to equity capital. As Bierman and Smidt [1975, p. 317] observe, investors may conclude that "the risks associated with owning a diversified portfolio of common stock are less than those of owning debt securities not protected from inflation." Such a result has obvious implications for corporate financing decisions.

Finally, if it is concluded that investigation into the CFPM is appropriate, two extensions of the present model are important. The first extension would expand this model to articulate with the other financial and operational models whose input it consumes. Otherwise we inevitably produce suboptimal decisions. In other words, marketing, production, and finance decision models should be appended.

The second extension would recognize that accounting procedures are not always in harmony with economically justified decisions. For example, a capital budgeting decision assumes certain cash flows. These cash flows are in part based on tax computations that in turn reflect depreciation schedules. But it need not be true that the financial statements are computed using the same depreciation schedules. (Similar statements could be made concerning the investment credit, research and development, goodwill acquired in acquisitions, and so on.) The point is that what appears to be a viable economic decision may have undesirable effects on financial reports of EPS, return on investment, and important financial statement ratios. While ideally, it might seem appropriate either to adjust accounting reports to reflect economic reality or to prevent them from having investment implications, neither solution is operationally practical. Hence some decisions, such as capital budgeting decisions, may need to be considered not only in light of their impact on both existing and other new investments, but also in light of constraints on what will be reported in the financial statements.

This is so for any firm, given generally acceptable accounting procedures, that is concerned with investor re-actions to income, loan sources concerned with financial statement measures of default risk, and government agency views concerning return on investment. This in no way should be interpreted as meaning that such groups should not be made more aware of the impacts of inflation on the organization and the failure of current financial reporting to reflect them.

In preparing these financial statements, the change in the measuring unit should be reflected. Managers, investors, government, workers, and other interested parties should be told what the results of operations are in constant terms.[1] If conventional reports are also desired, a position consistent with the FASB, these can also be provided.

---

[1] We avoid here three major issues: (1) whether the fact that information on inflation is available to the market from other sources negates the importance of reporting price-level adjusted data (an efficient market notion); (2) whether adequate measures of the change in the value of the dollar are available; and (3) whether inflation is sufficiently serious that the costs of reporting on a price-level adjusted basis are justified by the increases in social benefits.

Bibliography

Bierman, H., and S. Smidt, *The Capital Budgeting Decision* (New York: Macmillan, 1974).

Durbin, J., and G. Watson, "Testing for Serial Correlation in Least-Squares Regression," *Biometrika,* Vol. 37, pp. 409–428, and Vol. 38, pp. 159–178 (1951).

Horngren, C., *Cost Accounting: A Managerial Emphasis,* 3rd Edition (Englewood Cliffs, N.J.: Prentice-Hall, 1972).

Ijiri, Y., F. Levy, and R. Lyon, "A Linear Programming Model for Budgeting and Financial Planning," *Journal of Accounting Research,* Vol. 1, No. 2, pp. 198–212.

Johnston, J., *Econometric Methods,* 2nd Edition (New York: McGraw-Hill, 1972).

Floor Discussion

Spivey: I have a few slides which may expedite my comments. I have been helped a great deal by my colleague, Professor Dyckman, who sent me his comments on our paper before the meeting. These comments showed very clearly that in writing the first draft of our paper we were not as informative as we might have been. I hope my comments today will be an improvement.

Suppose one wanted to think about the effects of price level adjustment, not merely in the present or in the past, but in the future. In short, we're concerned with the question of how to incorporate expectations concerning price level changes into planning for the future. The corporate planning model we've used is an operational model currently in use by a public utility. It was developed by a team of about 15 people, two of whom were from the University of Michigan—my colleague was one, and the other was Lee Brummet of our accounting faculty, whom many of you know. This model was developed completely independent of any uses to which we are putting this model. It is quite a large one, and we were lucky to have an opportunity to run our experiments with the company's cooperation. In any case, the idea is that one uses this model to simulate or trace out expected future consequences, financial statements are developed, and they could be consulted by a manager in a feedback mode. It could in this way have some effect on management planning policies in the future.

It might be helpful to describe the model briefly. It has econometric forecasting modules. There is also a book depreciation module which calculates book depreciation with quite a large amount of detail. There's a tax calculation module. Information would come out of that and proceed into the simulation module in the program. There is an optimization model that examines financial ratios, and attempts to optimize heuristically certain quantities, and one then examines the consequences through the income statement, cash flows and balance sheet modules. This may give some idea of the extent and size of this model and might be helpful in assessing some of our results.

Rogge: Allen, does that forecasting model include forecasts of aggregates in the economy at large as well as—

Spivey: Yes, it would have to include a forecast of the unemployment rate over the relevant time horizon in the area served by the public utility. It would include forecasts of the inflation rate and other such endogenous influences.

Davidson: Would it include forecasts for the regulatory commission's reaction to these changing prices?

Spivey: Yes, and that's a matter we agreed not to discuss in relation to the forecasts.

Fabricant: When you said you made an estimate of the un-employment, did you pick on those estimates of unemploy-ment in the local area or some other Washington estimate of unemployment for the nation as a whole, or did you just estimate the whole business?

Spivey: That forecast was made informally, but one had available forecasts of national levels of employment, and, more importantly, estimates for the area served by the utility. This area would have unemployment rates that might well differ from the national average because of local pe-culiarities—yet it might depend to some extent on national influences also.

Now, very quickly, to give you some idea of the sequence in which this model operates, the model has independent variables and, of course, they have to be forecasted. As we caution students in our introductory statistics courses, one of the problems with all regression analyses is that they pro-vide forecasts of dependent variables, but the user must de-velop forecasted values for the dependent variables. The latter forecasts may be as difficult to make as the former. In the model we are using, one must forecast beginning bal-ances for the initial year—these go into the simulation mod-ule. Then other parts of the program generate the values of the other contingent variables which are independent in the typical sense, and then the values of the dependent variables are generated. There is also an optional subroutine which provides management with an opportunity to override the model and put in its own inputs and its own forecasts. The model has this flexibility—as any good model should. You can see that the flow of this logic comes down as indicated in the diagram, and finally we obtain the balance sheet, income and cash flow statements.

Now we've said we have three cases in presenting the statistical data in this paper. One we call the unadjusted case, where we make no explicit adjustment of any of the data as a result of change in price level influences. Essentially this assumes that there is no inflation and no change in the unit of measurement. Then we have the after-the-fact case, which our colleagues in management tell us is usually what is used in the corporate planning field: people tend to make forecasts for some period in the future in current dollar terms, and then after the forecasts have been generated, make an adjustment by predicting or projecting the implicit price deflator and applying this to the forecasts.

Ryan: Allen, at the point of each adjustment, does the procedure assume that for the balance of the period there will be no inflation? In other words, at the end of year one, in forecasting do you go back to the unadjusted base?

Spivey: What we do is we make a forecast for the year one and afterward, we simply adjust the balance sheet, income and cash flow statements for the inflation that took place during that year.

Ryan: But not for subsequent years?

Spivey: We repeat this for each of the future years, using the forecasted deflator. We call this "after-the-fact" for this reason because the model itself is not reacting to the changed monetary value. The model is always ingesting the dollars that are essentially in a historical cost form, and one trims them back "after the fact" at the end of the year with the projection of what the inflation rate might be in the given year.

Vancil: Let me try to understand that, too. I'm looking at Tables 1 and 2, where you have data for the unadjusted and after-the-fact cases. Just taking replication No. 1, is the $1.51 in 1974 stated in historical cost dollars or a mishmash of all kinds of dollars?

Spivey: That's the usual thing.

Vancil: Right, but on Table 2, the $4.94 is stated in dollars of what year? Does that reflect price-level adjusted accounting using a general index?

Spivey: For 1974.

Vancil: And then the $4.26 for 1975 is in dollars of what year?

Spivey: 1975.

Vancil: So you have not used a common index to make a comparison cost. I can't say that earnings per share 1975 are lower than 1974 unless I know the amount of inflation for 1974 or 1975.

Davidson: To go back to the facts of the after-the-fact case, is it right to say that each year management is surprised that there has been a price change in that year—that is, year one there is a price change and they discover that after-the-fact —and year two—well, after three or four years, you'd think they might be inclined to push over into the interactive.

Spivey: We are not prescribing any kind of behavior in any of these three cases. We are just saying, suppose one made forecasts for five years in the future, and then one simply after-the-fact in each one of these cases makes a discount. Our colleagues tell us that in the management field, when people use corporate planning models they tend to do it this way—a kind of after-the-fact adjustment.

Now the third case was one in which we tried to say, "Well, maybe we ought to try to intrdouce some kind of rolling adjustment so that the model, with its many inter-relationships, would interact to those changing numbers on a year-by-year basis." Now, of course, we're not saying that management behaves this way; this is not a behavioral model. We're simply saying these are three possibilities to think about, and we ask, "What are the implications of each as far as this particular model is concerned?"

Now, we have reported in our paper earnings per share only, and that's a somewhat slippery measure. It's already been exposed by the comments here today. There are many other things that one might want to look at and the model would permit one to look at. For example, one may wish to examine how fast revenues change when price level adjustment takes place, how revenue requirements differ under these cases or differ under other possible regimes that might be injected into the model. It might be possible to see how revenue requirements differ under various depreciation policies and how changes in pricing policies affect other aspects of the model, dividend payouts in the three cases, the changes that are induced in bond financing and equity and so on. The important thing, I think, that comes out of this —and our discussants and others may well wish to examine vigorously the implications of this—is the change in earnings per share in the three cases. They are marked, and, for example, the average here is 2.43 for the first year, 5.63 in the after-the-fact case and 6.36 in the interactive case, so there is a very big jump in earnings per share whenever these adjustments, however imperfectly we have attempted to accommodate them, have been made. What's happened here is that there has been a big jump in the earnings per share over what it was in the unadjusted case. Now, when we first saw these differences, we experienced considerable trepidation because we were sure that one of the doctoral students who was working with us had punched the wrong hole in an IBM card or stepped on it with a pair of golf shoes and that some mistake was involved. Most of the literature I had been reading on price adjustments in the popular press seemed to indicate that whenever one adjusts for price level changes, earnings per share always went down, and here the earnings per share went up markedly. This may have some interest for Sid Davidson, who has done a much more thorough comparative study on this issue.

Davidson: In fact, it's spelled out on this wide sheet of paper that has been distributed to everybody.

Spivey: And Sid has found out that the earnings per share of public utilities in all of the cases went up, after the price level adjustment.

Davidson: Following the FASB recommended procedure.

Spivey: Following the FASB procedure. Now let me make sure about this. The adjustments in depreciation had a negative effect but it was the positive effects in the monetary gains that caused this rather significant rise in the situation.

Now, we followed the FASB recommendations in allocating to the given year the realized monetary gains rather than holding them until a financial instrument has been repaid to your company, which I understand is the practice of the Indiana Telephone Corporation. Is that right?

Fletcher: The Indiana Telephone Corporation recognizes the gain on the bond debt when the debt, in fact, is reduced. Refunding doesn't count—that's a switch in creditors.

Spivey: In your calculations, your earnings per share came down after the price level adjustments.

Fletcher: Yes.

Spivey: Now, we set out to analyze these results statistically, and we had an enormous amount of trouble getting all the calculations done. We now appreciate our colleagues in accounting on the faculty of the University of Michigan in ways that we never did before, and I might say to Mr. Sprouse that to actually generate all the price level adjustments that are blithely recommended in the FASB report is a hell of a big job.

Dyckman: The first question I asked myself about this model as I read it was: Is it adequate to deal with the problem that the authors wish to address? And for many reasons, some of which they specify, I think it is not. In particular, it makes a very naive assumption about the way management reacts to inflation. Essentially the model assumes that management ignores inflation, that management pays no attention to it at all. Given the feedback mechanisms that usually exist in organizations, we would expect at least some partial adjustments by management for this sort of thing.

We would expect, for example, in capital budgeting models dealing with construction (an input to their model), that management would be concerned about inflation. It would be part of what they consider, and, if so, then to some extent management isn't stymied by inflation. This may be the case for utilities or it may not. I don't really know whether the managements of public utilities ignore inflation or whether they don't. But one way or another, it seems to me that that's a conclusion that can be tested empirically. We could see whether management makes decisions that ignore inflation.

As I read Professor Baxter's paper, I noticed that he, too, was worried about whether management really does respond to inflation and he has his views on that subject. My own perception without any empirical data would say that management does not ignore inflation.

But let's assume for a moment that we can ignore this problem and go back to the model itself and ask, "Does it really tell us what will happen if we recognize inflation and what will happen if we don't?" The answer is no.

First, many of the inputs to the model are the same. But if affected by inflation, the inputs should reflect this difference if the total inflation effect is to be determined. Second, only one set of regression equations is used. Yet a different set is required for the case where inflation effects are incorporated in the model than for the case where they are not. Finally, the only place where there's uncertainty in this model is in the regression equations which are used to estimate certain account balances. Yet many of the inputs to both models, including unemployment, the construction budget, and so on, would involve uncertainties, including the effects of inflation. This reduces the validity of the simulation.

Meiselman: I have read the paper by Professors Spivey and Wrobleski rather closely and look upon it as an experimental attempt to answer the question, "What difference would it make if corporate accounts were adjusted to price level changes?" The title of the paper suggests several important aspects of the more general question regarding the implications of alternative accounting systems for financial planning and management decisions in the context of uncertainty. In this sense, the paper is a welcome addition to the small but rapidly growing literature which has been spawned by the current era of inflation, by the growing awareness that inflation impairs the usefulness of information provided by conventional rules of accounting and ordinary market processes, as well as by the growing acceptance of the unhappy view that inflation is not likely to be eliminated in the foreseeable future.

The Spivey-Wrobleski paper has raised many more questions than it has begun to answer, but at the outset I must admit that I have great difficulty in evaluating the paper itself. The main reason is that the central feature of the paper, the model involving 800 different variables characterizing an anonymous public utility, is never presented. The only information we are given are the names of eight principal inputs for each year of the forecast period 1974 to 1978. You then see some items related to demand, such as the average number of customers to be served during the year and kilowatt-hour sales by major consumer class, and some items related to cost, such as the number and type of employees, construction expenditures and interest rates. (Fuel costs and rates themselves are not on the list, and there is essentially no reference to the regulatory authorities that set the rates.) If we have no way of evaluating the content of the models, which I take it are merely used as a convenient and available representation of a real-world situation, I cannot on my own trace or replicate the effects of either inflation or uncertainty on the accounts of the corporation.

In addition, because no management or consumer decision rules are presented, we also cannot evaluate the management and financial responses of the corporation. The change is either in the corporation's accounts per se, or the corporation's real economic and financial circumstances, which may or may not be reflected in these accounts. No outside information seems to be relevant. I am left wondering how and why changes in accounting procedures affect management decisions. Does management read and believe only the numbers their accountants give them? Does management suffer both from money illusion and the traditional accountant's nominal-value illusion? What of the customers?

We do know that accounting rules affect real as opposed to nominal variables in at least two important ways, but the paper does little to address itself to these questions. First, accounting rules have an especially important role in regulated industries because they influence such variables as the rate base and reported depreciation charges which regulatory authorities consider in fixing rates. The relationship between inflation and rates is essentially omitted in its entirety. Second, accounting rules also affect tax liabilities and, therefore, after-tax profits. This is especially true because, as you know, historic cost accounting in a period of inflation understates the cost of replacing inventories and appreciated assets.

In addition, although inflation is the principal actor in the drama, the forecast of inflation rates for the five forecast years of 1974 through 1978 is never revealed. Thus, we are left to wonder about the sensitivity of the results of the exercise to the inflation rate, including whether the recorded differences in accounting profit under the three accounting systems are the results of moderate inflation or large-scale inflation, or whether what the authors call the temporal coherence structure of earnings per share "reflect" the year-to-year variability of the inflation rates over the period or something else.

The paper is also addressed to the topic of uncertainty. There are several senses in which the term "uncertainty" is generally used in economic analysis. One reflects the fact that frequently we face real-world situations about whose outcomes we are partially or wholly ignorant, either because costs of additional information are too great—a situation which Milton Friedman once termed "avoidable ignorance"—or because information is essentially unattainable, which is to say, a situation of "unavoidable ignorance." Uncertainty implies a probabilistic statement. In the Spivey-Wrobleski paper, mention is made of uncertainty but there are no probability statements about alternative disturbances or forecasts for each year. Even where the alternatives are examined, where the alternatives are derived from historic data, there are no probabilities given. Therefore, when six alternative forecasts are given for each of the five years in the forecast period, I cannot interpret the forecasts because there are no probabilities attached to them except that there are suggestions that each is equally likely. Further, to go through the motions of several statistical tests of the entire 30 "results" of each of the three cases as if the 30 were independent observations is surely wrong, because each annual set of six alternative observations must be derived from at least partially similar disturbances plus essentially the same 800 variable model—instead of 30 independent observations.

Now, in addition, changes in year-to-year reported profits are not the same as uncertainty about profits. These changes in profits may be fully anticipated and correctly forecast with certainty. Thus, a forecast of perfectly stable earnings may be held with uncertainty, and stable earnings may turn up to be different from anticipated earnings and, therefore, incorporate some unanticipated profits.

Kohlmeier: When I heard of the paper, "Financial Planning and Management Decisions Under Uncertainty and Inflation," I had some anticipation of a discussion of questions like, "Should budgets be price-level adjusted?" "Should price level concepts be introduced into budgeting?" "Should price level concepts be introduced into capital expenditure analysis?" "Should such concepts be part of management decisions?" so that I am somewhat disappointed by the paper in view of its lack of discussion of these issues.

One of the basic assumptions of the paper is that the model is a reasonable representation of management decision-making, and I don't think that is at all correct. We are told the required input includes construction expenditures, and if you look at the recent experience of what's happened with electric utilities, one of the important management variables is delaying or deferral of construction. Another variable that we are told is required input is the number of operating, maintenance and construction employees, and one of the few discretionary variables available to the management of a utility is employment level. I could cite other examples of how the model does not appropriately represent management decisions. However, in a very narrow sense the model may simulate some financial activity, for instance, debt equity ratios, but even in that case not all types of financial activity are represented in the model.

In today's inflationary environment, no electric utility can show increases in earnings per share without frequent rate increases. We are told nothing about the nature of the regulatory process. You are really mixing apples and oranges when you say that we have earnings per share in dollars of '74, compared to earnings per share in dollars of '75, and so on; they should have all been adjusted to dollars of '78.

One other factor that hasn't been mentioned—most utilities in this country are regulated under principles which involve original cost. Commissions today, generally, do not allow price-level adjusted rate bases and they do not allow price-level adjusted depreciation. One of the tenets of accounting is that you do not admit assets on the balance sheet unless there is a likelihood you can earn or realize on them at some future period. Given the type of regulation we have, there is at least some question whether that is the case.

Finally, I have worked with many people who are involved in planning, and people find it very difficult to talk about explicit rates of inflation in the future. People do not relate to that very well, and they find it very difficult to talk about what it's going to cost to build a plant given a 6 percent inflation or given a 10 percent inflation. They think of it in terms of the specific prices of what they are going to build, and they will include a forecast at the proper place where there is implicit feeling that copper is going to go up this much and the components are going to go up, but to tell somebody to plan on the basis of a 10 percent inflation, people have very difficult times sorting out these basic concepts.

Spivey: Let me respond to several of the comments. I think they are well taken, and I appreciate them very much. First of all, about the points that Tom Dyckman has made about the responsiveness to the model, the relatively mechanical nature of the model and of the work that we have done. We chose to perform three experiments using the model. There is no reason why management, if it wished to participate in something like this, could not become more fully involved with this process and use the model more effectively as a policy assessment or policy alternative examination device to consider many other realistic possibilities. So I think one could respond to that.

Kohlmeier: I suspect that taking a look at Brazil and Argentina might be a more fruitful avenue of research, and how companies in that inflationary environment have reacted. What you find is that production ceases, that playing monetary balances of liabilities and assets is the name of the game, and that where you can make 50 percent by playing that game and 2 percent by improving production, nobody produces.

Davidson: George Terborgh, in your comment earlier, I thought you were calling for a reduction of the reported inflationary interest charges by the erosion of the principal of the debt. I probably misunderstood you.

Terborgh: I was suggesting an offset against erosion. That is, inflation could have been an offset against erosion.

Sprouse: I'm sorry, but I still didn't understand that point.

Terborgh: I was simply against debt erosion during the year because of the 10 percent premium and the propopsition as I was seeing it. Am I right, Sol?

Fabricant: Yes.

Sprouse: You're looking at the holder of the bond now, aren't you? From the terminology you're using.

Davidson: Is it easier to start out with the inflation all being anticipated and reflected in the debt rates?

Terborgh: Inflation premiums I don't think ever quite equal inflation rates, except accidentally and temporarily.

Fabricant: In order to make this point, I made the assumption that it was anticipated fully. Therefore, with a 5 percent inflation anticipated, you would be paying 10 percent, and the 10 percent then includes a 5 percent inflation factor which is, in effect, a sort of reserve item which will be offset later on against that gain.

Davidson: The 10 percent interest charge would, on the unadjusted statement, be shown as an expense. The adjusted statement then would offset that 10 percent interest by the 5 percent debt erosion so that on the adjusted statements, you would wind up with an effective interest charge of 5 percent. Now, there is a question of geography of where you show this 5 percent—Sol, if you don't mind, let me use some different rates, because when I have two 5's I always get confused. Let us have an interest rate of 6 percent, a 5 percent erosion factor, and an overall unadjusted cost of 11 percent. Your unadjusted statement would show 11 percent interest charges. Now, there is a question of geography of whether you ought to show the 5 percent debt erosion as a deduction from the 11 percent interest, or whether you ought to carry the 11 percent interest right straight across into your adjustments and show a purchasing power gain of 5 percent. But either way you do it, it seems to me the only way you can get the right answer, if the anticipated inflation rate turns out to be the actual one, the only way you can get the right answer using terms of measuring the effective interest costs is by picking up all of that money value change in earnings on the adjusted statement.

Terborgh: Well, I think you are right; it would not make any difference in the adjustments—they would come out the same way. It would still divorce reported earnings from their cash flow equivalent.

Sprouse: If income were to be equated with cash flow.

Terborgh: It is substantially so, now, after Inventory Valuation Adjustment. It is basically the cash flow available for real inventory expansion and for noninventory purposes.

Spivey: This conversation is fascinating, and it reminds me of a conversation I had at a cocktail party last Saturday afternoon. Several of my accounting colleagues were standing in front of me, and they were talking about the woes and the problems in teaching accounting. I asked, "What are they?" One said that the trouble is that students ask us what's right, and then we have to say that the experts disagree. We have experts here, and there are interesting disagreements. I replied, "Accounting differs from statistics in one important respect. If a student asks you in accounting if you know the right answer, you can say that the experts disagree, but in statistics, you can often answer correctly that no one knows the right answer." In your field, there are at least all sorts of answers. That's what I find is happening.

Meiselman: I would like to raise a question about the usefulness of starting out with a model that has 800 equations.

I've had some experience with large models that purport to predict the Gross National Product, and I have never gone as far as 800 equations. In view of the number of variables, it is very difficult to find what is going on inside the model, that is, interactions among elements of the model. When something goes wrong, very able, hard working people have a devil of a time to find out why the model doesn't track, or what is wrong. It is very difficult to evaluate so-called simple models with only a few variables. How can one have any confidence in the implications of a model when you have something on this scale? How can you know what's going on in there?

Spivey: Well, there are not 800 variables in this model. In any case, size itself is neither good nor bad. There are models in routine use in industry having much more than 800 equations. These can be interpreted and their content summarized for management. Indeed, I know of cases in which this is done, again on a routine basis, and in which the output is used by management effectively.

Meiselman: Perhaps, but with anything as massive as this, you run the risk of really not knowing what you're doing. The problem is reflected in a lot of questions that are now being asked about what some of these numbers mean.

Spivey: I think you make a good point. Often, the less one knows about something, the more equations are required to describe it, and I think this is a fundamental point that should be kept in mind. There are a lot of ways to make a fool out of oneself, and one can make a fool out of oneself in a simple way, and one can make a fool out of oneself in a sophisticated way.

Rogge: If we have equal knowledge among participants who care, does it make any difference what kind of instruction we give the accountants?

Fabricant: There may be costs that will be different in dealing with one set of rules as compared to another.

Rogge: I am not assuming that the answer to that is that it makes much difference. There is a strong tendency if a change can result there are certain results and they will change some of the parameters. Whether you give them the data in these dollars or some other dollars, they will change unless you are affected by money illusion.

Again, that's one of the questions, and I'm not implying a position on my part because I don't have one. I know when I work with the Public Service Commission, they will often say—the people with whom I'm working will say, it makes no difference whether you give them fair value or original cost data or reproduction cost data, they have an idea of how many dollars they are going to let you have and they'll just readjust the other accounts.

Index

A Note on the Type

This book was linotype set in the Times Roman series of type. The face was designed to be used in the news columns of the *London Times*. The *Times* was seeking a type face that would be condensed enough to accommodate a substantial number of words per column without sacrificing readability and still have an attractive, contemporary appearance. This design was an immediate success. It is used in many periodicals throughout the world and is one of the most popular text faces presently in use for book work.

The cuneiform inscription that serves as the design motif for our endpapers is the earliest known written appearance of the word "freedom" (*ama-gi*), or liberty. It is taken from a clay document written about 2300 B.C. in the Sumerian city-state of Lagash.

Book design by Design Center, Inc., Indianapolis
Typography by Typoservice Corporation, Indianapolis
Printed by Benham Press, Inc., Indianapolis